Letting Life Happen

A Personal Story of Guidance, Opportunity and Abundance

by Donald de Laski

With Preface and
Commentaries by

Mark Thurston

4th Dimension Press • Virginia Beach • Virginia

Co-published by
Personal Transformation and Courage Institute
Virginia Beach, VA
www.transformationANDcourage.org

and

A.R.E. Press
215 67th Street
Virginia Beach, VA 23451-2061

To contact Donald de Laski or Mark Thurston:
info@transformationANDcourage.org

ISBN 13: 978-0-87604-614-2

Front cover photography and design by
Michael Thurston

CONTENTS

Preface

The well-lived life is an inspiration to us all. A life story that is filled with integrity, courage and creativity teaches us all something about the possibilities of our own lives.

This has been my own experience hearing the life story of my friend Don de Laski. And it has been an honor for me to help him bring his biography into the form of this book so that it can be shared with others.

Although we are separated in age by nearly a generation, I have felt a special kinship with this man because of many common themes in our lives. For example, we were both born in Missouri, and both of us had boyhood homes in Takoma Park, Maryland—just over the state line from Washington, D.C. We both counted Hugh Lynn Cayce as a friend and mentor—a man who helped us appreciate the importance of meditation and helped us get a bigger picture of spirituality than we had been able to find in our church life. And—no small matter—we both love the game of golf, for recreation, friendship-building, and even as a metaphor for the challenges of life.

But why does one write his or her memoirs? No doubt one reason is the personal insight that comes from standing back and seeing the trajectory of one's own experiences—to experience the wisdom that can come with hindsight. Going through this soul-searching process is bound to lead to valuable insight for the author.

Others who write an autobiography may do so for the benefit of future generations, descendants who might deeply appreciate knowing the details of an ancestor's life. Don, though, has not seen this as a central purpose for his writing.

A third and perhaps most significant reason for writing one's life story is a way to connect to that which is universal in the human condition. For Don or any one of us who writes his or her life story, it allows the discovery of how we are all connected by common themes of what it means to be human. In writing his memoirs, Don finds the patterns that are universal in the human condition, and shares with us how he has tried to meet those challenges that we all face in one way or another:

- Being both blessed and challenged as a child
- Searching to find his real talents and then use them productively in the world
- Finding a life partner and raising a family
- Leaving one career and starting another
- Wrestling with what it means to have a spiritual life

These are just a few of the universal life themes that you will find in this book. Don's story documents how he has traveled these many phases in life. But his journey is merely his own, just as it is with anyone who writes a book of personal memoirs. And why would any of us as readers find value in someone else's story? Simply this: *We learn about our own lives by deeply appreciating the life experience of someone else.* It gives us perspective on our own successes and failures. It helps us understand our own hopes and dreams.

In many ways Don's story is the classic American success story. A boy is born in the Depression Era to a family that has a lot of love but is just getting by financially. Too young to have to go into World War II, he is nevertheless very resourceful and by the time he is 15 the family survives economically in large part because of the entrepreneurial business he has started. He goes off to a prestigious college, even though many are surprised that he would aspire to something so grand. After college he marries his first love and then settles down to start a career and raise a family. Eventually he decides to adapt his business to the changing opportunities in the world, and because of his resourcefulness and good timing, his business becomes a fabulous success. He retires a very wealthy man and dedicates a large portion of his financial resources to helping the world become a better place.

But that's not all there is to the story. Woven throughout the chapters of this book are other themes that give Don's life its unique flavor and which challenge us all to consider the place of spirituality, intuition, meditation, and divine providence in our own lives.

As Don and I worked together on structuring this account of his life story, we kept in mind *you*, the reader. We had a strong feeling for what would make Don's life story both inspiring and instructive. Instead of sticking rigidly to a chronological timeline, the book often takes a topic and lets it unfold over many years—such as spirituality or golf or sharing money. This means that sometimes it may feel as if the timeline sequence of Don's story is revealed to you in bits and pieces—that the narrative jumps over years without always having filled in the details. Please trust that in the end the whole story will have been revealed, but in a way that makes it easiest for you to relate it to your own life.

Another feature that we decided upon is a brief introduction to each chapter. We had deep and rich one-on-one conversations before Don would begin writing each particular chapter, and these deeper analyses seemed like they were worth capturing as a part of the story. And so, for each chapter, you will find a preamble that I have written. It offers a description of the principles and lessons to be found in that respective chapter, and it presents an invitation to how you might view your own life through the lens of Don's personal experiences.

As I now look back at the work that Don has done on recounting his impressive life story, I am touched especially by three themes that you will frequently encounter in this book—1) the presence of a spiritual world that impacts the physical world, 2) the place of money in our material lives, and 3) the importance of relationships. Just a few thoughts about these three.

First, Don's life so dramatically shows that there is an invisible hand of purposefulness in life. That force—whether we call it Spirit, or God, or angels (as Don often chooses to do)—is continually available to help us. Giving support and comfort. Offering guidance and direction. Of course that invisible hand of purposefulness is not going to do everything for us. We still have to do our part, and you are bound to be touched by Don's own industriousness, determination, and steadfastness in virtually every aspect of his life. But even such valiant efforts are never enough. Each of us also needs the intervening assistance of something bigger than ourselves. And you will find many inspiring examples of this in Don's memoirs.

The second point is money. Our society is quite ambivalent about financial matters. On the one hand, as a society we often seem to be obsessed with money matters. Just look at what is constantly in the newspaper or on television. At the same time, it is often very awkward to talk candidly about your own relationship to money. It seems quite personal—even a rather intimate topic that may feel like it is nobody else's business.

You are likely to be struck as you read this book with how honestly and openly Don is able to share his experiences with money. He didn't start out with much money in his childhood family. And in the early years of his adult life, he made only slow and steady progress being able to provide more and more financial stability for his family. It wasn't until the later years of his professional life that he had extraordinary financial success. Nevertheless, Don's life story includes open references to money matters throughout—not just in recent years as he and his wife Nancy gladly and generously shared of their abundance with good causes. This candid and frank way of approaching money—the matter-of-factness of it all—is a refreshing element of this book. I think it invites us all to see money as just one of many ways spiritual energy expresses itself in the material world.

The third point that strikes me about Don's life story is the central role of key relationships. Don is a soul who gets involved with people. You are sure to be touched by the way Don as a boy built relationships with his customers and created a thriving business before he was even in high school. Or how decades later he was intuitively skillful in hiring just the right people for his computer software business. And the way in which his philanthropy is really about relationships and doing good work in the world, all of it resting on the foundation of solid and trusting relationships.

In closing, let me say that my favorite way of thinking about Don's life story is through the metaphor of a fruit tree. The soil of his early childhood family and his home circumstances was rocky. But there was enough fertility in that soil so that the seed of his soul—with all its talents and capacity for love—was able to sprout like a young tree and take hold. With great determination and integrity of character Don's life grew and unfolded. He put down deep roots by connecting with solid communities, such as his church and the Boy Scouts. As an adult he was adventurous—studying expanded human potentials and holistic healing, and even committing to a disciplined life of daily meditation. His family life and his business thrived. Now that tree is in full maturity, and there are tremendous fruits of his soul journey in this lifetime. This book—with its wisdom and humor—is one such fruit, and there are many fruits still to come.

I think this book will inspire you, the reader, to find the patterns and themes of *your own* life journey. It may even move you to write *your own* memoirs—a deeply meaningful and soul-searching inner adventure.

Mark Thurston, Ph.D.

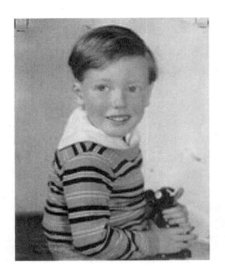

Don, age 4

Don, years later, in front of the house with the hammock on Ruby Ave.

Chapter 1

In the Hammock

It is very fitting that Don begins his memoirs with some very *personal reflections about his connections to the spiritual world— starting with the remarkable account of a life-altering experience when he was just four years old. That event was the start of a life-long alertness to how the invisible, spiritual aspects of life are continually available to anyone who is open-minded enough to receive such guidance and support.*

Don often thinks of the help coming from the spiritual world in terms of "angels." Woven throughout his life story are many examples of how they work for him—and perhaps even more importantly— through him. Although by his own admission he is no theologian, nevertheless he has a favorite way of putting it: "The angels work for the Holy Spirit."

But perhaps even more important than "what is an angel?" is the question of how angelic forces come to us and how they can impact our lives. Don's life story illustrates at least three primary ways that these invisible spiritual forces touch our lives and help us make our way. You will find these themes throughout this book, and each one is touched on lightly here in the opening chapter.

First, angels stimulate unexpected opportunities and synchronistic events. Over the more than seventy years of Don's life, angels have sent the right people to him at just the right time—such as Nancy whom he met in 1952 at Duke University and who became his wife in 1955.

Second, angels provide guidance and help, especially in times of stress or turmoil. More often than not, the spiritual support that comes in these difficult times does not magically make the problem go away. But the angels show the way through our challenges, and Don's life story has many such examples, some of which are highlighted in this first chapter.

And third, angels lead us to mentors—that is, key people in our lives through whom angelic forces can work. They have come into Don's life with perfect timing, just when he needed them.

❀

I was four years old in 1936, and I lived on Ruby Avenue in Marblehead, Massachusetts, an oceanfront town in the northeast suburbs of Boston. I had been an asthmatic child since the age of two. One day as I was just getting over an asthma attack that had come on suddenly, my mother told me to go lie down in the hammock in the backyard and just have a rest.

There I was, looking up at the sky and contemplating all of the various cloud formations. Suddenly a door opened in the middle of a large cloud, and a loud voice said, "Hello, Donald. I love you."

I don't remember much of what my response was to this Voice, but I know I told the Voice that I wanted to come up there and be with him. He replied that that would happen much later, but in the meantime he had a lot for me to do. He also promised that he and his angels would always be with me.

In retrospect it now seems unusual that all this didn't particularly excite me. It just all seemed so "normal." But looking back now as an adult, I have often wondered about the huge impact of this brief encounter with the invisible world of the Holy Spirit. Surely, this experience has in some way given me an inner knowing that no matter what happens, everything will be all right. In fact, I think this was the point in my childhood where I truly became happy. Up until then I was crying all the time, whether it was in my crib because my mother wouldn't come and get me, or at the dinner table because I didn't want to clean up my plate.

From time to time something will happen in my life to take me back to that event at age four, which was in so many ways pivotal and formative. For example, just recently in 2006, Nancy (my wife of fifty-one years) and I were at our winter home in Indian Wells, California. It was a Sunday morning, and we were participating in a Bible class at our Presbyterian church. The group was studying

Chapter 14 of the *Gospel of St. John,* and we came to a very telling verse. Jesus promises that the Father will bring us the Holy Spirit to be with us and to teach us. Reading those words, suddenly my own experience "in the hammock" as a young boy came rushing back to me. In biblical language this was surely the Holy Spirit that had spoken to me.

Angels Work on Large and Small Scales

I have also found that these angels do *not* limit their activities to major concerns. For example, when we were living on Laurel Street in Fairfax, Virginia, my neighbor noticed that whenever we went anywhere, we always had perfect weather. He asked me to let him know about all of my travel plans so he could make his arrangements for the same times. Another example of angels working in small ways is parking spaces. Someone always seems to pull out just when I need a space. For example, in May of 2006, my wife and I were in New York to see some Broadway shows with a group from Indian Wells. On a free night my nephew, Don, drove us to a nice restaurant. Just as he was about to let us out so he could go find a place to park, we noticed a parking meter right in front of us. The meter required a quarter for every ten minutes, and of course no one had any change. But the meter was broken and wouldn't take our money anyway. So we left the car there, and three hours later when we returned everything was fine.

The next night we went to see *The Pajama Game,* a really great show. We had made arrangements for a limousine to pick us up since my wife didn't walk very well. When we came out, the limousine was not there, and it's very difficult to find a cab in New York City after a show. Suddenly, a cab pulled over right beside us, and three ladies got out. As I grabbed the handle to the door, one of the women said, "You guys are really lucky tonight." But I don't think it was luck; I think it was an angel helping us out.

But more important, I am certain that angels have had a very profound influence on major turning points in my life. Here are three examples that I describe in more detail later. In Chapter 5, I tell about how a friend asked me when I was 15 to look after his egg business while he was on vacation. This activity led to a thriving business which supported my parents and me for several years.

As a young man I unsuccessfully applied for a number of jobs that I describe in Chapter 8. Each of those potential jobs would have forced me to move out of the Washington D.C. area and would have changed my life considerably. Something was directing me to stay put in the city where I was already living because that is where my destiny was to be found.

And at the end of that same chapter, I tell the story of how I bought an accounting practice—all because my father-in-law knew someone who knew a widow who was trying to sell her deceased husband's practice. It was an improbable set of circumstances that I can now see was being guided by a higher power. In fact, I had always planned to be a corporate executive, never dreaming it would be in my *own* corporation. I think that in all three of these situations my angels were at work.

Angels Have Led Me to Mentors

In reading this book you will be introduced to many people who played a key role in my life, and I think that angels were very much involved in bringing us together. Probably the angels were also involved by influencing me in the books I read, such as *The Sleeping Prophet*, a biography of Edgar Cayce by Jess Stearn. This led my wife and me to attend many seminars in Virginia Beach, Virginia, at the Association for Research and Enlightenment (A.R.E.), an organization dedicated to carrying on the Cayce works. At one seminar I met Hugh Lynn Cayce (son of Edgar Cayce) who became a mentor for me, helping me first with my meditation practice, and giving me ideas for a church discussion group for teenagers that I was starting back home. At another seminar I met Mark Thurston, and decades later it was he who suggested I write this very book and who has been serving as my editor and co-author.

Some of the A.R.E. seminars were led by Sid and Mary Counsel Crane who ended up moving to our area and joining our church.

They were very instrumental in helping me start a discussion group at our church which in turn led to many other outstanding experiences mentioned in Chapter 12.

On another occasion, I feel that the angels led me to yet another book which greatly influenced me. It was entitled *Sadhana* (meaning, "Realization of Life"). In Chapter 3, I tell the remarkable story of how this very book was a favorite of my grandfather's and how the angels brought it to my attention.

I was even led to a spiritual teacher of my own—Guru Maharaji. I found him by running across a reference to him in my *Duke Alumni Register*, which I hardly ever read. Following the path that he laid out for me was extremely important in my life; and many of Maharaji's followers, including my son, became employees of my business.

Another prominent example of angelic help came from a reading which I received from a clairvoyant in Santa Fe about twenty years ago. It helped me to get a whole new understanding of my difficult relationship with my mother—a topic that is documented in several of the early chapters of this book. The clairvoyant startled me with her guidance—which I think was inspired by angelic forces. She said to me, "Don, your mother made you who you are." In other words, I was guided to see that all the challenges and problems with my mother had forced me to be strong and independent—qualities about myself which I am very glad I now have.

Doing the Angels' Work

I feel that I have often helped the angels do *their* work, and it gives me great joy whenever I can be an instrument of divine purpose. On many occasions in my life, I think that the angels have led me to specific people and I have been given the opportunity to make a meaningful difference in the lives of those individuals. For example, in the final chapter, I relate how Mark Thurston and I are both in the process of realizing our soul's purpose by the program we are setting up at George Mason University. Also, while following Guru Maharaji, I became very much involved and instrumental in a number of businesses which have provided a large portion of Maharaji's support to do his work worldwide.

And also, I am so thankful that the angels led my son to join me in my business; and, of course, he has also greatly benefitted from our business relationship. According to the philosophy in the Edgar Cayce material, many souls select the families into which they are to be born, with the soul entering the fetus soon after the first trimester. Maybe the angels encouraged my wonderful children to join our family.

In some of the most stressful and scary times of my life, angels have showed me the way. Two times it happened with a major health crisis, which I will describe later in detail. One instance was my wife's life-threatening ectopic pregnancy. The circumstances which led to her escape from death were, in my opinion, surely the work of invisible angelic forces. Just as surely, I had a very serious health crisis with pancreatitis, and I believe that I survived because the angels intervened.

Deepening My Relationship with Angels

From my studies and my personal experiences, I have come to understand that angels are not human souls, but instead they are creations of God intended to help humankind carry out our individual soul purposes. Angels give me so much love that I can't help but believe that they know me personally. In fact, even as I was in the process of writing this book, I received a life reading from a well-known clairvoyant who spontaneously began to describe the influence that angels have had on my life. She described one angel in particular, characterizing it as having a feminine vibration and giving her the name Axena, pronounced "Ah-ZEE-Nah." Axena complained to my clairvoyant that I didn't talk to her enough, so in recent months I have increased my communication. In talking to the angels I always thank them, and then I ask them for directions to do God's will.

I have often wondered whether the angels give me more attention than other people. I really don't know, but I do think that it helps to give credit where credit is due, and I would not have become the man I am now were it not for this kind of angelic support. It has been my observation that most people credit a good experience to luck, coincidence, or their own hard work. Not me. I say thank you to the angels, and I believe they like being appreciated.

Don's mother, Onda Odon Warnock de Laski

Don's father, Edgar Gustav de Laski

Chapter 2

Mom and Dad

Mother and father are the starting point for one's life—not just biologically with the genes we inherit and the physical bodies we are given. Each of us is also shaped profoundly by the strengths and weaknesses of our parents. We "inherit" from mom and dad a whole array of attitudes, emotions, perspectives, beliefs, hopes, wounds, and dreams. Here is something that is just an inescapable part of life for every one of us—the elements out of which we spend a lifetime shaping an identity are largely the ones that come from mom and dad.

Don's mother and father were like the parents of all of us. Both of them had lovely gifts and strengths—qualities that were there for Don to absorb and make his own. His mother's hard-working determination. His father's philosophical bent. In the same way, his mother and father were both wounded and stuck. And therefore, Don had to find his way through blocks and limitations that came from growing up in the midst of his parents' disappointments and frustrations.

As we will see in the many chapters that follow, Don has had many wonderful accomplishments and successes in his life. Each one of them grew out of the foundation of his early life and the impact of his parents and the extended families on both sides. In this simple and straightforward narrative of Chapter 2, there are many names and people, and the reader might find it hard sometimes to keep track of everyone's place on the family tree. But more important is to get a sense of the energy of Don's ancestors. This is the "soil" in which his life germinated, took root, and grew. We start to understand this one life by appreciating its foundation. Just as surely, we understand our own life story by stepping back and taking an objective view of our ancestors.

❋

I come from a line of strong women. My maternal grandmother, Jennie May Warnock, was born in 1871 and gave birth to 11 children, two of whom died in early childhood. Those who survived eventually gave me a considerable array of aunts and uncles. From oldest to youngest they were named Cline, Crete, Onda (my mother), Garth, Dwight, Arloween, Lyle, Anna Jane, and Oscar (who was always called "Junior"). Grandma really liked to come up with unusual names.

My mother, Onda Odon Warnock, was born in 1899 in Portland, Indiana, and she was named after an Indian missionary. Because her older sister was a victim of polio, in many ways my mother came into the role of "oldest daughter" and had many responsibilities for helping raise a family as big as this one. And because of my grandfather's unusual and progressive attitudes about women and education, my mother and her sisters all received a college education, something that was a big deal back in those days.

My grandfather Oscar Warnock was born in 1868. In 1910, when my mother was eleven, he had moved his family to West Lafayette, Indiana, largely because of his strong desire for the children to have the opportunity to attend college. This was especially the case for my aunt Crete. Polio had stunted her growth and left her with a serious limp. Grandpa felt that getting a college education was going to be the only way she could make a decent living. And, of course, the other children in the family also went to college, but Crete's college education was the prime reason why my grandfather moved everyone to West Lafayette. Eventually, my mother and all her siblings graduated from Purdue University—all except my Uncle Cline, who wanted to concentrate on making money.

Although my grandfather's main job was administrator of an orphanage, he also spent time and money in helping Cline establish a very successful creamery in Bucyrus, Ohio. I can still remember dipping my finger in a large vat of butter at Uncle Cline's creamery. It was June, 1935, at the time of the funeral for my grandfather.

My mother's strength and determination were big factors in

helping her childhood family get by. She was given not only significant duties taking care of the younger children; she also helped run the dormitory of Purdue University students, which made up a part of their home. The responsibilities related to those live-in students added a lot of work to her life.

My mother was a very accomplished and ambitious young woman. She graduated from Purdue in 1920 with a degree in nutrition. She was very attractive and had a serious boyfriend named Dexter. He wanted to marry her, but she turned him down. She said it was because he was Catholic, but it was probably because she wanted to go to New York and make money. My mother, like her brother Cline, was very much into making money.

Soon after getting her university degree, my mother got a job as a nutritionist at a large department store in New York City. It had three restaurants, and she did all the buying for the restaurants, in addition to supervising all the restaurants' staff. Her salary rose to $6,000 a year, and she took great pride in sending money home to her family in Indiana.

In 1927 when she was twenty-eight years old and very successful in her career, she met my father, Edgar Gustav de Laski. Although I don't know a lot about their courtship, it must have seemed to her that Edgar would make an excellent match. I'm sure she loved my father very much, and the fact that he had a well-paying job as a consultant and was from a wealthy family living on Park Avenue was icing on the cake.

Just a year after meeting, they were married at the Church of the Transfiguration, also known as "The Little Church Around The Corner." It's such a unique place, and we even had a chance to visit there as a family when I was a teenager. Since its founding in the mid-19th century, this church has been a leader of the Anglo-Catholic movement within the Episcopal Church. While this movement often is associated with elaborate worship, it also has stressed service to the poor and oppressed from its earliest days. The founding pastor, Dr. Houghton, built a congregation that cut across class and racial lines, sponsored bread lines to feed the hungry, worked vigorously for the abolition of slavery and harbored runaway slaves during the Civil War. It was certainly a historic spot for their wedding.

My mother probably thought she had the perfect marriage. In 1928 Dad got a job at Ford, Bacon, and Davis, working as an economist and market analyst. That meant moving to Webster Grove, just outside of St. Louis, Missouri. My mother quit her job when they got married because in those days married women didn't work unless they needed the money. They got a nice apartment in Webster Grove and bought a fine Hammond piano since Dad liked to play. A year after the stock market crash and the beginning of the Great Depression, my brother Edgar Gustav was born. A year later my father lost his job, and I was born.

We had no money. My mother and father went from being very well off to becoming penniless overnight. I don't know any of the details of why my father's parents didn't help out. My mother told me that she had asked her brother Cline for help, but he wanted no part of it. This seems very strange because my mother had sent money home to her family for many years before she was married.

My mother tried to get back her old job at the New York City department store, but they had filled her position with three employees. She had assumed that a husband with a good job and from a wealthy family would be able to take care of her financially. In fact, my father's family did provide some assistance. I don't know what my parents would have done if it weren't for my father's aunts in Swampscott, Massachusetts. They were quite rich and said they would help out if we would move near them. So when I was a baby, the family moved to Marblehead, Massachusetts.

It was quite a turning point for our family in terms of the role played by my father. In almost no time he had gone from a seemingly promising career into a situation in 1933 where he would never hold the same job for more than two years. This led to lots of tension between my mother and father for many years. I can remember many episodes of my mother getting extremely upset with my father. For example, one time he went out and bought a car—an old beat–up thing—and it seemed so foolish to her when she found out, that she physically boxed his ears. She would yell and scream at him, and he would put up no defense, probably because he felt ashamed of the family's financial condition. In fact, she did quite a bit of yelling and screaming in the first five to ten years of my life, and I often felt caught between them. It often felt to me as a boy that I was the glue holding the family together.

My Father and His Side of the Family

My father Edgar Gustav de Laski was born on March 9, 1892 in Paris, France where his parents were visiting. He was the oldest of four sons, his three younger brothers being Arthur, Ralph, and Bert, the youngest. In many ways my father was a very private man. He spoke very little about his childhood. He did say that he grew up around New York City, and he mentioned a couple of times that he had his own car when he was in high school. So the family must have been pretty well off.

Dad went to Cornell University at both the undergraduate and graduate levels. He majored in philosophy, got well into his graduate training in philosophy, and had plans to become a professor. But before he got his Ph.D., he left Cornell and took his first job as a business consultant. It's too bad he didn't become a professor because he certainly wasn't a businessman. Years after he gave up his Ph.D. studies in philosophy, I found and read some of the papers he had written back then. He would write stories about the nature of things, but I didn't get the sense that he had a *passion* for anything, and I suspect that is why he dropped out.

My father certainly loved me. But he never did anything physical with me like sports or hikes or anything else. In fact, my brother was more of a "father" to me than my own father was. But Dad and I would talk quite a bit, and sometimes it was even about spiritual things. He never seemed to have anything especially profound to say. He was a man who seemed to largely be disappointed in how his life was going.

Whatever wealth might have been in my father's family as he

grew up did not make its way down to him. When my paternal grandfather died sometime in the late 1920s, my father never received anything from the estate.

Although I was born after the passing of this grandfather, I do have vivid memories of my father's mother, Emily de Laski. I was with her on several occasions in New York, and I attended her funeral when I was 16 in 1948. The only inheritance that my parents received from her estate was a pearl necklace. The youngest son Bert lived with his mother all his life, and he probably got most of the estate. He was a big spender, probably gay, and an alcoholic. In 1970 my dad got a letter from the state of New York announcing that Bert was in a state poorhouse. The letter requested help from my father in supporting Bert, but my Dad never answered the letter. In fact, he never paid much attention to any of his brothers. And, I met them only on rare occasions.

I realize now just what a turning point the Depression was for my father and so many others like him. It was particularly difficult for my father since he had always been an intellectual and had never held any kind of a manual labor or clerical type job. He spent a great deal of time typing job applications, generally in hopes of getting a job as a marketing analyst for the U.S. Government. In fact, he had success in getting jobs, but he was always let go after the two–year probationary period.

When my father got his first government job in 1941, things got better. Nevertheless, there was still a pattern of instability for him with employment. He would go from one assignment to another, with unemployment periods in–between. My mother seemed to accept the fact that she really couldn't rely on him for long–term security. She would often say that she never knew a family that would so frequently go from rags to riches and then back to rags. But she did appreciate how some of his government assignments led to unusual opportunities to live abroad, and she particularly liked my father's foreign assignments to Japan, Ethiopia, and Cambodia. I got in on the first of those, and my fourteen months living in Japan during my high school years proved to be an important period in my life. But thereafter, my parents' foreign adventures were on their own because I had started my own independent life.

One Very Special Relative

In most ways I was closer to my mother's side of the family throughout my growing up years. But I feel a deep connection to one relative on my father's side—my grandfather Albert de Laski, who died just a few years before my birth.

I am very proud of him. He went to sea when he was 15 and enlisted in the Union Army at Lynn, Massachusetts on December 5, 1863. He was honorably discharged on July 30, 1865, two months after the Civil War came to a conclusion. His official mustering out papers describe him as follows: Age 21 years; height 5 feet 5 1/2 inches; complexion, light; eyes, brown; hair light; place of birth, Sebec, Maine; Occupation; sailor.

We have copies of some of the letters he wrote to his sister in Massachusetts. One letter from Fredericksburg, Virginia is dated May 14, 1864, and it describes a battle in which he fought. Some of his friends were killed and wounded there. Later he, too, was wounded and sent to a field hospital, followed by a transfer to a general hospital in Alexandria, Virginia. While in these hospitals he wrote many other letters to his sister.

My father kept these letters and showed them to me and my children. They were very neatly written and had little sketches along the margins. He always signed his letters, "in haste." My daughter always liked this, so she and her cousins would sign their letters to each other the same way.

After the Civil War my grandfather Albert made a lot of money as an inventor. My father told me he invented a machine for making hats. He also did something to improve the fabric in tires. We have a copy of a patent, dated June 8, 1899, which reads "First and sole inventor of the new and useful improvement in flat woven tubular fabrics."

There was another side to my grandfather which I am very thankful that I found out about. It almost didn't happen, though. When my parents were moving from Virginia to Florida in 1972, a

lot of their memorabilia was thrown out. But one little book entitled *Sadhana* (meaning, "the realization of life") by Rabindranath
Tagore was given to a bazaar for the Providence Presbyterian
Church. I just happened to come along, saw this book, and I
bought it for forty cents. The book has 164 pages, divided into
eight chapters entitled as follows:

The Relation of the Individual to the Universe;
Soul Consciousness;
The Problem of Evil;
The Problem of Self;
The Realization of Love;
The Realization in Action;
The Realization of Beauty;
The Realization of the Infinite.

Rabindranath Tagore was from the Bengal region of India, and
he became a world-renowned poet, philosopher, visual artist, play-
wright, novelist, and composer whose works reshaped Bengali literature and music in the late 19th and early 20th centuries. He
became Asia's first Nobel laureate when he won the 1913 Nobel
Prize in Literature. Here I had discovered that Tagore was writing
about the very kinds of topics that I had become interested in.

Many of the pages in this book I recovered had sentences underlined. After I had read about three chapters of the book, I was
leafing through the front pages, and a beautiful signature jumped
out at me, "Albert de Laski, Feb 26, 1914." From that time on I have
felt that my grandfather Albert's spirit has been looking out for
me. It's mind boggling to think that when both of us were about
50 years old, we were interested in the same philosophy. It also
appears that the sister to whom Albert was writing was the same
aunt who helped my father when he lost his job. Maybe before
my grandfather died he told her to look after Edgar and his family.

Just looking back at this book *Sadhana* rekindles my enthusiasm
for reading it again. And I have made a commitment to study once
again the very pages of esoteric and metaphysical wisdom that

my grandfather felt were so important to his life nearly one hundred years ago. These are surely principles for my own study and for sharing with some of my spiritual friends.

Tagore's philosophy is very similar to mine even though I consider myself a Christian and Tagore was Hindu Brahman. My grandfather underlined the following paragraph,

> Though the West has accepted as its teacher him who boldly proclaimed his oneness with his Father, and who exhorted his followers to be perfect as God, it has never been reconciled to this idea of our unity with the infinite being. It condemns as a piece of blasphemy, any implication of man's becoming God. This is certainly not the idea that Christ preached, nor perhaps the idea of the Christian mystics, but this seems to be the idea that has been popular in the Christian West.

This theme of the oneness of Eastern and Western thought is right at the heart of my own philosophy of life. And nowadays I have quite a few Buddhist friends. Our belief systems seem to be the same. Through our meditations we try to become one with God; and we understand Jesus to be only one of a great lineage of teachers which includes Buddha, Mohammed, and Krishna. I can see that Rabindranath Tagore's book inspired me to start an extensive study and practice of the world's religions. I have my grandfather to thank, and I can feel how an ancestor can have a direct impact on the generations that follow him.

Don with older brother Ed, ages 4 and 5

Don as the youngest paperboy award-winner for
The Washington Evening Star. His brother Ed is the tallest
boy in the back row

Chapter 3

Growing Up

The first dozen years of anyone's life is pivotal. Patterns are shaped and qualities of the personality emerge. But just as the child is being conditioned by all those external forces and situations, just as surely something of the child's own essence even starts to peek out. Seeds of what will come later begin to show themselves early, such as an aptitude for business or a willingness to be a self-starter.

Don grew up in the Depression Era, and yet his narrative pointedly does not refer to these enormous economic or political forces that were impacting America in the 1930s. The child's world is smaller. It is the only way that he or she has ever known the world to be.

As you read these anecdotes and reflections from Don's first dozen years, think about your own biography. Who were the key people in your life who supported you—people like Don's uncle who gave him a taste of what it was like to have a man in his life who would do things with him? What were the times in your childhood when you felt like you really "belonged" to some group or community—some situation where you felt seen and appreciated? And what was the wound in your family structure that meant that you didn't get certain things that a child genuinely needs—wounds such as Don's father's inability to be a provider or Don's mother's fragile emotional state that made it hard for her to give the needed space and trust to a growing boy.

These kinds of challenges largely shape our character. Don—just like all of us—either collapses into those wounds in our adult life, or as grown-ups we find an inner resiliency and courage to find an internal way to fulfill what wasn't coming from the outside world.

❀

I think that I was a very happy child, even though I had prob-lems such as asthma and a very emotional and controlling mother, which caused me a lot of stress. In spite of my asthma, I led a very active life although many times my mother used my asthma as an excuse to tell me what to do. For example, once when I was six, I got very upset when only my brother got to go on a ski trip with the other kids we knew. My mother wouldn't let me go because she was afraid I would have an asthma attack.

My earliest memories go back to when the family lived in Mas–sachusetts. I can remember being three years old at our first home in Marblehead. It was a bright yellow house and had a sandbox at the side. This is surely one of my earliest memories, and I can vividly recall crying in the sandbox. My mother asked me what the problem was, and I said that I had no one to play with. She replied, "Why don't you play with Donald de Laski." Perhaps this memory stuck with me because my parents always expected me to be my own playmate. In looking back over my childhood, I cannot remember my parents ever playing with me, except my father occasionally reading me a bedtime story.

When I was four years old, we moved to another home in Marblehead, this one on Ruby Avenue. I remember pulling a wagon with my father, helping him to deliver eggs to customers— a budding interest in business that would blossom by the time I was a teenager. In fact, small entrepreneurial activities were a part of my early growing up years. My parents also bought and sold turkeys at Thanksgiving, and I remember being in the basement helping them pluck turkey feathers.

Crying and Asthma

Much of my childhood was against the backdrop of my asthma. I have another clear memory of walking to a nursery school with my mother. At this school we each had a mat that we put on the floor for an afternoon nap, but I took my nap on a table because my mother was afraid that the dust on the floor would cause an asthma attack. One day during naptime, I was playing with a cord from a window shade, and I knocked down a flowerpot. The teacher spanked me and made me sleep on the floor. I immediately got an asthma attack, and my mother had to come and get me. I don't know whether the asthma was caused by the dust on the floor or the spanking. I didn't continue going to that nursery school, and my parents couldn't really afford it anyway.

I remember crying a lot in those days at Marblehead. When I woke up from my nap, I would cry for a long time in my crib waiting for my mother to come and get me. She would always say she was busy and ask me, "Why can't you play with the toys in your crib?" After she finally came and got me, she would put me in my playpen. Today my younger son David has two sons. When the boys were little, David's wife Syd was always near a monitor. She could always hear them when they awakened, and then she got them immediately. And of course, they never had a playpen. (However, I guess that for most families, the modern day playpen is the television.)

I also cried a lot at the dinner table. My mother expected me to clean up my plate, and I was a very picky eater. I would throw up a lot at the table. I must have driven my mother crazy. Today I have six grandchildren. Ironically, until the age of ten, all but one of them have been picky eaters. They would eat whatever they wanted, rarely cleaned up their plates, and nobody seemed too worried about it.

Something had happened in me by the time I reached age five. I don't remember what might have led to this dramatic change, but from that age onward I don't remember crying anymore—even in situations where crying might have been normal. For example, we had a little white dog that got run over by a car. My brother and parents cried a lot at the loss, but not me. I remember saying that it was the dog's fault because he shouldn't have been in the street. Perhaps up to the age of five I had cried often because I wanted attention or as a way of standing up for myself when I didn't want to do something. It doesn't ever seem to have been out of unhappiness, and, in fact, I don't even remember being unhappy. It is possible that the experience that I had "in the hammock" at age four connected me to a deep source of inner happiness and knowing. Only decades later did I come to realize that crying can have a valuable place. Today, I even envy people who can cry when they are sad. When my loved ones have died, I have never been able to cry.

It has become my belief now that keeping emotions pent up inside myself is what aggravated my asthma as a boy. Instead of crying, I would get asthma attacks. And to this day, I find that other people that I meet who are asthmatics seem to be very un-emotional on the outside—they keep their feelings hidden. I have never heard this expressed by any asthma physician, but instinctively it feels true to me. In fact, my mother's nervous breakdown when I was two-and-half coincided almost exactly with the beginnings of my asthmatic condition. Although I don't remember her breakdown, it was probably a tremendously stressful situation for me and might have caused me to keep my emotions inside.

The Move to Indiana

Moving was a recurrent theme in my childhood, and when I was five years old we went to live with my grandmother in West Lafayette, Indiana. I don't know whether it was because my mother wanted to get away from my father, or if the rich aunts stopped supporting us. My mother, brother, and I lived in one bedroom on the first floor of my grandmother's home. I went to nursery school, and again I got spanked because I crawled under a table and was chewing on some alphabet cardboard squares called anagrams. I was always something of a cut-up in school, and I think it was because I wanted attention.

I really liked my grandmother. She got up early and worked all day, including her job running a student dormitory. She is still a powerful character in my memory. For example, one day I was in the basement talking to one of the chickens that was in a crate. She came downstairs, opened the crate, picked up that chicken by the neck and twisted it. The chicken said, "awk" and that was the end of him.

After about six months in West Lafayette, we went back to join my father in Scarsdale, New York. He had gotten a decent job in

New York City, and we temporarily moved into a big house with the Wyman brothers, who were friends of my dad. But we soon moved yet again, renting a little house of our own on Mt. Joy Avenue. The only thing I remember about living in that house was playing with a wasp's nest in the back yard and being badly stung. I had a severe asthma attack and had to be rushed to the hospital.

We were there less than six months, and my father lost his job again. My poor mother screamed and my father, as usual, was very morose. During this period we had been attending a little Dutch Reformed church down on Central Avenue in Scarsdale. The pastor invited us to come and live with his family in the manse. Can you imagine being so poor that you have to move into the pastor's house?

One vivid memory from this period is stealing a dime out of the collection plate. I felt so bad about having done this that I confessed to the pastor, and he forgave me.

Happier Times

In late 1938 my mother showed her real fortitude and business acumen. There was a very large house on Old Army Road which belonged to the Frank family, and the New York World's Fair was about to begin in April, 1939. The Franks, who were members of our church, were getting ready to close their house and go to Europe for over a year. My mother persuaded our pastor to talk the Franks into letting us live in their house and use it as a tourist home while they were away.

I can remember going down to Central Avenue with my father and helping him nail up the tourist sign. The tourist home was an immediate success. People would come from all over the world and sit on our long front porch. Mother would serve breakfast to everyone. She even hired a maid to help out.

I loved this house, and I had a pet rabbit that I would chase all over the 20–acre estate. There was also a pond that I would wade in. One day I collected about thirty frogs and put them in a barrel, but by the next day they were all dead.

The Franks collected old carriages, and my brother and I played a lot in the carriage house. We also walked every day to the Edgemont School where I attended kindergarten and part of the first grade. It was a beautiful, wooded-path walk of about one-and-a-half miles. My mother didn't worry about me because my brother Ed was always with me. He was only fifteen months older than me, but he was much taller and very strong. He helped bridge the gap left by my inactive father—that is, my brother was always encouraging me to participate in games. After about three months at the Franks' house my father got a good job in New York City. We must have had a lot of money then because I remember my father buying my mother a fur coat, and we also got a used De Soto automobile.

When the Franks came home in early 1940, we moved to a house on Evansdale Road on the other side of Central Avenue. I was eight years old now and rode my bike everywhere. My best friend Larry and I would wade in our boots in a number of ponds where we caught many pollywogs and frogs. One day my mother got very mad at me. She yelled and screamed and slapped me around. She said she called me for lunch, and I didn't come. I don't even think it was lunchtime—she was just being unreasonable. My mother couldn't get used to letting me be on my own, and she was frequently arbitrary and illogical like this.

Radio entertainment was another big part of my life in this era. About 5:00 p.m. my brother and I usually started listening to radio serials. I remember *Superman, Flash Gordon,* and *Death Valley Days.* My father listened to *The News with Gabriel Heater* and my mother loved *One Man's Family,* which eventually became the longest running serial drama in American radio broadcasting history.

One day my father brought home a little puppy in his pocket. It was black and a cross between a cocker spaniel and a fox terrier. We had a lot of fun playing with him, and we named him Chips. More about Chips in a later chapter because he became a key part of our family.

I also rode my bike to the Edgemont School, which was about

three miles away from our new home. While in the second grade, a little girl and I played the leading roles in a school play, "The Bluebird of Happiness." The play was about our search for the blue-bird, and we were on the stage for almost two hours. It was my dramatic debut, and it took some courage to be on stage for the first time. I loved this school. It was a place where I was seen and known, and I had a lot of friends. It was my best childhood experience of feeling like I "belonged" to the group. One small example: in early 1941, I came down with pneumonia and was out of school for about six weeks. When I came back to school, I remember how glad everyone was to see me. We had a little party, and the children had prepared displays about what they had learned while I was gone.

In the years thereafter, with all of our moves and new schools, I would always be "the new kid" and have very few friends.

Relatives

My Aunt Anna Jane came to visit us. She was about 25 years old, and my mother's youngest sibling. We had a lot of fun riding our bikes together. She was living near her mother in West Lafayette, and when she got ready to leave to go back to Indiana, she invited me to go with her for part of the summer. We went on an overnight Pullman train. I wanted to play cards with her, but she said I had to wait until we got in the bunk because if the conductor saw me playing cards, he might suspect that I was not under six years old. Children under six could travel free with an adult if they slept in the same bunk. Even though I had recently turned nine, I was very small and scrawny.

One reason I wanted to make this visit to West Lafayette was because my uncle Lyle would be there at the same time. He came to Indiana every year because his wife, Eleanor, was also from West Lafayette. He adopted me and treated me like I was one of his boys. He took us all to a beach at a nearby lake. I was not used to having a man doing things with me, and it felt very good. His oldest son Bud Warnock was the same age as I, and we cousins had a great time hanging out together.

Another memorable family member from my mother's side was Uncle Oscar. We all loved him, and everyone called him Junior, even though he was about five feet three inches tall and weighed about 350 pounds. He lived with my grandmother, and he ran a pool hall. In the back room there was always a poker game, and the house collected 25 cents a hand.

That summer of 1941 is so memorable for me because it underscores how important family is for me. And it reminds me of how I always felt connected to my mother's side of the family but not my father's. Over the years I have kept in touch with all these relatives with whom I had so much fun that summer. Uncle Oscar (Junior) died about ten years later. My brother Ed was a pallbearer at the funeral, and because Uncle Oscar still weighed 350 pounds, the casket was really heavy. Uncle Lyle died in his late sixties of cancer. Many years later in 2004, my wife and I and my sister-in-law Nancy Lou (my brother Ed's wife) went to Michigan to visit Uncle Lyle's son Bud and Bud's son David. We three men played two rounds of golf. We also visited Aunt Anna Jane who was about ninety and remembered everything about my childhood.

Moving to the Washington, D.C. Area

Near the end of 1941 my father got a government job in Washington, D.C. and we moved to Erie Avenue in Takoma Park, Maryland, just across the state line from Washington. My brother and I walked about two miles every day to school where I attended the second half of the third grade and fourth grade. We weren't allowed to ride our bikes because we walked along Sligo Creek Parkway which was too narrow for bicyclers. I remember that I had a problem in this school because we were learning to write in long hand and in Scarsdale everyone printed through elementary school. My brother was in the sixth grade and therefore his handwriting for all his life was always like printing.

Ed and I each got a paper route delivering *The Evening Star*. My brother's route was a couple of miles away so he used his bike. My route was in our neighborhood, so I used a wagon. My route became very concentrated. When I first started, it was five square blocks, but I got so many new customers, it soon became only three square blocks. It was also very concentrated because the houses were big, and had many families living in them. Sometimes I would deliver as many as five papers to a single house. I eventually had one of the largest routes which was about 130 customers. I made about $30 a month. All the time I was growing up I had my own money which gave me a great deal of independence. I never remember getting an allowance, and I would buy Christmas and birthday presents for the family.

Chips would always go with me on my route. He knew where all my customers were, and he would wag his tail at them when they came out to get their paper. On Sundays I had to start my deliveries at 6:00 a.m. At my mother's insistence my father would go with me. On Sundays the papers were much heavier, and we had to make several trips to the drop-off station. A couple of times in the winter we had to put the papers in boxes on sleds. It was a rare instance in my childhood up to that time in which my father and I worked on something together.

At first the route manager for *The Evening Star* wouldn't let me collect the monthly subscription price from each customer because I was too young. Eventually I talked them into it. I'm glad I did because I got a lot of tips at Christmas time—about $200. I think a lot of people felt sorry for me because I was so thin and scrawny.

On Erie Avenue we lived next to a Seventh Day Adventist college and church. Most of our neighbors were Adventists, and they were always trying to convert us. Since we weren't involved with any other church, we went to some of their meetings. The Adventists are big believers in the second coming of Jesus Christ, and some believe that when that happens only the Adventists will be saved. I had a neighbor friend named Melvin. One day he came over and started walking away with my football. When I asked him where he was going with my football, he said that Jesus was coming soon and since I wouldn't be here then, he might as well take the football now.

Even though I have criticized my mother considerably in these memories, I should add that I always knew her main concern in life was the welfare of her boys. One of the best decisions she ever made was when she decided to move her family from Takoma Park, Maryland over into Washington, D.C. At that time the Washington schools had the reputation of having the best school system in the country. Since the schools were run by the federal government, the teachers were federal employees. So in the summer of 1943 we moved just a mile or two to Whittier Street in Takoma Park, D.C. My parents first rented and then bought this house a few years later. It would be their principal residence for the next twenty-five years. I was ready to stay in one place for awhile. In fact, for those first ten years of my life I lived in eleven houses. For the next sixty-eight years I have lived in only ten houses.

Now I was a fifth grader, and my school was about a ten block bike ride to the corner of 5th and Dahlia Streets in Takoma Park. Even though my brother Ed was only fifteen months older than I, we were two grades apart in school because of when our birthdates fell. He had just started seventh grade at Paul Junior High School and had to take the bus because it was about six miles away, across many busy streets. They didn't have school buses in Washington D.C. in this era, so school children used commercial transportation and could get bus passes which cost just three cents each way, substantially less than the normal ten cent bus fare.

In fact, transportation was an issue for everyone in my family in 1942. When we first moved to Whittier Street, we didn't have a car, and I usually walked the three blocks to the store with my mother in order to help her to carry home the groceries. In those days it was normal to have milk and bread delivered at the door, but my mother refused because it was a few cents cheaper at the store. This, of course, made our burden walking home with groceries that much greater.

I got a paper route right after we moved. Since my delivery neighborhood was about five blocks away, I was going to need to use a bike, and my old one was not going to be at all adequate. I knew that I needed a new one very badly and that was not going to be a simple matter. Because of the War, everyone needed a special permit to buy a bike. Fortunately, because I was a paper boy, I qualified. The new bike was for *business*, not pleasure. When I got it, I was so proud of my new bike because it was the nicest one at my school and in our neighborhood.

I had started taking piano lessons while living on Evansdale Road in Scarsdale, New York, and I decided to start again. Altogether I took lessons for about six years, I could never play by ear, but I got pretty good at reading music. I would usually practice before dinner and Ed would frequently want to sing songs with me. I can also remember us singing "Rudolf the Red Nosed Reindeer," plus "She'll be Comin' Round the Mountain When She Comes," and "When the Red, Red Robin Comes Bob, Bob, Bobbin' Along."

It was about this time, when I was ten years old , that Ed and I seemed to start building a very close relationship. Before then I was too young to appreciate him, and I took him for granted. Subsequent chapters will mention how we played and worked together in Boy Scouts, the egg business, finding a job at Jewel Tea, and working in real estate. When I was about 15 we attended Christian Endeavor (CE) at the Presbyterian Church which is a young people's social group. One night Ed wanted to delay our walk home by stopping in at the Park Pharmacy to play the pinball machine for half an hour. When we got home there were 25 people waiting for me, and they all sang happy birthday. He and my mother had arranged this surprise birthday party for me.

Looking back over these first eleven or twelve years of my life, I think all these early changes in residence did two things. First, this variety of different homes now helps me recall many of my childhood experiences and details of when they happened. Second, and even more importantly, I feel that all those moves helped me become more successful. I had to learn how to cope with new situations. Traumatic as it sometimes felt as a young boy, it strengthened me in a way that I could appreciate only many years later.

Don (back row, farthest right) and his Boy Scout
troop from the Takoma Park Presbyterian Church

Making an Eagle Scout award to one of his Scouts

Chapter 4

Boy Scouts and Lessons in Leadership

As we are growing up, we all need experiences through which we build self-esteem, along with a sense of personal proficiency and the capacity to achieve goals. For some young people that comes through athletics, the arts, or academics. In Don's life the Boy Scouts provided a vital opportunity to accomplish goals, attain levels of achievement, and to find community with other boys. Scouting did for him exactly what it was created to do.

So too were the Boy Scouts a chance for Don to develop leadership skills—both as a boy stepping into leadership roles among his peers, and also to give back to Scouting by serving as a troop leader when Don was in his 30s. In choosing to step forward and resuscitate a dying troop, Don was able to honor all the wonderful things that happened for him as a Boy Scout decades earlier. But leadership has its temptations, too—including a tendency that we sometimes have to hold onto a position of authority even after its time has really passed. Don knew when this period of adult leadership had run its course, and he was able to relinquish and step out of leadership when the time was right—a quality of leadership that we can all aspire to nurture.

In the setting of wartime Washington D.C.—living in a new neighborhood, and having a new paper route—a very important adventure began for me. I decided that I wanted to be part of the Boy Scout troop at our Presbyterian Church. Actually, I made this decision and wanted to be a Boy Scout even before I was old enough to join. This troop had the rule that you couldn't become a member until you received your Tenderfoot badge. However, even before a boy would turn eleven, it was permissible for him to start working on the requirements and achievements necessary to eventually become a Tenderfoot. So, I got started on the various things I had to learn and do, and when I turned eleven on February 1, 1943, I immediately qualified for my Tenderfoot badge, and I became a member of Boy Scout Troop 33, Takoma Park, Maryland.

Camping Adventures with Our Patrol

The troop was made up of several patrols, and in the summer of 1943 a new patrol was formed, and my brother Ed was appointed patrol leader. Our patrol had about eight boys in it, most of whom lived in our neighborhood. The entire troop had meetings every Wednesday night, and we went on a troop overnight camping excursion about every six weeks. In addition, our patrol would go on an overnight by ourselves about once a month, even in the winter.

Our group of eight boys would head out on these patrol overnights, riding our bikes with our packs on our backs, ready for a new adventure. Our dog, Chips, would generally ride in the basket of my brother's bike. Especially for wintertime overnights, we had a favorite place. On a previous hike we had discovered an old abandoned cabin deep in the woods about eight miles out New Hampshire Ave., north into Maryland. We kept coming out to this place for our hikes in the winter because this shelter meant that we didn't have to carry tents on our bikes.

Naturally my mother always worried about me going on these hikes, but she knew that Ed would look out for me. Our patrol members became outstanding campers. We cooked some pretty good meals. Hot dogs were not allowed, but we would do burgers with onions. We would also have bacon and eggs for breakfast.

Chips really enjoyed these campouts. He would go rummaging about the woods and be gone for hours at a time. A little excitement occurred one night when we were sleeping outside in our sleeping bags. Chips was sleeping in the bottom of my sleeping bag with his nose stuck out of the zipper. Suddenly there was a lot of barking, and Chips came straight out of my sleeping bag, running across my face. Ten seconds later he came running back into the sleeping bag. All of us got up and found eight wild dogs encircling our camp and snarling at us. We threw rocks at them, and they soon left.

But on another occasion there was a near disaster with Chips. On this particular hike, as we prepared to go home, we couldn't find Chips. We called and called. One of the boys said he saw a man getting into a car with a dog that looked like Chips. Eventually we went home without him. We were all very sad, and when we got home my mother cried. Even though she was always complaining about Chips, she really loved him. She was always the same way with me. She felt that by complaining she was making me a better person.

But there was a happy ending to the story of Chips' disappearance. Three days later my mother came into my room in the morning and said she had a surprise for me. I went downstairs and there was Chips, in his bed sound asleep. His fur was matted with burrs, and his feet were all bloodied. My mother said she had heard a faint scratch at the door at four o'clock that morning, and she got up and let him in. Chips slept for two days, and of course we never knew where he had been.

Skits

On troop hikes the various patrols were each asked to put on skits in the evening after we had made camp and had our supper. One time my brother came up with an idea for a skit which he called "Truth or Momo." It was a variation of the then popular radio quiz show called "Truth or Consequences." In the skit, I was the first contestant, and I got the question right. When the next contestant—another member of our patrol—gave the wrong answer, the emcee pronounced, "Then it's time for Momo." My brother came out snarling, dressed in a black cloak, and dragging his right foot. The second contestant screamed as Momo carried him off. For two or three minutes we heard blood curdling screams and hollers from the woods. The skit made an impression on all the boys in the troop, and from then on my brother was called "Momo."

This kind of boyish playfulness was a memorable part of Scouting for me. On another occasion one of our patrol members, Willis Volkmer, wanted to do a skit by himself, but he wouldn't tell anyone what it was. In the skit he announced that he was being chased by a monster, and he was trying to get into a locked house. He pulled out his key chain and tried the first key. It didn't work. Neither did a second key. In fact, none of the keys seem to fit. Finally he comes to what he calls "de Laski"—"de last key" — which fits fine and he is saved from the monster. Everybody thought this was pretty funny. To this day, when I meet someone new, I sometimes tell them they can remember my name by pulling out their key chain and going through each key until they come to de Laski.

Scouting as Personal Growth and Transformation

Scouting was, of course, much more to me than just these fun-loving times with the other boys. Boy Scouts gave me a framework for learning about myself, developing new skills, and achieving goals. I knew all along that I wanted to become an Eagle Scout. I have always been ambitious, and once I start something I always want to finish it.

Boy Scouts have a series of achievement levels. After Tenderfoot comes, in order: Second Class, First Class, Star, Life, and finally an Eagle Scout. Those last three levels involve earning merit badges with specific skills. Star requires five merit badges, Life requires five more, and Eagle requires twenty-one altogether. Some of the merit badges are required such as cooking, pioneering, first-aid, bird study, and life saving. In cooking we had to build an oven out of clay and bake a meal in it. In pioneering we had to build a bridge over a ravine using ropes.

Many of these merit badge tasks came easily for me, but I had a very big problem getting my life saving merit badge. I was not a good swimmer because of my asthma. I would go down to the Ambassador Hotel swimming pool, and a very large woman would give me lessons. She would be the one to determine if I met the requirements and could be awarded my life saving merit badge. My problem with my asthma was that I couldn't hold my breath long enough. She would pretend she was drowning, and I was supposed to jump in and save her. The only problem was that she would end up saving me. One day she had to give me artificial respiration. She finally passed me and I was able to achieve my life-savings merit badge. But I think it was probably out of sympathy.

After about four years in the Boy Scouts, I finally received the rank of Eagle Scout. I don't seem to remember anything about the ceremony itself, but I took great pride in what I had worked hard for and achieved. Over the years I have learned something about myself, though. Accomplishing something always makes me feel very good, but compliments from others don't mean a whole lot to me, except compliments that come from my family.

I've always been very grateful to the Scout Leaders at Troop 33. I think that experience was very important in my development. Since I was very small and sickly as a child, I needed Scouting to enhance my self-esteem. But as important as this was in my own life, I realize that nowadays it would be very difficult to have a Boy Scout troop like the one we had in the 1940s. In today's world there is so much emphasis on organized sports and other kinds of commitments that it is extremely difficult for an eleven-year-old or a fourteen-year-old to have the kind of experience I had.

Years Later: Giving Back to Boy Scouts

Boy Scouts took on a new dimension for me as a parent, and I had a chance to give back to Scouting by coming into a leadership role. In 1966 my parents and our family were living in Fairfax, Virginia, and we attended the Providence Presbyterian Church. The pastor, Rev. Holmstrup, heard from my father that I had been an Eagle Scout. He came and told me that the Boy Scout troop at the church was falling apart. He wanted me to please come and be the Scoutmaster. I agreed, provided that I got some help from other members of the church.

As it turned out, one member, Jay McConnell and a mother of one of the boys were both of a great help. They did all the paperwork and tended to the administrative details. My job was to run the meetings and go on hikes with the boys. I brought a different spirit to those outings than the boys had been used to. In previous campouts the troop leaders would set up a picnic table and do all the cooking while the boys played baseball. On the first hike I made it very clear that each patrol would do its own cooking. What a calamity at first. The boys were totally disorganized. They made very few plans, and one patrol even ended up with nothing to eat except chocolate pudding. Of course, it was partly my fault because I had erroneously assumed that this troop was just like the one I had been in twenty–five years earlier in Takoma Park, Maryland. I discovered later that many troops in our area were just like this one at Providence Presbyterian Church.

For the next six weeks, the Wednesday night troop meetings were dedicated to camping instructions such as cooking, meal planning, and packing. The next campout was a huge success. What I saw once again was that the patrol method really works— about eight boys working together to make things happen for the benefit of the group. From then on, I discovered that I didn't have to bring my own food because all the patrols invited me to join them at their meals.

I also had some additional leadership join me. Within three months, three outstanding scout leaders showed up and wanted to participate. They all said they had heard about our troop from friends of their boys. It was about this time in my life that I was beginning to realize that my angels were working for me. All four of us as leaders got along very well.

We had a troop overnight hike once–a–month, and I went along for about half of them. Bagley's Farm was our favorite campground. Dr. Bagley and his four medical partners were clients of my accounting practice. His farm had a large pond for boating, fishing, and bird study. It also had a deep running creek which was great for swimming. On Sunday mornings we always had a little church/Sunday school service. I would give a little sermon and frequently we would have questions-and-answers among the boys and me.

When he was only nine, our older son Kenneth started going on some hikes, and he joined the troop when he was eleven. He became a member of the "Rat Patrol" which was made up of his friends from our immediate neighborhood. We didn't do patrol hikes as I had done as a boy with my patrol, but sometimes I would go on a hike with our family and some of Ken's friends.

One year we hiked the C&O Canal from one end to the other. It extends along the Potomac River for about 160 miles from Georgetown in Washington D.C. to Cumberland, Maryland. When the canal was built in 1845, it was originally intended to go all the way to Pittsburgh. Our Boy Scout troop's trip was broken down into six segments, each of two or three days of hiking, with the segments completed several weeks apart. After the completion of each segment, a scout received a patch for his uniform sash.

For this multi-part adventure along the C&O Canal, the troop leaders—including me—prepared talks about the historic spots we would be visiting. We all felt like soldiers in the Civil War, particularly at Sharpsburg, Maryland—site of a famous and bloody Civil War battle on September 17, 1862—also known as the Battle of Antietam.

Camp Goshen

Every year the whole troop would go for a week to Camp Goshen, a Boy Scout camp in the Shenandoah Valley, about twenty-five miles southwest of Staunton, Virginia. I went every year, and at least one other leader would also go. The parents particularly liked it because they could get rid of their kids for a week and go somewhere else themselves. One year we had a new scout who had just turned eleven, and he had never been away from home. The first day at camp he came to me crying and said he was sick and wanted to go home. I called his home and found out that his parents had gone to England for a week. I told the boy he would have to hang in there for a few days and we would see what we could do. I then met with the patrol leaders and said they had to make this kid happy. They did a great job and the boy was fine. This kind of camaraderie and support is what I think Scouting is all about for the boys.

Since we had a mess hall at Camp Goshen and meals were prepared for us, the boys had more time to participate in various activities such as boating and swimming. Most boys worked on merit badges. This was a perfect opportunity to earn the more difficult badges such as cooking and pioneering.

There were about six troops at Goshen at any given week. Each night all the troops would get together and have a big campfire. Every night a different troop put on a skit. One year our troop put on the "Truth or Momo" skit that my patrol had done in 1948. It went over really well. It made me wish that Ed could have been there to see it.

I went to Camp Goshen for six consecutive years, and I enjoyed it every time. In my final year something rather momentous happened for me. I was in my tent smoking cigarettes, and some of the older boys were with me smoking, too. I had been a smoker since my freshman year in college and had tried to quit several times. One of the boys said "Mr. D., would you please buy me some cigarettes? I'm all out."

I replied, "No. You boys shouldn't be smoking."

But this boy was not going to let me off easily, and he came back with, "But you smoke. Why can't we?"

Without thinking I said, "I'll tell you what, as of this moment I have quit smoking." And I threw my cigarettes into the field. It was a dramatic gesture, but it was seemingly lost on at least one of the boys who promptly went and salvaged them for himself.

It wasn't until after they left that I realized what a commitment I had made. I can see now that I quit that day because I was feeling guilty about smoking with the boys. And this decision seemed to have a big impact on at least some of those boys. On the bus trip home they sang a song about Mr. D. giving up smoking. And the following week at troop meeting, everyone was asking whether I had taken up smoking again. Some of the boys were even taking bets. Knowing that, there was no way I could start up again. But within a week, I had no desire to smoke again. Was this angels at work again? These days, whenever I'm talking to someone who says they want to give up smoking, I tell them this story and suggest that they tell all their friends that they have quit. If you keep it a secret, it's too easy to start up again.

Scouting Comes to an End

But things were now coming to a point of closure for me with Scouting. The following spring I gave it up because it felt like something was coming to a natural end, and I needed to be able to gracefully accept that fact. Most of the boys I was close to had dropped out. Many of the boys had stayed in until they were sixteen, which was quite unusual. In fact we weren't getting many new, younger scouts because we had too many older scouts, and the young boys didn't feel at home with our troop. There were also quite a few new troops starting up in the neighborhood, so we weren't really needed. We had a little ceremony and everyone said goodbye. Many of the older boys who had dropped out came by and expressed their appreciation.

Scouting made a big impression on my life—both as a boy and then as a grown man. Early in my life, before I was a Boy Scout, I didn't have many friends because we moved around so much, and I was always "the new kid." I was also very small and not very athletic, and that made it hard to feel like I fit in. But Scouting helped me make friends, and it gave me a lot of self-esteem. I also learned how to become a leader and got experience in caring for other people.

One of the most important lessons I learned about leadership is that it's often like a two-sided coin. On the one hand a good leader must be strict and provide structures that will be respected. But on the other hand, a good leader must focus on the well-being of his followers. I have discovered that when people know that their leaders are fair and looking out for their best interests, they are likely to cooperate. I have tried to keep this in mind throughout my business career and fatherhood.

Chapter 5

Making Money: Age 10 to 21

Ever since he was a boy, making money was a natural part of Don's life. He wasn't afraid to deal with money, and he always saw business as an honest way to serve the needs of people and to earn a living to support his family. In fact, his story is quite remarkable in that it was his businesses that kept the family afloat when he was a teenager.

Reading these stories of Don's various business adventures—and that's how they always seem, true adventures of being creative in the world—you cannot help but be struck by this boy's tenacity and willingness to take prudent risks. Whether it's going door-to-door to sell magazine subscriptions or building a miniature egg sales empire in Washington, D.C., Don's life shows a remarkable quality of trust. He knew that if he would work hard and trust the invisible hand of Spirit—the angels—then economic success would be the result. Sure there were bound to be challenges and tests, even ethical dilemmas, such as a dishonest produce manager wanting Don to join him in cheating.

Money is energy. And by keeping a clear ideal of honesty and industriousness, business is simply a creative way of working with the universal Law of Supply. And by bringing one's own integrity to that monetary energy, the Universe supplies an abundant return.

The stories in later chapters of this book involve considerably larger sums of money than do the stories here from Don's childhood and teenage years. But the pattern is set in Don's early ventures into being a young businessman. Everything that followed in his adult life came from the intentions and hard work that he demonstrated early on.

❀

I didn't keep my paper route very long after moving to Whittier Street. It was too restrictive on my time, considering all of my Boy Scout activities. But instead of the paper route, I started a magazine subscription sales business. I had read somewhere about how you could send away and become an agent for a company that handled a variety of magazines. I thought that would be a good way for me to make money, and so I went around just in my neighborhood, and I knocked on doors to sell magazine subscriptions. I could make three or four dollars from a successful sales call. I also kept a file which showed when people's subscriptions would be running out, so I could go back to them for renewals. I think this sales business lasted for only about a year.

I also made money taking care of lawns. I took care of our own yard, and took a personal interest in making it look good. Then I began to pick up accounts with other people in the neighborhood, most of them had fairly small yards that wouldn't make it too hard for me with my old push lawn mower.

But one customer stood out. She lived farther out and would come and pick me up—driving out to get me and taking me to her estate, where I would use a power mower. I really liked this because I had never used a power mower before. While I was working she would bring lunch out to me, and I would get to take a swim in her pool, too. This was high living for a 13–year–old who never had a whole lot of money. And the $5 she would pay me each time was good money.

Getting Jobs in the World of Business

By the time I was fourteen, I began to look for jobs working in commercial establishments. I was old enough now that I could be hired for work like this. First I got a job in a furniture store. My job was to go around and dust the merchandise. And I was never much of a nit–picking kind of duster. I would dust off all the furniture in the store in thirty minutes, and then I would stand around and watch the customers talk and shop. I think the manager thought I wasn't working very well, so he fired me—not the last time I ever got fired!

Next I got a job in a hobby shop. I was always into building model airplanes and frequently went to this hobby shop in Takoma Park. One day on a whim I asked the owner for a job. I said, "Gee I like it here. Would you like for me to come work for you?"

I was really pleased when he answered, "Yes." He paid me 75 cents an hour. My friends would come and visit me while I was there, and we would just talk and have fun. It was a great job for me, and good for the owner, too. He really loved having me because I would come in for a few hours around dinnertime, and this would free him up so he could go home for dinner or take his wife out.

However, my mother would sometimes get mad at me because she had other things for me to do, and the hobby shop job interfered with our dinner hour. It just seemed like another instance of my mother's unreasonable nature. In fact, I really helped my parents out a lot, and it didn't seem fair that my mother would try to undermine my work commitments at the hobby shop. At home I was taking care of the yard, and not just doing it as drudgery but taking a real personal interest in it. I remember even building a concrete wall to separate two flowerbeds, just to make things look more beautiful. But my mother depended on me, and it was hard for her to share me with an employer. For example, I might have to leave the house to get to my job at the hobby shop, and she would say I couldn't leave until I finished raking the leaves. I would get all upset and very frustrated. Then I would leave and go to work anyway.

I not only was taking care of the lawn at home (for free), I also started a small tomato garden at home, with maybe just half a dozen plants at first. For some reason that I don't fully understand, I was always interested in tomatoes, and for a couple of years I had a small garden there at home before I started expanding it into a business. By the spring of 1947, when I was a 15–year–old and in the 9th grade, I had ideas to go big time and make big

money. The man across the street owned a vacant lot. I went over
and knocked on his door and asked him if I could make use of
that land for the summer. He agreed and even let me use his hose
and water hook–up. That year I cultivated a thousand–square foot
tomato patch with two hundred plants. I went over to the garden
almost every day to weed and water. I was very proud of my crop,
and I made some nice profits from this small business—with the
landowner, of course, getting all the free tomatoes he wanted!

The Egg Business Revisited

In June of 1947 our family found itself in the egg business
again—this time with me older and wiser than during my stint as
a 4–year–old helping Dad. A friend of the family from church, Mr.
Petersen, had a brother in Iowa who sent him eggs every week.
Mr. Petersen sold these eggs to customers who came by his house
to pick them up. He wanted to go on vacation for three weeks and
asked me to take care of these customers while he was away. Four
cases of eggs were sent to our house each week, and I sold them
for one dollar a dozen. Each case had 24 dozen eggs, and I made
about 20 cents a dozen—nearly $5 a case. This almost $20 *a week*
was a lot better than the $30 *a month* I used to make on my paper
routes, and a lot easier than caddying or selling golf balls.

The first week of selling eggs for Mr. Petersen I had about half a
case left over, so I put them in my wagon and peddled them
around the neighborhood. Remarkably I sold them all just along
one block of the neighborhood, so I asked Mr. Petersen's brother
to send me two extra cases the next week. These were easily sold
and thus the de Laski egg business was born.

The following month my tomato crop started bearing fruit. I
would put them in the wagon and sell them along with my eggs.
The tomatoes, though, took some extra care between harvesting
and sales. I remember spreading the tomatoes out on the cellar
floor because if I kept them in a basket, they would crack as they
went through the natural phase of swelling after being picked. Of
course, even though I didn't want the tomatoes to crack, the swell-

ing was a good thing as far as I was concerned as a businessman. As they swelled they got heavier, so there were fewer tomatoes per pound if I kept them around for a few days. Plus the customers got a juicier tomato.

Meanwhile, the egg business continued to grow. My brother Ed had an old red car, and he established a route in another neighborhood and sold a couple of cases each week. Even something that started out just to be fun turned into an opportunity to expand the business. Ed and I went to a lot of baseball games to see the Washington Senators at Griffith Stadium, near Howard University. In those days kids would come up to you when you parked your car for a game, and they would offer to watch your car for 25 cents. We would always park in the same place and got to know a lot of the people around there. One day when we went to a game, Ed happened to have about ten dozen eggs left in the car. After the game was over, we sold all them in a few minutes. From then on, Ed and I would drive down there once a week and we would each make about $20. This was a totally black neighborhood and these eggs were much better than those available in the local grocery stores. We would also give customers credit for one week's purchases. I don't remember ever losing any money by giving credit.

I don't know what caused things to change in years later, but in 1947 we were never afraid to wander around the streets and knock on doors in a black neighborhood. I was just a 15–year–old kid and always had a couple hundred dollars in my pocket.

We continued selling eggs throughout the following school year. When I turned 16 on February 1, 1948, I bought an old Studebaker for a couple of hundred dollars, and was able to sell some eggs wholesale to a restaurant and some delicatessens. Somewhere along the line we started to buy our eggs from Wayne Shetler, a distributor who brought the eggs in from Pennsylvania. We started to "candle" the eggs which involved holding each egg up to a special lantern and giving it a twist. If you could see the yolk go around in the egg, it meant that the white was not firm and therefore the egg was not fresh enough to be a "double A". If you could see blood, the eggs had to be discarded, which happened about

1% of the time. It would take us about 15 minutes to candle one case of eggs.

By the end of that spring, as I was finishing 10th grade and my brother the 12th grade, we were selling about twenty cases a week and making about $100. Ed and I serviced our routes and Mom did a lot of the candling. In April my father had left for a job with the Government in Tokyo and in June we closed down the egg business and went to Tokyo to join him.

For three months Ed and I did a lot together. Ed had taken typing in high school so our father was able to get him a government job. We did a lot of exploring the countryside on bikes and several evenings a week we would go to the officers' club and have cocktails. I was only sixteen, but no one seemed to care. We would frequently double date with two sisters, Katey, age 21 and Marty age 18. Ed would go out in the park and make out with Katey while Marty and I would stay behind and philosophize. Ed was frequently fixing me up with girls, but I was always too scared of them to do anything about it until I met Nancy at Duke.

That September Ed decided he should go to college so he enrolled at the University of Arizona, and I spent the next year and a half visiting various places with my parents, such as Osaka, Nara, and Karazawa. When we returned home in January of 1950, we stopped by the University of Arizona to visit Ed. We met one of the deans, and he said Ed would be right in, but he could not be found. My mother was, of course, very worried and upset, but we had to go on home without knowing where Ed was. When we got home Ed was waiting for us. He explained that he knew he was flunking out, so he and a friend made plans to hop on a banana boat to South America; but in the end, Ed just hitchhiked back to Washington, D.C. In looking back, I find it to be very strange that that there was no communication among the family on what was going on, but that's the way Ed was.

With this return home from Japan in January, 1950, I was now a senior in high school, and the family decided to start up the egg business yet a third time. We called Wayne Shetler and he was willing to work with us again. It was a good thing we did this because my father wouldn't get another job for over four years. Ed enlisted in the army, so it was just my parents and me. We focused primarily on wholesale customers, but I did set up retail routes with some of the kids in the neighborhood. At first our best customers were two Jewish delicatessens. We made deliveries three times a week and all the eggs were " double A" quality. I did the sales solicitations, Mom did most of the candling, and Dad made a lot of the deliveries. One thing nice about the wholesale end of the business was that once you got a customer, follow-on orders were made by phone. There wasn't any issue on price because egg prices were regularly quoted and Mr. Shetler adjusted his prices accordingly.

An Ethical Challenge and Expanding the Business

We also got a very large supermarket for a customer, to which we sold about twenty cases of eggs weekly. A friend of mine in high school was a very talented cartoonist, and he created a poster for this supermarket. The cartoon showed a farmer in a rickety old truck with egg cartons and chickens. The caption said "Direct from the Farm to You."

Then something happened to show me the dark side of business dealings—the potential for dishonesty. One day the produce manager at this very same supermarket wanted to make a deal. He wanted me to charge him weekly for five cases of eggs more than I actually would be delivering. He said that the two of us would split the overcharge. Even though this man was a good business friend of mine, I was very insulted that he would think that I would do this, because I immediately knew that I would not cheat. He said it was a common occurrence, and everybody else did it. He even implied that if I didn't go along with the deal, I might lose him as a customer.

He really gave me no choice. I wasn't about to start being dishonest, and I also wasn't willing to lose this supermarket as a good customer. So I put on my coat and tie and went to the main office and told them all about the deal being offered to me. The management there thanked me, fired the produce manager, and gave me more business after eliminating one of my supplier competitors.

That summer I also got back into the produce business—this time on a much bigger scale than merely selling the tomatoes that I had grown across the street. I would drive about 80 miles in our big old Hudson to southern Pennsylvania and buy corn, tomatoes, and cantaloupes. Getting the tomatoes had one complication, though. All the farmers in that area had contracts which provided that their total crop would be bought by Campbell Soups, and the farmers were not allowed to sell to anybody else. But several farmers let me pick tomatoes after the Campbell pickers had left. They charged me about 75 cents a "pony" (half a bushel) which I could sell for about $4 wholesale to my egg customers. A day's trip to the farms would generally net about $100.

Making Money During College Years

My going off to college didn't mean the end to the business I had started. Our family still depended on that income. So in the autumn of 1950 as I went to Duke University, things simply changed in terms of who did what. Ed was discharged from the army because he was having asthma problems; so he came home, enrolled in the University of Maryland, and helped my parents with the egg business. Mom, who had always been a good businesswoman, got all the orders, with Ed and Dad making deliveries and doing the candling.

The summer after my freshman year, I was back to the egg business, and Ed established an egg route near the University of Maryland. As I recall, the family was now making about $10,000 a year.

At the end of my sophomore year at Duke, I got a summer job at the Takoma Park swimming pool. I was in charge of the refreshment section which included ordering all the supplies. I made 95 cents an hour and had one assistant. This was a very easy 40-hour-a-week job. I was able to help my parents with the egg business during the evenings and early mornings. One of the toughest jobs in the egg business was carrying the egg crates from the alley to the cellar for candling, and then back to the garage to load the car for delivery. The crates weighed about 50 pounds and the distance each way was about 50 yards.

The business continued until the fall of 1954 when Dad got an overseas assignment in Ethiopia. We were in debt to Wayne Shetler for about $5,000 which he forgave in return for us turning over our wholesale accounts to him.

After my junior year at Duke, my summer job was with the Jewel Tea Company. Ed was working in their warehouse, and he told me about the job opening. Jewel Tea was headquartered in Chicago, and they had grocery routes throughout the country. The products were all staples and included coffee, tea, cookies, and crackers. The route men would take orders for delivery two weeks in advance. My initial job was to fill in for route men when they were on vacation, which meant I had a different route every two weeks. But they lost a route man in Alexandria, Virginia, and I was asked to take over this route on a full time basis.

I got to know my customers very well, especially a group of Japanese army wives who had married G.I.s while they were in Japan. I knew a few Japanese words, and we would talk about my time in Japan. By the end of the summer I had doubled the size of my route. Jewel Tea gave me a bonus and offered me a job, after I graduated, as an assistant manager for $6,000 a year. I turned them down because by this time I had decided to become a CPA. But, they must have been pretty impressed with my performance to have made this offer. In fact, after graduating from Duke, it would take me four years before I was making as much money as they had offered. But I was more dedicated toward enhancing my professional development as an accountant, rather than being a corporate manager.

In looking back on those early years of making money, I am certain that I had a lot of help from my angels in all of these business activities. If Mr. Petersen had not asked me to help him with his brother's eggs, I would have never started the egg business. Or the idea of a 15-year-old growing and selling tomatoes in the city. The inspiration for doing that seems to come from some place in myself beyond logic.

When I stop and try to understand this kind of help from the invisible side of life, I know I am not the only one to whom it's directed. I suspect that most people are being offered assistance from angels, but maybe they ignore it and focus their energy instead on the negative side of what's happening to them, such as their poor health or unemployment. My own life experience has shown me there is a better way—and that means being hopeful, trying hard, and being open to the help that comes in surprising ways.

Don as a boy, and with his brother Ed

Don, age 14, with his family at their home on Whittier St. in Washington, D. C.

Don at age 5 with his brother Ed, who is 15 months older

The brothers at age 30 and 31

Don and Ed at age 50 and 51

Don at 17 on the boat trip coming back from a year and a half in Japan

The family home on Whittier St. in Washington, D. C.

Arial view of West Campus, Duke University, 1954

Student management team at WDBS-Radio at Duke.
Don (third from left) is business manager

Portrait photographs of Nancy and Don in 1956,
One year after their marriage

Moments after the wedding ceremony

Don with his kids at Nags Head, North Carolina in 1981

Family portrait in 1983

Don's parents in 1976

Feature article about Deltek in the Washington
Business Journal, with overlay picture of Ken and Don
used in Deltek's information brochure

Childhood family home on Erie Ave.

Nancy and Don 50 years later in front of their first apartment home

Family home on Hidden Creek Dr.
as painted by Nancy de Laski

Jim Gordon, M.D., with kids in Kosovo

Don and Nancy in 1987

Don and Nancy's home in Great Falls, Virginia
on Deerfield Pond Court

Chapter 6

Golf: A Game for All Ages

Sometimes we find an activity or hobby that becomes like a metaphor for life. For Don this has been golf—an activity that was certainly recreational and good exercise for him over the years, but something that came to symbolize the journey of life, with its camaraderie, personal challenge, competitive engagement, and sense of adventure. As Don's personal friend and author Tim Gallwey writes on page 8 of The Inner Game of Golf, "What other game [than golf] invites such tension and mental anguish? Like one's own children, golf has an uncanny way of endearing itself to us while at the same time evoking every weakness of mind and character, no matter how well hidden . . . We either learn to overcome the weaknesses or we are overwhelmed by them. Few games provide such an ideal arena for confronting the very obstacles that impair one's ability to learn, perform, and enjoy life, whether on or off the golf course."

Whether or not you are a golfer yourself, you can find in this chapter some of the themes and principles that we all have to learn in life. Those principles include honestly playing within the rules, striving to reach your own personal best without comparison to others, and accepting how life is a combination of skill and lucky chance.

❀

In the summer of 1946 when I was 14, our family went to visit my maternal grandmother in West Lafayette, Indiana. We were used to going out there about every other year, but my father usually didn't go because he was either working or looking for a job. It was always great to see Uncle Lyle, his son Bud, and Junior (Uncle Oscar); but unbeknownst to me at the time, this year with them would be something special—my introduction to a game that has been with me ever since.

That year everyone went to my mother's birthplace, Portland, Indiana, for a family reunion. Junior was driving his big Cadillac. My grandmother was in the back seat, and she kept saying how fast all the other cars were going by—but actually, Junior was driving about ninety miles an hour! The reunion was at the Elk's lodge, and no alcohol was served, but the men kept going to the back of the lodge where the alcohol flowed. When we got back to West Lafayette, Junior took Bud and me out to the golf course. Junior was so fat he had to stand a long way from the ball in order to see it. Junior lasted only six holes, but that was enough to hook Bud and me for the rest of our lives.

As soon as I got back home after this trip to Indiana, I started playing golf at the Rock Creek Municipal Golf Course. My best friend at school, Eugene Carusi, also took up the game. I was passionate about golf from the start, and I took a lot of lessons from the teaching professional at the course, Al Price. What's more, I intently studied a book by Ben Hogan entitled *Power Golf*. I wanted to find some of the secrets that would make me into a good golfer. Hogan emphasized how it is important to snap your wrists as you meet the ball. I got pretty good at this, and I was able to hit the ball as far as Eugene, even though he was bigger and stronger than I was.

Covering My Expenses as a Golfer

It costs money to be a golfer, and since I didn't have my paper route anymore, I caddied at the golf course in order to cover my expenses. I would "double-up" with two customers simultaneously and carry both bags for eighteen holes, and that would make ten dollars. I generally caddied for a group of policemen who were always there regardless of the weather. I remember caddying one time even while it was snowing, and I had to sweep the greens so the golfers could putt. If my golfer won money in the betting among the group, then I would usually get a five dollar tip.

I was resourceful and found a variety of ways to make money

around the golf course, not just caddying. For example, I would make money by selling golf balls for a dollar each. The trick was to first *find* the balls. Rock Creek Municipal had more than one course, and the fourth hole on the "A" Course was very narrow. I quickly discovered that this was good news for someone like me trying to find lost balls. The tee shots of most players would roll down into a hollow and into the woods where there were a lot of leaves. I would pretend to help look for the balls of people in the group for which I was caddying, but I was really trying to find lost balls from previous players so I could sell those balls.

But sometimes I went a bit further in my effort to create inventory for my used golf ball sales business. I usually saw clearly where tee shots went on that fourth hole, but sometimes I wouldn't tell anyone. If the ball was declared lost, then I knew I could retrieve it later. I remember one time I even went so far as covering a ball up so no one would find it. After we gave up looking for the ball, the golfer left and I put it in my pocket. Later I felt pretty bad about this, and I didn't do it anymore.

In fact that one episode of my not quite telling the truth stands in contrast to the strong sense of courtesy and fairness that the game of golf taught me. I remember one instance in particular to demonstrate this fact. Eugene and I invited our eighth grade math teacher, Mrs. Middlemas, to play golf with us. She had just started to take golf lessons, and we took good care of her out on the course. Admittedly, this was in contrast to what she might have expected because Eugene and I cut up a lot in school, and we had a bad reputation. Out on the golf course Mrs. Middlemas was totally surprised at how nice we were! In fact, she later told all the other teachers about this new side of us, and she even called our parents with compliments. As I think back over this, I can see and appreciate how golf is a wonderful thing for teenagers because it teaches them common courtesy.

But golf was not only giving me lessons in courtesy, it was also a great source of physical exercise for my body. In looking back I find it hard to believe how much walking I did back then. When I went to the golf course after school—which was about twice a week—I would walk a mile from school to the course, play a round of golf which would usually be at least four miles, and then walk home another two miles. Of course, I do remember getting very tired, especially for that final two miles on the walk home. Luckily when I played on weekends, it was a little easier because I could use my bike for the roundtrip from home to the golf course.

Competitive Golf

I played a lot of golf that summer when I was 14, and I entered the ninth grade at Coolidge High School, eager to try my hand at some competitive golf. Eugene and I had become pretty proficient for teenagers, and we were shooting in the mid–80s. We joined the high school golf team, and a new side to my golf life began. The neatest thing about this was that we played all the best courses in the Washington area. We played twice a week starting in the spring and teed off about three o'clock. The Coolidge High School team won about half the time, but it didn't seem all that important to me. I was thrilled with being able to play on these excellent courses and to have the camaraderie of guys my age who loved golf, too.

The following summer those of us on the team went to golf clinics once a week. We would have a lesson and practice in the morning, and then we played eighteen holes in the afternoon. Each week the clinic would be held at a different private golf course. These golf clinics were organized by Frank Emmet, who later organized similar clinics in other parts of the country. He came to be known as "Mr. Junior Golf," and today Tiger Woods has greatly expanded this program. I feel blessed to have been touched by a visionary man like Frank Emmet who realized what a positive influence golf can have in a young person's life.

Our oldest son Ken was introduced to golf when he was about 14 years old. He never got as excited about it as I had, but he has enjoyed it as a social outlet, and does so even to this day. From my own experience as a young golfer and from being a father, I have come to believe that parents should encourage their children to take up golf. These days children are focusing their energy on baseball, football, and soccer, and this pays off primarily when the child is an outstanding athlete—but even then, only for a very short time. Golf, on the other hand, is a game that anybody can play. It can be enjoyed for the rest of your life, and it's a lot easier to play a decent game of golf if you start when you are young.

Golf in Japan

In the year and half I lived in Japan during 1948 and 1949, I played a lot of golf. I would usually ride my bike about five miles each way to the golf course. It was in Japan for the first time that I actually *had* a caddy rather than *being* the caddy. It cost two packs of cigarettes for eighteen holes. American cigarettes were a normal means of exchange, and each American was allowed to buy one carton of cigarettes per week which cost a dollar at the PX. We could sell a carton on the Japanese black market for 1,000 yen. The official rate of exchange was 360 yen to the dollar, so by using cigarettes we got almost three times the normal rate of exchange, which came in very handy for supporting my golf expenses.

I even had a unique golfing adventure as a byproduct of my health challenges with asthma. Early that summer of 1949 I was starting to accumulate a lot of mucus in my lungs, and so my doctor suggested I go to the mountains. Another blessing of asthma! We went to Karizawa, which was about 200 miles west of Tokyo and stayed at a lovely resort hotel. Americans could go to the best resorts and hotels for about $3 a day. We each had our own room and my father came to visit every couple of weeks. I played golf about five times a week and always had the same caddy. He was a teenager and waited patiently for me every day.

After a little more than a year in Japan, we moved back to Washington D.C., and I returned to Coolidge High School, where I became the captain of the golf team. By now I had become even more skilled, and I was shooting in the high 70s. All that golf I had been playing in Japan had started to pay off.

Golf Begins to Take a Backseat

That spring and the following summer I played very little golf except for the high school matches. I had a lot of other interests (especially a wholesale egg business that was described in the previous chapter), and I had gotten used to much better golf courses than Rock Creek, so it was hard to get up enthusiasm for playing at my old municipal course. It had been my starting point, but my life and my golf game had moved on. But because Rock Creek Municipal was where I had first discovered my passion for the game, its memory has stayed with me over the decades. In fact, many years later—in 2002—out of curiosity and nostalgia, I played nine holes there with my friend Scotty Wright. Sadly, only half the clubhouse was left, the once well-groomed tees were mostly dirt and awkwardly sloped, and the fairways were nothing but weeds. Even the greens had deteriorated and were now slightly below average. We only saw one other person playing. I think the city has let the course go downhill because it gets very little play.

My golf life changed by the time I finished high school and went off to college. At Duke University I had planned to play on the university golf team, but then I found out that most of the team members were par shooters, and I didn't have a chance. In fact, golf became a much less important part of my life while at college and during the early years of my career. I played golf only a few times a year, and that was just socially with friends and relatives.

Golf Returns: Country Club Life

With the success of my career, however, golf came back into my life. In 1962 as I passed the milestone of turning 30, my wife Nancy and I were living in our first house in North Springfield, Virginia. We joined the Fairfax Country Club, which was about five miles away. A non–stock membership was only $400 and dues were $50 a month which included unlimited greens fees. Golf carts were now being used by most people, and they cost about $10 a round for two people.

Belonging to a private country club was a whole new experience for the two of us. We went to many parties and played in quite a few bridge tournaments. Nancy and I had been playing bridge since we were in college, so we were happy to have a regular place to play. Since people our age didn't play much bridge in those days, most of our friends at the club were at least ten years older than we were. What's more, bridge became a connection to the golfing community at Fairfax Country Club. Most of the people I played golf with were people I had met at the bridge table.

However, after about fifteen years we dropped out of Fairfax Country Club because the fees went up a lot, and we were no longer using the club very much. I remember one pivotal moment for me: It was a beautiful Saturday morning, and I was looking for my ball after a bad slice into the woods. I suddenly exclaimed to myself that I didn't need this nonsense and would rather be camping with the Boy Scouts. It was time for a change—and not just because golf had lost its sense of adventure and magic for me. Nancy and I were also getting tired of playing bridge there at the country club. Instead of being romantic, we would lie in bed arguing about how we played the various hands that had been dealt to us. (In fact, since leaving Fairfax Country Club, we haven't played bridge more often than a few times a year.)

And so, for more than a decade, golf significantly diminished in my life. But in 1988, when I was 56, I decided I wanted to start playing again. Golf is like that; if you've ever played a decent game, it's very hard to give it up. It's also good exercise and a great way to be involved with friends. I've noticed that men generally need an excuse to get together, and a game of golf can be just that. Women, on the other hand, enjoy getting together to have lunch and jabber.

With this newly rediscovered desire to play golf once again, I joined Westwood Country Club in Vienna, Virginia which was about a fifteen minute drive from our house. The initiation fee was $17,000 and the monthly dues were $250 a month, but it felt like a good investment in something that had been so important in my life earlier. One nice thing about this period of my golf life was having a dear friend who would play frequently with me. Don Lee was my first employee at my accounting firm, and Don was also a member of this club. We played golf together all the time, forming a lifelong friendship that continues to this day. Even though there was a long hiatus in which I lost touch with him for 25 years, I was so happy to learn recently that my former employee and golfing buddy was doing very well operating his own office supply company.

In 1992, we moved to our current home in Great Falls, Virginia, but it was twenty minutes further from Westwood Country Club, so I joined the nearby River Bend Country Club. There was a waiting list at this club, and so I didn't become a full member for five years, so in the meantime I continued my membership at Westwood. Our son Ken and his family lived nearby, and he was also a member at River Bend, so this gave us a wonderful chance to play together more often and to include other friends. There's nothing much better in the game of golf than getting to play with one of your own children.

River Bend was also the site of one thrilling moment in my golf life. In 2000 I got a hole-in-one on the 150-yard third hole. I was playing with a guest, Fred Farmer, who was a longtime friend from college years. In celebration of my hole-in-one, the club gave free drinks to everyone in the restaurant and bar, and I was awarded a cute plaque.

Golf also played a role in how Nancy's and my life unfolded—even leading us to the place that is now our home for five months of every year. In 1990 we were visiting our younger son, David, in Los Angeles, and we decided to drive out to Palm Desert and spend a few days at the Marriot Resort Hotel. They were offering a $75 cash rebate to anyone who would tour their time-share facilities. We went ahead and took the tour, ending up buying two units for $17,000 each. Conveniently, each unit had a nice guest room and bath which could be locked out and made separate from the rest of the unit; thus we could stay two weeks annually for each unit. Of course, many people who bought these time-share units went to different places all over the world each year, but we always went to Palm Desert for four weeks a year. We were beginning to build some ties to the southern California desert and its way of life.

Our best friends from Virginia, Frank and Mary Carter, also bought a time-share unit. They had recently taken up golf so we played a lot together. Most of the other people I played with were strangers who were staying at the hotel. During the second winter in our time-share, I started playing in the Frank Sinatra Celebrity Golf Tournament, and I continued to do so for the next ten years. Each golfer paid $3,500 to play, but we got about $1,200 in various gift items such as golf bags, shirt, etc.—all of which was donated by various companies for this charity tournament. The proceeds went to support a center for abused children, which was established and operated by Barbara Sinatra. Each team had a celebrity and an A, B, C, and D player based on handicaps. On the second day we would get a different celebrity. I played with Robert Stack (Elliot Ness) twice and Ron Masak, of *Murder She Wrote*. Robert was about 80 years old and played a pretty good game. And Ron was at least as memorable. He always had a big group following him because he was always telling stories. But the Sinatra Tournament was about more than just golf. We had a big gala each night, and Frank Sinatra would sing.

Golf Leads to a New Home: The Vintage Club

By this time in my career, I was almost fully retired, and so Nancy and I decided it was time we joined a country club and spend most of each winter in Palm Desert. The weather in the desert is perfect from November through May, and we liked to be near our younger son, David, who has lived in Los Angeles since college.

In November of 1997 we went to Palm Desert to go country club shopping. By that time our business ventures were going extremely well—more about that in later chapters—and we had the financial resources to pick a really nice place for ourselves. Several years earlier we had met a couple, the Tappans, who were members of the Vintage Club, and they had told us that they would be happy to sponsor us. We had heard this club was the best in the Desert, so we went by the sales office to check it out. They put us up in a condo for four days while we looked around. I played three rounds of golf with some of the members, and we ate at the club, all for free.

There were two 18-hole courses—the Desert Course and the Mountain Course—both perfectly manicured with many waterfalls and flowers. I had never seen golf courses like these two. After looking at only two other clubs we decided on the Vintage Club, even though it was much more expensive—a $175,000 initiation fee and annual dues of $17,000. For $850,000 we picked out a 2,700 square foot, two-bedroom condo facing the first hole of the Desert Course. The house was put in escrow while we went through the process of being approved. The sales office threw a little party for us so we could find two more sponsors. Herb Boyer, founder and CEO of Genentec and Jim Berry, who I had played golf with, agreed to be our sponsors, along with Dave Tappan. Bill Gates and his father are also members of the Vintage Club, but they were not at the party.

We returned home to Virginia and the membership committee checked our references and mailed a notice to each of the 476 members. The notice included our other club affiliations and addresses, and it asked for any positive or negative comments from the members. Since nobody knew us, we didn't have any problem. A month later we were told that so far there was no problem, but we still had to come out and meet each of the seven members of the membership committee.

In early January we drove out in our 1992 Mercedes and stayed at our Marriott time-share unit while we went through the interview process. One of the interviewers was Sally Nordstrom, wife of the grandson of the founder of Nordstrom Company, the fashion specialty retailer. A week later we were approved and we settled on our house and moved in. This approval process reminded me of when I was rushed for the Sigma Phi Epsilon fraternity in college. Some people who went through the same steps we had to go through complained and were insulted by the process.

Of course they were generally turned down. I've often wondered what Bill Gates went through.

After three years in that home each winter, we were ready for a change, and we moved to a 3,800 square-foot patio home which cost $2,300,000. It had a private pool and an extra room which I used as an office and an extra guest room. And then, three years later we moved again at the Vintage Club, this time buying a 5,900 square-foot house for $4,500,000. In the back there was a nice covered sitting area with a large grill and a beautiful pool and spa. Even though we could walk out onto the golf course, we had a lot of privacy. We had a very large master bedroom and dressing area. There was a very nice guest room, plus my office which had a pull out couch for guests. There was also a detached casita with separate bath and cooking area. Everything was furnished exquisitely in a kind of desert décor. It's very easy to move at the Vintage Club because most places are totally furnished. With this house, we had about seven overnight visits a year from friends and relatives who stayed about three to five nights.

With our life at the Vintage Club during those retirement years, golf once again became a significant part of my life. I played 18 holes about five times a week. About once a week I played with a regular foursome. And David took up golf, so we played twice whenever he came out. Golf provided fellowship with other club members, plus a little bit of informal competition, too. There was always a little tournament about twice a week with about 25 people who would each put up $20.

Golf, though, never became something for Nancy and me to share. She took a lot of lessons and tried hard, but finally she quit altogether. She often said that she found the game very boring. If I played the way she did, I would be bored, too. But she was involved in a lot of other activities, including her artistic expression through painting, as well as membership in a book club and a Bible study group. Nancy was always into the weather and the main reason she liked to go to the Vintage Club was the incredible weather. From November to May the lows are in the mid-fifties and the highs are in the mid-eighties. The humidity is low and there is very little rain.

Playing golf at the Vintage Club was golf at a whole different level than I had ever experienced before moving there. Tee times are not required because there are two courses and only 475 members. We had our golf carts in our garage at home with all our clubs and necessary accessories, so all we had to do was get in our cart and drive five minutes to the course. Because everyone owns a home here, we were always playing golf with people who lived in the area and not strangers or people who rent. It made it more like a big family.

I played in quite a few club tournaments, one of which was called the "Bandidos." Members not only had a stake in winning themselves, but they could also bid to buy half of each other's teams. You paid $1,000 and automatically got half of your own team, and you could also bid for the *other* half of your own team or someone else's.

One year's tournament—the third annual "Bandidos"—was especially memorable. My partner was Bill Gross, a multi–billionaire who ran large bond funds. Bill has a beautiful $30 million home overlooking the sixteenth green on the Mountain Course. The first day of the tournament was 18 holes, played as "best ball," meaning that the team score for each hole was the best score on that hole for either player on the team. The second day was again 18 holes, and this time both golfers counted all their strokes. The third day was a playoff in which the three best teams of each of the six flights competed. (Each "flight" was a skill level, so that each team could be in a flight with other players of about the same proven ability.)

Bill and I each had about an 18 handicap—an average of shooting one over par for each of the 18 holes on the course. That is just about exactly what we shot on the first two days of that year's tournament. This qualified us for the 3–hole playoff the following day in which we would be competing with other teams from all six flights. The "equalizer" was that because of our handicaps of 18, we were entitled to six strokes altogether that would be subtracted from our score.

As we teed up on the first hole, Bill was so nervous he dropped his club then knocked his ball in the water. Luckily his next tee shot was fine. I hit a good drive off the tee, but then I had bad second and third shots. My fourth shot went over the green and into the sand trap. I hit it back onto the green and ended up with a seven for the hole. Bill hadn't done much better than me on that first hole. After his poor start of hitting his tee shot into the lake—costing him a two shot penalty—Bill ended up on the green and two putted for a six. So after that first par-4 hole, we had already used up five of our handicap strokes and were one–under–par, instead of the six–under–par that our handicap strokes had allowed us to start with.

The next hole was a par-3, and we both hit our tee shots 30 feet from the pin. I sunk my putt for a birdie, and he two–putted for a par. We headed off to the third and final hole with a joint score of two–under–par. On that last hole, a par-5, Bill sunk a thirty–foot putt for a birdie 4, and I managed to get bogie 6. Our final score of two–under–par won the tournament by one stroke. We divided $35,000, and we each got a big trophy. We gave our caddy a $2,000 tip, which he used to go to college, and we never saw him again. The other golfers in the playoff received between $5,000 and $15,000. Golfers love to win money on the golf course regardless of how much money they already have in the bank.

Two years ago was another memorable moment for me at the Vintage Club. I hit a four wood on the 190–yard par three fifth hole on the Desert Course, and it went in the hole. Another hole-in-one! Instead of getting a plaque, I got $5,000. This money came from a special pool created by the golfing members and spouses who pay $10 every time anyone gets a hole–in–one. I've always participated by putting my $10 into the pool, and this time I won.

In more recent years I have not played golf as often when I am back in the Washington, D.C. area. The weather between mid–May and November is frequently too hot or it's raining. Sometimes I get together with Ken or other friends for a game, or I might go out to the practice tee. Many of my friends at the Vintage Club tell me that when they go home for the summer months, they also play very little golf even though they are a member of another club. The reason is probably not just the weather back home. The course and the overall situation at the Vintage Club are so good that we lose interest in playing golf anywhere else.

As I get older, I'm trying to play golf for the sheer enjoyment of it and not worry about what I shoot. I have a friend in Santa Fe, Rick Phillips, who used to be a facilitator for the Transcendental Meditation teacher, Maharishi Mahesh Yogi. He's a very good golfer, and he says golf to him is a Zen game and that one should frequently meditate on the golf course.

Another friend of mine, Tim Gallwey, says pretty much the same thing on page 14 of his book *The Inner Game Of Golf*. "The secret of gaining control over our bodies lies in gaining some measure of control over our minds . . . Thus, the challenge of golf lies as much in the relatively unexplained aspects of the Inner Game of Golf as it does the Outer Game . . . The only question is whether we are playing the Inner Game consciously and whether we are winning it or losing it."

Chapter 7

College Life and Finding a Wife

Each of us is special, and each has a life's destiny. Leaving home and going out into the world—such as what happens to an eighteen-year-old heading off to college—is a unique time for self-exploration. It's a scary time, too, when a young person "leaves the nest" and starts to be known simply for who he is as an individual, and not as part of a childhood family.

Don's life story tells of a young man looking to find what makes him unique. By some standards maybe he didn't seem so special. His high school counselor discouraged him from even trying to get into a top-notch school, labeling him as only middle-of-the-road as a student. And once Don proved the counselor wrong and made it into Duke University, he found that he was rather "nerdy"—to use his own self-description—someone who hardly matched the archetypal "big man on campus." But what is lovely about this part of Don's biography is the way that he discovered many, many things about himself that were extra-ordinary. In his own way he became his own kind of "big man on campus"—someone who was respected by students of both genders for his honesty in relationships, someone whose entrepreneurial spirit rescued the campus radio station from obscurity, and someone so full of devotion to the woman he loved that he won her heart.

As you read about Don's life between the ages of eighteen and twenty-three, think back to those years in your own life story. The details of your life are no doubt quite different, but you can probably find the same themes—finding a way to "be seen" in the adult world, finding the courage to make commitments, and trusting that your life really does have a destiny.

❊

I never thought much about where I wanted to go to college, but my mother wanted me to go to Duke University. She knew they had a good hospital, and she was concerned about my asthma. The counselor at Coolidge High School told my mother that I would never get into Duke because my grades were only slightly above average. Nevertheless, my mother and I wrote a long letter setting out all I had accomplished, and to our surprise I was accepted.

I found out later some of the reasons why Duke accepted me. First, Coolidge was one of the most respected public high schools in the country. Also in my favor was that I had a rather unique business background, and I had lived in Japan where I was active in school activities. Fortunately, at that time Duke didn't require SAT exams, which was good for me because I typically did not do well on exams of that nature. Duke prided itself on selecting well-rounded applicants from many parts of the country, and apparently I fit what they were looking for. Financially, it was within reach for us, too, with a yearly tuition of only about $1,500 a year including room. In contrast, by 2010 this annual tuition and housing had reached about $50,000.

First Impressions of the Campus

I had applied to and got accepted by Duke University sight-unseen. Months later when I showed up on campus I was awe-struck. I first drove onto campus with my parents a few days before the start of my freshman year. The grounds were so remarkably beautiful. As you drive in, you face the very large and famous Duke Chapel, which is especially beautiful to see lit up at night. The Chapel is known for its grand façade, soaring roof, and lovely stained-glass windows. As the University describes it with freshmen like me in mind, "The tower rises above the trees, providing a point of reference for disoriented first-year students."

The academic facilities seemed equally impressive to me as we drove through campus that day. Classrooms are on both sides of a long quadrangle to the right of the Chapel. At the far end of this quadrangle is the campus entrance to the Duke University Hospital. Student dormitories are on both sides of a long quadrangle to the left of the Chapel, with the stadium and athletic fields beyond the far end of this quadrangle. The Duke Gardens are on the right just before reaching the classrooms. And creating a unified feeling for the campus, all of these buildings are made of stone. The engineering and physics buildings are made of brick and are a short walk behind the Chapel. All of this is referred to as the West Campus. The East Campus is about two miles away and has women's dormitories and additional classrooms.

In 1950 as I started my freshman year, the West Campus dormitories were for men and the East Campus dormitories were for women. All of the freshmen men lived in one quadrangle called Kilgore. As I began, the University had only about 4,000 undergraduate men and 1,000 undergraduate women, plus about 500 women in the nursing school and about 1,000 graduate students.

I signed up for a course of studies toward a bachelor of arts degree, with a major in accounting. During my first two years at Duke, I was required to take mostly liberal arts courses. My freshman courses were algebra, chemistry, psychology, religion, English, and Spanish. Each course met three times a week, and chemistry also had a three-hour lab weekly. We also had to have gym three afternoons a week which would involve swimming, track and field, wrestling, tumbling and various exercises. This was really good for me. In my freshman year my weight increased from 118 to 130 pounds.

Getting Into the Rhythm of Campus Life

Overall I enjoyed my first semester at Duke. I felt good except for one bout with illness. In the early part of my freshman year I got mononucleosis (mono). This was a common ailment at colleges and was referred to as the "kissing disease." I wasn't doing any kissing at that time, so I probably got it from my roommates—but not from kissing them! My lungs became filled with mucous, and I got a low-grade fever every afternoon. At the same time, my asthma was pretty bad. I went to the Duke University Hospital which was right on campus, and I asked for some prednisone. The doctor sat me down and told me that they give prednisone and other steroids only to old people to keep them alive. He pointed out that the adrenal glands become dependent on steroids, and the immune system could be severely damaged. Instead, he prescribed some antibiotics and admitted me to the hospital in the student section. For two weeks I walked to classes from my hospital bed. My mother always wanted me to go to Duke because of the availability of good medical care, and it seemed to be paying off right here in my first semester.

I fell into the routine of student life. Most mornings I had an 8:00 a.m. class, but that was not bad because I could walk to class in about five minutes and pick up breakfast in the cafeteria along the way. Most of our grades were based on the final exams, and about half the freshman class of men would flunk out each year. Back in the 1950s most major universities operated this way. Fortunately, I got through that first year with about a C+ average.

Athletics was a big thing on campus, even back then. We all looked forward to the Saturday afternoon football games. In those days the Duke football team was usually nationally ranked, and we had a pretty good team in my freshman year, winning seven games and losing three. It was really exciting when we beat our biggest rival, the University of North Carolina Tarheels. This large rivalry was due partly to the fact that Duke was regarded as the "Yankee School of the South," bringing in students as it did from all over the country, but especially from the mid-Atlantic and New England states.

The main thing that happened in my second semester was joining the Sigma Phi Epsilon fraternity. Rushing cannot begin until the second semester, and only for those students who have at least a C average. All fraternities are located in dormitories on the West Campus, and they each have a main meeting room and a card room, the cost of both being paid by the fraternity members. I met a Sig Ep named Art Judd at a Sunday school class that I attended with my father, who had come down to visit. This was the only time I attended Sunday school while at Duke, but I wanted to impress my father. The fortunate byproduct of that one Sunday at church was my friendship with Art, who invited me to a rush party at the start of second semester. The Sig Eps were a small fraternity, and they were pretty desperate to find new members. I was a pretty nerdy guy: five feet eight inches, 118 pounds, glasses, and attending Sunday school.

During the rushing parties it was customary for some of the brothers on the first floor to serve drinks to selected rushees. Art put the word out *not* to let de Laski see the alcohol. After I became a Sig Ep, the brothers were very surprised to find that I was a pretty good party boy. I had had a lot of experience with my brother at the officers' club in Japan.

Once I was in the fraternity, I had a very nice social life. I was still very shy and nervous around girls, but my fraternity brothers got me a lot of blind dates. I had more blind dates than the other brothers because the girls I liked would always turn me down when I asked them out for a second date. After our dates the guys in the fraternity would have a few drinks and play bridge in the card room. The next morning I would frequently fall asleep in my 8:00 chemistry class. I realized near the end of the year that I didn't know any chemistry, so I went to the library and studied for three solid days, starting at page one of the text. Remarkably, I did well on the final and got a B in the course.

In my sophomore year I lived at the Sig Ep dorm, and my roommate was Newell Yaple from Columbus, Ohio. One time his sister came down to visit, and I had a couple of dates with her. I fell madly in love and wrote her a lot of letters after she returned to Ohio. On spring vacation our family drove up to Bucyrus, near Columbus, to visit my Uncle Cline. I got dropped off in Columbus to visit Newell's sister. We had a date, and she very sweetly explained that she had a regular boyfriend. I must not have been too upset about this rejection because now I can't remember her name. What's more, putting my love interests first had not gone over well for that family trip. I heard reports from my brother that

Uncle Cline was angry that I didn't visit him.

Another connection from fraternity life also proved to be very important to my college life. One of my fraternity brothers named Neil Andon was involved with the Duke radio station—WDBS. This station broadcast music and school news by cable to the dorms on the East and West Campuses. One of the students working at the station was David Hartman, who later became the first anchor on the ABC television show *Good Morning, America.*

I had no aspirations myself to be an on-the-air broadcaster, but I knew where my talent lay, and I agreed to become the business manager. The only income the station had was a few thousand dollars a year from the University for supplies. I put together a volunteer staff to solicit ads from the local restaurants and clothing stores, who were all very enthusiastic. All the students wanted WDBS to broadcast the "away" football and basketball games because the local stations would not do it. I figured that since the cigarette companies were giving away free cigarettes in the cafeteria lines, they might go for this. Sure enough, Chesterfield Cigarettes put up over $25,000 to pay for the travel expenses of our radio announcers at the football and basketball games. I was a real hero. In the Duke annual that year, the page about WDBS had the caption "From Rags to Riches."

In the middle of all these negotiations on behalf of the radio station, I got a letter from my mother explaining that she could not send me my usual $100 a month because she didn't have any money. But I knew I could find a way to deal with this financial setback. A lot of students had part time jobs which paid about 75 cents an hour, and so I got a job at the Duke Hospital typing doctors' reports. I still can remember many of the reports which ended with the words, "so and so expired at such and such a time."

This job at the hospital meant that I needed to make some changes. I went and told Dr. Fearring, dean of student activities, that I could no longer be business manager of WDBS because I needed to work. He didn't want me to leave, so he got me a $2,000 loan, which I paid off after I graduated. I was a very slow typist and was about to be fired anyway, so it's just as well that I found a way to quit that job at the hospital.

In my junior year I continued working with the radio station and participated in many social activities. The fraternity frequently had a "cabin" party. We weren't allowed to have drinking parties on campus, so we would go to a cabin in the woods with our dates. The favorite drink was "Purple Jesus," a mixture of grape juice and gin served in a punch bowl. Many of us would drink too much and puke in the woods. Others would bring blankets and make out in the woods. The University required chaperones at all student activities, but we could always find an alum who would look the other way.

Meeting Nancy

At one of these parties a new fraternity brother named Deno Pantalockus had a blind date with a freshman named Nancy Panossian, who was from Arlington, Virginia. Although I had met her at a freshman mixer at her dorm, I really didn't get to speak to her very long. I liked her a lot, and after getting Deno's permission I called her for a date. Nancy and I went to a movie and started dating on a regular basis. Twice a year Duke had what is known as "Joe College Weekend." Well-known bands and performers such as Les Brown and Vaughn Monroe would perform at Friday and Saturday night dances, plus a Sunday concert. With Nancy now in my life, this would be the first time I would be going to this event without a blind date.

That autumn, as Nancy and I had started dating regularly, Duke was having a great football year, having won their first five games. A number of my fraternity brothers were planning to drive up to Charlottesville to see Duke play the University of Virginia, another undefeated team. It just so happened that Nancy needed a ride to Fork Union, just outside of Charlottesville, where her family was having a family get–together.

It turned out to be a big weekend for me. First Nancy and I watched Duke beat Virginia 21 to 7. (In fact, it was on the way to a championship season because even though Duke lost the next two games to Georgia Tech and Navy, they finished up by beating North Carolina and won the ACC championship.) After the game, Nancy spent the night in Fork Union, and I stayed at the Sig Ep house there on the campus at the University of Virginia. They was celebrating homecoming and they had a huge party. There was a conga line which included townspeople and local farmers—the line going throughout the campus and into all the fraternity houses. I had never seen so much drinking. I had heard that UVA was a very big party school, and the next morning I had a pretty bad hangover to prove it. However, I still managed to pick up Nancy in Fork Union *and* meet her parents. That was a big event for me. Her father was probably a little bit leery of me because he wanted his daughter to find a nice Armenian boy at Duke, and I certainly did not match that expectation.

I had never really had a girlfriend before. I had had a few nice dates, and sometimes I would worship a girl from afar. For dates in those first two years at Duke I was always very bashful; and at the end of those dates I would usually try to get the two of us involved in some profound conversation—which really did not advance my social life. But things were changing now for me in the autumn of my junior year with Nancy. About a week after our trip to Charlottesville, she and I went out on a movie date. Afterwards we were sitting outside of her dorm in my car, and I reached over and gave her a kiss. From then on I knew I wanted her for the rest of my life.

Nancy and I dated a lot that year. I confessed my undying love for her and offered her my pin, but she wanted to date others, too. I was lucky in that she did not have a boyfriend at home. That meant that during Christmas, spring break, and the following summer—when both of us returned to the Washington D.C. area and our respective homes—I had her all to myself. Nancy gave me a lot of self-esteem from the boy-girl point of view. She was (and still is) very beautiful, and she liked me a lot. Up to this time I thought that pretty girls didn't like me very much because I was small and skinny and they preferred strong, good-looking men. But with Nancy I discovered that I could make up for my small size by being able to carry on interesting conversations about attitudes and emotions.

But I also had in–depth conversations with many of my fraternity brothers. One of my best friends was Bryce Douglas who everyone called Doug. One day he admitted to me that he was gay, which is the first time I had heard the word "gay" in this context. Gays in college usually stayed "in the closet" until after they graduated. Doug told me a lot about his experiences and introduced me to a number of other gays at Duke. He referred to me as his sister, which in gay jargon means a close friend who is heterosexual. Doug explained to me that homosexuality was generally caused by having a very dominant mother and a father who did not get involved much in the raising of the children. This situation was referred to as mamism. I definitely grew up in this situation, but I was lucky to have an older brother who was a good role model. I don't think this theory about the cause of homosexuality is very prevalent today.

Nancy and I did a lot of dating the summer after I had just finished my junior year and she, her freshman year. As I mentioned in a previous chapter, I had a job working for Jewel Tea Company, doing delivery routes in Alexandria. At the end of the day I would drive my truck over to Nancy's house in Arlington and pick her up. I thought we were having a lot of fun that summer, but as it came time to get ready to head back to Duke, she announced to me that she wanted to break up, but remain good friends. This was very crushing to me, but I could understand her situation. She had just turned nineteen and had had very little experience with men other than me. I knew she loved me a lot, but she frequently said that since she was so lucky the first time around there was no telling what else was out there. She was so beautiful I knew she would have no trouble getting dates.

Sure enough, once she was back at Duke for her sophomore year, she soon had a regular boy friend named Frank Greene. I would frequently see them together at the Duke football games and the dances on Joe College Weekend. Even though I was very sad, I remained positive and knew that someday Nancy would be

my wife. I remember one time I had a date with a very nice looking student who knew Nancy. We were sitting in my car outside
my date's dorm waiting for the curfew, and suddenly it became
quite obvious to me that she was hot to trot. I explained to her
that I was in love with Nancy and that I was waiting for her to get
tired of dating other men. This date was very impressed, and it led
to a long conversation about true love.

Nancy had really meant it when we broke up and she said that
she wanted to remain good friends—it hadn't just been a brush-
off line. During this period when she was dating others, I would
visit Nancy whenever I could, and we would frequently have long
telephone conversations. Calls had to be made from phone booths
in the dorm, so we would establish a time after curfew. One of us
would call the other, and she would slink down in the booth so no
one could see her. We would talk for a long time, and she would
tell me all about her dates. Since she told me that intimacy with
her dates did not exceed kissing, I figured that I still had a chance.

Finally I won her back, and on Valentine's Day Nancy accepted
my pin. The rest of my senior year was complete bliss. Not only
was Nancy now committed to me, but also I was elected president
of Sigma Phi Epsilon. Dean Cox asked Nancy and me to be the
chaperones at the annual Sig Ep Ball in Raleigh, N.C. for our fraternity branches at Duke, Wake Forest, the University of North
Carolina, and North Carolina State University. I took this assignment very seriously. In fact, that night at the ball I had to say "no"
firmly to a fraternity brother who was invited to spend the night
in the room of a freshman girl. This grown-up side of me started
to be recognized in many other ways, too. For example, many of
Nancy's friends soon started coming to me for advice concerning
their boyfriends, and I became known as Uncle Don.

Graduation and Getting Engaged

Of course, during this period my life was not just my social life
and my work at the radio station. There were also academics. Most
of the classes I took in my junior and senior years related to ac-

counting since that was my major. I was allowed only one elective, and I chose a graduate course on Eastern religions. I picked this one because when I lived in Japan I had visited many Buddhist temples, and I had long been interested in reincarnation. In retrospect, I can see that this one elective course had a strong impact on my life. In contrast to most all my other classes in college, I felt very comfortable in participating in class discussions. My professor was Dr. Braibanti, and twenty-five years later he was still teaching at Duke and our daughter Kathleen was one of his teaching assistants. Visiting Kathleen at that time, I stopped in to see him, and I told him how much his course had meant to me. He remembered me well and really appreciated my compliments.

In retrospect, I can see what an important mentor figure Dr. Braibanti was for me. I believe that my angels guided me to take his course as my one and only elective in my final years at Duke. He inspired me about the study of Eastern religions, and his open-mindedness and scholarship helped me in my adult life to feel safe in shaping my own personal understanding of spirituality, which blends what I see as the best in Western and Eastern religions.

I graduated from Duke with a C+ average and my parents and brother came down for the graduation. Ed had graduated the day before from the University of Maryland. It was quite a weekend to celebrate for my family.

College life quickly transitioned to work life. In June I went to work for Ernst & Ernst as a junior accountant at an annual salary of $3,600. Back in those days, aspiring CPAs had to serve as apprentices for three years at very low salaries with lots of overtime. But I was highly motivated to get my career going, in part because of my hopes for getting married.

During that summer Nancy and I talked a lot about marriage. I knew that Nancy was very much in love with me, but she wasn't ready to disappoint her father. He had his heart set on having an Armenian son-in-law, even though both this first and his second marriages were to non-Armenian women.

This conversation between Nancy and me concerning disappointing her father went on *ad nauseum*. So one day I went down to the Hecht Company, a department store in Washington, and made credit arrangements for buying a diamond engagement ring. The next day, on the way out to dinner with Nancy, I stopped at this store and told Nancy to come inside because I had a surprise for her. I took her to the jewelry counter and told her to pick one out. She looked at the diamond rings and finally said "I'll take this one." We went back to her house to announce our engagement and invited her parents out to dinner to celebrate. From the back seat, I can still remember my future father–in–law saying, "It's never too late to change your mind, dear."

Nancy decided to go to summer school at George Washington University so she could graduate a semester early, and we set a wedding date for January 1956. About three months later, we decided we didn't want to wait that long and thought it would be better if we got married in the early summer of 1955—the plan being that Nancy would then return to Duke for her last semester as a married woman. But first we had to get permission from Dean Brinkley so that Nancy could still live in the dorm. Up to that time a married woman had never lived in a Duke dorm. Fortunately I knew the dean quite well because she served on the board of the Duke radio station. She told me that she didn't want anyone to see any of "her girls" enter a Durham hotel with a man. After I promised that I wouldn't come within a hundred miles of Durham while Nancy was at Duke, she gave her consent.

In the summer just after I graduated from Duke, my father got a two–year government assignment in Ethiopia. The only employment he had had in the previous five years was his assistance in the egg business. So my parents rented out their house and moved to Africa. I moved into an attic apartment at a friend's house in the neighborhood, and I started attending George Washington Law School at night. I wasn't really planning to become a lawyer, but I needed something to do with my time. In looking back, I now realize how important it was for me at this time to be engaged to be married. My brother had married a year earlier and, with my parents gone, I probably would have been quite lonesome and would have had to worry about who I was going to date. Since I was about to become a married man, I needed to focus my attention on my career.

Our Wedding

Nancy finished her junior year at Duke, and we were married on July 9th, 1955 at the Mt. Olivet Church in Arlington, Virginia. My parents felt bad that they couldn't be there, so they asked our minister, Rev. Shearer from the Takoma Park Presbyterian Church to participate in the ceremony. They even sent us $300 for our honeymoon. I was amazed at the number of people who attended the wedding. More people will attend a wedding in which both husband and wife are young and from the same area. There were many of our friends from college as well as the neighborhoods in which we grew up. Five of my friends from college showed up. And we had lots of relatives from both sides, including my Uncle Dwight who drove from West Virginia. However, Uncle Dwight and his family missed the wedding itself because they forgot about the time difference. In those days many farming communities, such as southern Virginia and West Virginia, did not go on daylight saving time. But at least they got in on the reception.

Nancy and I left the reception at about ten o'clock, and on our way to the Poconos we stopped at a hotel in Baltimore. I had brought a large cooler with a bottle of champagne on lots of ice. On the way to the room it leaked all over the floor. The next morning the bottle was almost full. We couldn't put the cork back in the bottle so we had to throw it out. Our honeymoon was on a beautiful lake at a place called Vacation Valley. Since we were both in our second week of a six-week summer school and taking two courses, we had to do a fair amount of studying during the honeymoon.

After our honeymoon we moved into a one bedroom apartment for $75 a month at Colonial Village, in Arlington, Virginia. I went back to work at Ernst & Ernst, plus my night school classes at George Washington Law School. And Nancy returned to summer school during the day at George Washington University. I found it was easier and less expensive to use the bus than to drive since the bus ride was only about 15 minutes. This is the only time in my life that I ever used a bus on a regular basis. That fall Nancy returned to Duke and found a ride to come up to Arlington about once a month, plus we saw each other at Thanksgiving and Christmas. And hard though it was, I lived up to my promise to Dean Brinkley not to visit Nancy at Duke.

Chapter 8

Early Married Life and Starting a Career

There is no "owner's manual" for a marriage. Each couple has to discover for themselves what makes them a couple and how they weave together their talents and hopes for the future. Don and Nancy's early married years were in the late 1950s, a time culturally that is different in many ways than what we see in the 21st century. Back then, there were clearer roles that men and women were expected to fill—the husband as career-oriented bread-winner, the wife as mother and homemaker. But even within those roles there was considerable room to be creative and discover what it means to live cooperatively and lovingly with another person. Marriage truly is a workshop for soul growth. It is also important for a couple to have a network of support—such as through family—in which to meet the setbacks and the unexpected opportunities that arise.

These are also years for starting a career—with all its "starts" and "stops." We can sometimes get an inkling of what our future holds— what it feels as if we are called to be and to do. For example, Don felt strongly that he wanted to be part of something in which he would really be making a difference. And yet those intuitions and feelings sometimes do not manifest in quite the way we expect. Destiny usually has its own plan and purposes for us, and the best we can do is stay flexible, hopeful, and creative as opportunities arise.

❋

Having completed all her course work, Nancy returned from Duke in January, 1956. We were both glad to end this period of being married but living hundreds of miles apart. Once back in the Washington, D.C. area, she got a job as a secretary at the Equitable Life Assurance Society at an annual salary of $3,900, the same as I was making at Ernst & Ernst after my first annual raise. Her office was near mine, so we could frequently ride together into the city on the bus in the morning. We decided that we would live on my income and save her salary.

We enjoyed doing things with my brother, Ed, and his wife, Nancy Lou. We already knew a lot of their friends, and it seemed like someone was always having a party, which frequently included playing bridge.

Sometimes these same people would get together at Ed's house for a special party, and Ed would always organize some games. We frequently played charades; and another popular game was "hide the objects," where a list of about 12 small items were hidden in a given area (maybe two rooms) and the people would write down where each item was located as they found them. Each item was supposed to be in plain sight and not inside of anything. Another popular game involved the name of a different well-known person or character being pinned on the back of each person. We could see the identity of everyone else, but we couldn't see our own. Then each of us would try to figure out who we were by asking questions of each other and getting clues from the 'yes" or "no" answers.

Of course, Ed was already a key person in my life, and it became even more special with the birth of his first child. A year after Nancy and I got married, Ed and Nancy Lou's son was born, and they named him after me. Now there was another Donald de Laski in the family. What's more, they didn't just stop with another Donald. Over the next three years, two daughters were born, Sally and Carol Sue. Then, after a lapse of four years, he and Nancy Lou had three more children—Paul, Andrew, and Ellen. By then we had started our family too—more on that in Chapter 9—and for years the two families did many things together. For example, we would take turns going to each other's house about once a month—which usually meant lots of kids in sleeping bags and on sofas at night. Sometimes the two families would go on overnight camping trips, and every year we went to Ocean City, Maryland together. During the year all of the kids would save their money so they could spend it at this oceanside resort.

Family vacations were also with Nancy's side of the family. We went on several vacations with my in-laws, Aram and Mary, and we also had dinner at their house almost once a week. There was a frequent family ritual: After I prepared the charcoal fire in the outdoor fire pit, Aram would cook lamb shish kabob. He trained me on how to do the meal. This was a wonderful way for us to build our personal bond. I would never be the Armenian son-in-law he had once dreamed of, but he was discovering that there were things about me he did appreciate, such as becoming his apprentice for a family cooking secret.

As he taught me, first you buy only the lower half of the leg of lamb and cut fairly small pieces all the same size. (That leftover meat is then cooked in the kitchen with string beans for a very nice lamb stew.) The lamb pieces are placed on the skewers with nothing else. Then you put whole, medium-sized tomatoes and onions on separate skewers. When the onions and tomatoes are well cooked over the fire, you put them in a bowl and remove the charred skins with a glove. The flames from the coals are sprinkled with water to prevent the lamb from becoming charred as it continues to cook. Finally, the lamb is removed from the grill when it is a little pink inside. In this country, restaurants generally serve lamb too rare. If it cooks longer, it is more tender. This was all great fun, and I was learning that I could be a pretty good cook.

During these early married years before we had started our family, my parents came back into the picture. In May, 1956, they returned from Ethiopia as my dad's government assignment ended. They moved into an apartment down the street from us.

In June we all went down to Duke to attend Nancy's graduation. She had already finished her course work some six months earlier, but had to wait until June to actually graduate. After the ceremony, we went to a small mountain resort in the Smoky Mountains to celebrate. One day during this trip, my father and Aram were in the swimming pool together. It was a sight to behold. My father had very thick glasses and was almost blind without them. On the other hand, Aram was deaf if he wasn't wearing his hearing aid, due to a bout with malaria when he was a teenager. And so, my father couldn't see Aram, but was shouting for him. Aram sees my father even though he can't hear him, and Aram waves to him. But my father can't see Aram waving, and Aram can't make out what my father is shouting. When they finally found each other, they just decided to stay close together. They told this story for many years thereafter, and they explained to anyone hearing the story that "only together were they a complete person."

That autumn after Nancy's graduation, my parents got another two year assignment in Cambodia. Even though it meant moving again, this was great because they were finally enjoying financial security. My father was making a very respectable $12,000 a year, building a government pension, and renting out their house in Takoma Park. It was a windfall to them that government employees overseas got free housing.

A Revolving Door of Jobs

The year 1956 also had some changes for me with my work and law school career. Right after Nancy had finished all her course work at Duke, I decided that I would drop out of law school, so I did not take any classes during the winter/spring semester nor the summer session. I wanted to enjoy married life, and with busy tax season coming up at Ernst & Ernst, I could see that it was just going to be too much if I was in law school, too. But by the autumn I decided to finish my law degree. I was half way through, and I have always been the kind of person who likes to finish what he has started. The same thing was true in attaining eagle scout and in writing this book.

The following June—that is, now in 1957—my three-year apprenticeship with Ernst & Ernst was over, and I decided to get a new job. I wanted some kind of a corporate position and hoped to use some of my legal training. My wife's cousin, Scotty Wright, was personnel director at Vitro Corporation. It was a familiar place to me because I had done an Ernst & Ernst audit for them. Scotty asked me to interview for a position in their government contracts department. They thought I was perfect for the job and agreed to pay me $6,000 a year. I gave them permission to call Ernst & Ernst for a reference, but when they found out I was earning only $4,200 a year, they said that government regulations would let them pay me only $4,800. (I found out later that under the circumstances this was incorrect). So I turned Vitro down and, in turn, Ernst & Ernst fired me. It was hardly the way I had planned for things to go when looking for a new job.

Things *seemingly* still didn't fall into place very well for me. I was unemployed about a month and then took a job with Bond Bread to work as an accounting manager trainee. However, after one month they had to let me go due to budget problems. Next, I worked for a discount appliance dealer called Fieldermans. But within two weeks of taking that job, I got a call from The American Psychological Association (A.P.A.). Here was a contact from the past bearing fruit. While working with Ernst & Ernst, I had given A.P.A. some ideas on how to mechanize their accounting by using their Addressograph machine. They wanted me to overhaul their accounting department and also do an analysis of all their other departments. This was to be a part time job from 9:00 a.m. to 3:00 p.m. and was to last for 18 months with an annualized salary of $6,000—the same pay as my previous two full-time jobs.

My luck was changing. This was the perfect job because at 3:00 p.m. I could walk six blocks to law school, do my homework, get something to eat, go to class at 6:15 and grab the bus home at 8:30. If any of those previous jobs had worked out, my life would have been totally different. In looking back, I can see that I was never upset during this time of unemployment and short-lived jobs. I always had a very positive attitude and knew that whatever was happening was all right.

Steady Success Begins to Emerge

When Nancy and I were engaged, we frequently talked about children, and it was a foregone conclusion that when we got married we would have at least two children and probably three. Two years after we were married we got down to business, and Nancy soon became pregnant. About a month before the due date, the gynecologist told us that the delivery would be induced because Nancy had a rather rare blood type (AB–negative). This was a security measure to guard against any kind of an emergency that might arise. Thus Kenny was born by appointment on March 7, 1958, exactly nine months after Father's Day.

I couldn't name him Donald because my brother gave that name to his first son. I wondered about naming my first son after my brother, but I really didn't like the name Edgar all that much. However, Nancy and I agreed it would make a good *middle* name. In spite of this, in the years thereafter, my brother always called our son "K. Edgar."

Life changed for us with Ken's arrival. (More about that in Chapter 9.) Nancy had quit her job as most new mothers did in those days, and we had to dip into our savings because we couldn't quite live on my $6,000 salary. And sometimes we had to be creative as parents in order to be able to maintain some of our favorite hobbies.

For example, in those days we were still playing a lot of bridge, but it wasn't realistic to take a baby to a large bridge event. Instead we went to the home of Don and Fran Pearce once a week, and took Kenny in a basket. Don worked with me at Ernst & Ernst, and the Pearces shared our love for bridge. We devised a way to play tournament–like duplicate bridge. (This is where you and your partner compete against other pairs who have the identical cards at another table in the meeting room.) We came up with a way to simulate that kind of tournament competition. We got sixty sets of playing cards then dealt out sixty sets of hands, putting each set in a special holding board made for this purpose. We could play a dozen or so sets of hands on a given evening, and then about six weeks later—enough time for all of us to forget the particulars of that set of hands — on another bridge playing night those same hands would get played, but this time the Pearces would have the cards the de Laskis played earlier. It was all great fun and gave an air of stimulating competition to the evenings.

I was now a young father and things continued to unfold with my career. As planned, my job with A.P.A. ended in the fall of 1958. I applied for a job with a government contractor in Harrisburg, Pennsylvania. Nancy and I traveled all the way up there for an interview, and we were very disappointed to find that they had already filled the job. They were very apologetic and paid my travel expenses. They had tried to get a hold of me the night before, but we had spent the previous night in Baltimore at the in-laws of my brother Ed.

I was frustrated at this setback, but I was soon to be reminded that when an obstacle blocks the intended path, there is usually something better coming. Surely my angels must be at work, steering me toward the right job. It's fortunate the Pennsylvania job was no longer available because soon thereafter I got a position with a division of RCA Service Company in Alexandria, Virginia. I was hired as a contract accounting specialist, reporting directly to the division administrator. My annual salary was a nice raise to $7,800. This was a good fit for me because of my government accounting experience with Ernst & Ernst and my legal training.

Before long I started to make my mark there. I really got the attention of the home office when I was the key person negotiating a multi-million dollar add-on contract with Raytheon. Afterwards, they wanted me to come to work for them at the home office in Cherry Hill, New Jersey, joining their contracts group. But my boss in Alexandria wouldn't let me go because he said he needed me too much. Blocking this promotion made me so upset that I started looking for another job.

A Law Degree, CPA License, and New Home

In June of 1959, I graduated from law school and Nancy got pregnant again on Father's Day. What's more I earned my CPA license that month. The intensive exam was tough, and it was only on my fourth attempt that I finally passed all the parts.

Since Nancy was expecting, we decided it was time for us to buy a house. We found just what we wanted in an area called

Sleepy Hollow in Fairfax County. We signed a contract for about $20,000, applied for a mortgage which would require a 10% down payment, and gave notice on our apartment. A month later the mortgage company turned us down because my $7,800 salary was inadequate to support the monthly payments on what the mortgage would be.

Discouraged but sure there was something else out there for us, we moved in with Nancy's parents and started looking for another house. A few weeks later Aram called me and said he found a house which sounded like what we were looking for. There was one problem: it was about to go under contract. We would have to act quickly if we were interested. Nancy was unavailable at the time, but I hurried out the same day. It was a three- bedroom house on a slab with a car port and a beautifully shaded one-third acre lot. The price was only $14,000 and had an assumable $10,000 mortgage. The owner was even willing to take back a $2,000 second mortgage, making it even more affordable to a young one-income family like ours. I told the owner we would take it, but Aram suggested I let his daughter see it before I committed. The agent said he would hold it for us until the next day. When Nancy saw the house without me the next day, she immediately called me and said "Buy it."

This was the first home of our own. When we moved in, I made quite a project of fertilizing, mowing, and landscaping the yard, and of course I had my tomato patch. On March 7, 1960 we gave Kenny a special birthday present—a six-and-a-half pound baby sister named Kathleen Mary. The fact that both their birthdays were March 7 was not specifically planned. What looks like a coincidence may really be an example of synchronicity and have a deeper meaning about the connection between Ken and Kathy.

Becoming My Own Boss

I got a nice job in Washington, D.C. as chief financial officer and contracts manager for Welex Electronics Corp., a division of Halliburton with annual sales of about $3,000,000. My annual sal-

ary was $9,000. In this job I greatly increased my technical knowl-
edge on government contract accounting. I also managed a staff of
three people which was a new experience for me. Soon it became
quite obvious that I was a key person at Welex. Everyone came to
me for everything relating to accounting, contracts, and administration. Since all of these people were earning $20,000 a year, I
naturally expected a significant raise after the first year, but I was
given only a $900 annual salary increase. Even though I made it
very clear that I expected a higher salary, the chairman, Walt Greer,
would not relent. It would prove to cost him a very valuable employee, and his stubbornness would prove to be expensive for
him.

About this time a very significant thing happened that turned
my career from working for others to working for myself. My father-in-law's neighbor had a friend, Frank Chase, who had recently died. He had had a small CPA practice in Arlington, Virginia,
and his widow was now attempting to sell it. After some negotiations, in November, 1961 I bought the firm for $6,000 which was
considered to be the fair market value of the furniture and fix-
tures. I also agreed to pay 20% of fees for the next seven years
derived from clients of the firm at the time of my purchase. Back at
Welex, Mr. Greer was very sorry to see me leave, and he felt that
Welex needed me so much that he agreed to pay me my current
annual salary of $9,900 for a year-and-a-half to come in two days
a week to help them make the transition.

In looking back I'm surprised that I began practicing accounting. I had always assumed that my future would be as an officer in
corporate America, even though I was very entre-preneurial as a
boy and a young man. I wanted to be part of a significant organization, and I felt that it was unlikely that I could accomplish this
as a practicing accountant or lawyer. Since I did not have much
money as I was growing up, I was very conscious of doing things
that would hopefully lead to making a decent income. That's why
I went to college and majored in accounting and why I went to
law school. But the angels were planning something beyond my
dreams. Not only would I become part of corporate America and

earn a good income, but my family would own the corporation and become quite wealthy.

The Young Couple

These first five years of married life were busy and rewarding times. Nancy and I were both working hard—in our careers and in building a home life. I knew before we got married how much I loved Nancy and how much I wanted to spend my life with her. And it was also wonderful to find out that she is extremely easy to live with. For example, I was deeply appreciative of just how adaptable she was willing to be when I considered taking jobs in Cherry Hill or Harrisonburg. She would never say, "Oh, I don't want to go there." For something like this, she was always willing to trust my judgment about what was going to be best for us and our family.

When I was unemployed on two separate occasions when Kenny was about one year old, Nancy never got upset or worried—certainly a lot different from my mother when my father lost his job. Sometimes I think that Nancy's confidence in me gave me more confidence in myself.

Chapter 9

Fatherhood and Family Life

There is no greater blessing or challenge in life than being a parent. Helping to bring a new life into the world is a miracle unto itself. But each day of being a father or mother presents some opportunity anew for creativity, healing, and meeting oneself. In fact, it is within the bonds of a family that we best get to know ourselves— our weaknesses and foibles, along with our gifts and capacity for greatness.

In Don's life story there was no doubt in his mind that he wanted to be a father. Once he had found the woman he hoped to marry, then his thoughts naturally turned to having a family. And he and Nancy were blessed with three unique and very talented children. But as parents have discovered for centuries, each child is different—each requires a unique way of being supported, loved, disciplined, and appreciated. There is no single formula for being a good parent, even though there are principles and spiritual laws for good parenting— many of which Don discovered with the "on-the-job-training" that comes from being twenty-six years old and suddenly having a little boy come to live with you and your wife.

*One key principle is the importance of giving each child **"space to be"**—that is, trusting that there is wisdom and deep purposefulness within the soul of your child, and—if given space and nurturance— that child can blossom and flower. Don and Nancy's parenting style demonstrated lots of appreciation for this simple truth.*

*Another crucial principle is the importance of **family rhythms and rituals.** The child finds a sense of safety and support within those meaningful family patterns—such as vacation trips yearly to a special spot or the discipline of caring for a family pet.*

*Perhaps most important is the principle that **we really do need each other**, and what better place to learn that soul lesson than in a family. And this surely means much, much more than just the many* *ways that a child is dependent upon a parent. As we will see from these stories of Don's parenting, it is the father who needs the child, too. And this is illustrated with special poignancy when a parent grows old, and the one who was once the "dependent child" switches roles and then becomes like the parent himself to his own mother or father. That helped to transform Don's relationships with his own father and mother.*

What a deep and wonderful mystery is revealed to us through fathering and mothering.

❀

All the time that I was growing up, my only real ambition in life was to have a nice family and make enough money to enjoy a slightly better-than-average standard of living. This was no doubt due primarily to the fact that I grew up in the Depression with an unemployed father and an overly-stressed mother.

When I became a father, I was very happy because it meant that one of my two major goals in life had been accomplished. Now all I had left to do was to make more money.

During those years when first Kenny and then Kathy were infants, I was not very involved in being a father. I think I changed a diaper one time. Nancy was home full-time, and I figured that was her job. But a year after Kathy was born, Nancy began typing tax returns at home, and now she was working on both fronts.

Until 1962 I was commuting every day into Washington D.C. to work at Welex. In May of 1962, I was asked by Welex to conduct an audit in North Carolina, about forty-minutes' drive from Nags Head beach, so I took the family with me and commuted between Nags Head and my audit site. A vivid, early memory of Kathy is her dancing around in our motel room without any clothes on and me singing "There She Is, Miss America." It was just one of many highlights to this, our first family adventure to the beach—something that was to become an important part of our family rhythm each year.

One thing that is special about being a father is the chance to discover how each of your children is special and different in so many ways. So in 1963, when we moved the accounting practice office into the house at Gresham Street, I thankfully began to see quite a bit more of the children. Kenny was a very happy boy and always did what he was told. Kathy, on the other hand, fussed a lot, and I remember swatting her on one occasion. But Kathy was always a very proactive person. When she was only four, she got all the kids in our neighborhood together and organized a talent show and invited all the parents. While at nursery school, she was the self-appointed assistant to the teacher, who proclaimed that she wouldn't know what she'd do without Kathy's help.

About this time the kids were talking about getting a dog or a cat. I explained to them that we couldn't do that because of my asthma, but the real reason was that I didn't want a new dog to replace fond memories of my childhood dog, Chips. But one day in the spring I brought home two baby ducks from the pet store, and we named them Heckle and Jeckle. They became full-grown in a couple of months. They would strut together all over the neighborhood and sleep in the bushes behind our house. In the early fall we took them to Lake Accotink and let them go.

Schooling Choices

Parenting means lots of things to me. The example of Heckle and Jeckle shows how sometimes a parent needs to stretch a little bit and find some creative way to say "yes" when the automatic reaction is to say "no." But equally important, a parent must be willing to stand up for sons and daughters, and to take the initiative when a child's well-being is at risk. For example, in the fall of 1965 Ken was starting the second grade at a Fairfax City public school, which was going to be a new school for him. He had done very well in the first grade at his previous school, and he especially liked to read.

But we saw very early in that autumn of second grade that Ken seemed unhappy at his new school. Nancy and I scheduled a teacher's conference. We discovered he was reading "Dick and Jane," which was the same thing that Kathy was reading in her *kindergarten* at Fairfax Christian private school.

We decided immediately to put Ken in a private school. We set up a meeting with Reverend Thoburn, the principal and owner of Kathy's school. He introduced us to his son Mark who was also in the second grade. He read for us from the King James Version of the Bible. We were very impressed, and we registered Kenny immediately, even though the cost was about $1,000 per year. Fortunately, the following year the State of Virginia instituted a program that paid $250 a year for any child going to private school—although this provision lasted only several years. The curriculum at Kenny's new school included religion and classes in German. One year they produced *Rumplestiltskin*, and Kenny had the leading part.

The kids attended this school for four years, and when they left Kenny went from having just finished fifth grade right into seventh. In the same way, Kathy skipped over fourth grade and went directly into the fifth grade in public school.

The Family Expands

We were always open to having a third child, but Nancy had already had a miscarriage in 1962. In April of 1966, we decided to try again. One night Nancy complained of a severe pain in her lower abdomen, and the next morning she said it was worse. She didn't have a regular doctor, so I took her to my internist, Dr. Pascoe, whom I saw on a regular basis for my asthma. He said it was possible that Nancy had an ectopic pregnancy. When I told him we were trying to get pregnant two weeks ago, he set up an emergency appointment with an obstetrician upstairs.

Within minutes we entered his crowded office, and the re-

ceptionist motioned for us to come on back to the doctor's office. After a brief examination the doctor told us to meet him at
the hospital in half an hour. All the people in his office were
told to go home. When we arrived at the hospital, the orderlies
were waiting for us. Nancy told me later that as she was being
wheeled down the hall to the operating room, she was passing
out.

After about two hours the doctor came out and said that
Nancy was fine. He explained that sometimes the fertilized egg
cell gets caught in the fallopian tube and starts to grow, causing
the tube to burst. In this instance the large end of the tube had
burst, and blood had been spewing internally since the previous evening. He went on to say that if we had been just one
hour later, Nancy probably would not have survived. I've always felt that this was another instance of synchronicity and
the angels being on our side. If I hadn't had asthma, I wouldn't
have had Dr. Pascoe, and if he didn't have an obstetrician friend
upstairs, we might have been too late.

The doctor also said that since Nancy had only one fallopian
tube left, her chances of getting pregnant were cut in half. But
we tried again in the fall, and David was born on July 3, 1967. I
felt very blessed that David came along these many years after
Ken and Kathy. And years later, when the two older children
had begun to start their lives on their own, Nancy and I still
had David at home with us.

Family Adventures

With the family expanded and needing more space, we
moved to our new house on Laurel Street. That house had lots
of potential for a young, growing family, and we finished off
the basement, creating a large office for my accounting practice. Working from home also happily meant that I saw a lot of
the children, and I became very much more involved in their
upbringing. Nancy and I almost always agreed on things related to the children's upbringing; and even if she did not agree,

she never interfered. I've always felt that in raising children it's very important that parents maintain a united front on matters related to the setting of rules and discipline.

Kenny was very easy–going and never caused any trouble, but frequently Kathy would come running to me and say, "Kenny hit me."

In response I would look her over and say, "I don't see any blood." After more fussing on her part, I would add, "OK, both of you go to your rooms."

In a similar pattern, sometimes the kids would tussle about in the back seat of the car, and then Kathy would cry out, "Kenny hit me."

Defending himself, Kenny would reply, "She hit me first."

Kathy, of course, would have a counter–argument, "But you hit me harder than I hit you." I always knew that Kenny was very good to Kathy, and I always tried to exhibit a certain sense of humor in these confrontations and not make a big deal out of them. I also didn't want Kathy to rely on me to settle her disputes.

Every summer, starting around 1970, we would go to Ocean City, Maryland with my brother Ed's family. We would generally rent houses next to each other for about $700 a week. The kids would have saved their money all year just to spend during this vacation time on the boardwalk. While the older kids were out doing stuff together, Ed and I would sit on the beach, watch the little ones, and drink Bloody Marys. I remember him frequently saying, "I wonder what the poor people are doing." To me this meant that Ed was saying something that we both felt—we had reached a level of affluence that we could only have dreamed of when we were growing up.

Ocean City was not our only family vacation spot. Several times before David was born, the four of us went to Myrtle Beach, South Carolina for a different sort of oceanfront adventure. These trips south had become an important family tradition for us, but it was not going to be easy to keep this up when David was just a baby. For Christmas, 1967, the solution was to have my parents take care of the baby, and the rest of us drove off to Florida. We opened Christmas presents in Ocala in the motel, and the next day we took a ride in a glass–bottomed boat. We took a tour of Busch Gardens and saw lots of animals in their natural habitat. We also went to Cypress Gardens and collected shells on Sanibel Island.

After driving through the swamp on the Tamiami Trail, we arrived at Miami Beach. We left the kids with their grandparents, Aram and Mary, at their condo for three days, while Nancy and I took a cruise. Kathy wanted to go with us, and she kept saying, "I wanna go with you, Baloo." We had just seen the movie *The Jungle Book*, and the lovable bear character Baloo stuck in her mind. The cruise ship wasn't much, but we loved Nassau and its beaches. The kids behaved themselves with Aram and Mary, and I think that experience was good for everybody.

Reflecting on those adventures from decades ago, Kathy told me recently that her favorite trips were the ones that just included Mom and Dad and the children because it made her feel close to everyone.

Even when we were in our typical work–a–day rhythm, there were important family times. For example, our Laurel Street home was only a five–minute drive to the Fairfax Country Club. In the summer I would play golf in the morning, and then join Nancy and the kids at the pool. She would take them to the pool almost every day during the summer. Ken took a few golf lessons and started playing a little bit when he was twelve, but he spent most of his time with Boy Scouts and Little League baseball, where I would occasionally umpire. I was, of course, very happy that he started up my favorite game, golf. It is something that we'd be able to enjoy together, and something Ken would be able to enjoy all his life.

After Ken graduated from high school in 1976, we quit the country club because I was so much involved in other things that I wasn't using it enough to justify the cost. (To this day, I always feel bad if I spend money unnecessarily, no matter how much money I have. And I think this was one way of teaching my children respect for money.) As a little girl Nancy had taken ballet lessons from the time she was five, and now Kathy did the same thing. I went to most of her ballet programs and always thought she ranked at the top of her class. She was certainly the most beautiful.

We also took some ski trips to Vermont and West Virginia. Nancy and I weren't very good, but the kids had a great time. Ken was outstanding because he was very well-coordinated. One time I was a chaperone for a ski trip that Kathy's junior high school took to Vermont. Kathy was embarrassed during the trip because she thought I was too strict.

I believe that good parenting has a lot to do with teaching children financial responsibility. I was always trying to figure out ways that Kenny and Kathy could earn money. I gave them a small allowance and a bonus of $5 for every report card "A" they got in school.

There were also some small-scale entrepreneurial opportunities. For a long time we used the girl living across the street as a baby sitter, but when Kenny and Kathy were 13 and 11, I let them baby sit themselves and David for one dollar an hour. In addition, Kenny would make money mowing our lawn and other lawns in the neighborhood. I was very proud of him when he managed to get a donut route from a friend of his. Krispy Kreme would deliver them to our door, and Kenny would deliver them throughout the neighborhood. This route earned him about $10 a week. It reminded me of little business ventures I had run as a boy. I was especially proud of how Ken had done this totally on his own.

Sometimes parenting requires a little creativity when dealing with money matters. When Kathy was 13, she would start telling us at the dinner table what she wanted for Christmas, even in September. She was very much into the clothes she wore and would go on *ad nauseam* telling us what she needed. Finally I got so tired of hearing this stuff I said, "Kathy, how much do you think we spent on your clothes for the past twelve months?" She said she didn't know, so we did a little research and agreed that a fair estimate was $900 a year. From that time on she received a clothing allowance of $75 a month. We excluded major items such as overcoats, and we would still give her a few items for birthdays and Christmas, but everything else had to come from those funds.

She soon discovered that she could get more clothes if she made her own, so this led to Kathy becoming an accomplished seamstress. This arrangement lasted until Kathy finished college and the amount stayed the same. I told my stockbroker about this arrangement and he said he wished they had done this with their daughters because his wife had many serious battles with them about clothes. Some mothers are very controlling with their daughters, particularly when it comes to buying and wearing clothes. But Nancy and I never tried to control any of our children.

Family Pets

Our "extended family" has often included pets. One day I came home from a Boy Scout camping trip at Bagley's Farm with a little mallard duck that I had found, and we named him Seymour. David would run around with Seymour in the basement and hold him on his lap. We recorded an audio–tape of David talking to Seymour. After about four months we discovered that Seymour was a girl because she started laying eggs. She would spend all her time sitting on these eggs, but since they were not fertilized they wouldn't hatch and they would get rotten. Since we kept taking them away from her, she would lay them in the neighbors' yards. Finally she gave up and let us have her eggs. Nancy even sold some to a decoupage artist.

The whole neighborhood loved Seymour, but that autumn I decided that we should return her to Bagley's Farm. We rowed out to a group of ducks, tossed Seymour over the side, and sadly started rowing back. The other ducks immediately swam away, and Seymour came after us, half running, half flying on the water, and quacking very loudly. She then ran up and got in our car. Dr. Bagley explained that Seymour didn't know she was a duck and she would have endangered the other ducks on the lake from hawks, and therefore they rejected her. She was a lot different than Heckle and Jeckle because they had each other, and she only had us. And so, home she went with us.

Seymour became an integral part of our lives and was the most talked about pet in the neighborhood. One night, three years later, I heard a big commotion outside in our backyard where Seymour lived. I went out to investigate and was confronted by a large, hissing raccoon and Seymour was lying on the ground. In a few minutes, Seymour died in my lap. I was very sad, but I was particularly mad at the raccoon. The next day we held a funeral service and many of the neighbors attended.

On another occasion years later, Kathy was the one who came home with a new pet. Getting ready to leave for school one morning in her senior year of high school, she heard a meow under the hood of her car. She discovered a little kitten curled up against the carburetor. I told the kids we could keep him, but because of my asthma, he would need to be an outside cat. We named him "Carburetor," and he was a member of our family for the next thirteen years.

He would hunt and eat rabbits, squirrels, and moles. One time he killed a rabbit almost twice his size and deposited it in the window well. When he was through eating it, there was nothing left except the fur. Carburetor loved to play with moles, and we would sometimes watch him knock them around for half an hour before he would bite into them.

Once I heard Kathy scream when Carburetor presented her from his mouth a dying mole with its blood squirting all over the place. But once Carburetor himself almost died from a squirrel's bone that he was eating. The bone had pierced one of his lungs. The vet had trouble giving him a shot because his muscles were so strong. After we had had Carburetor for thirteen years, he disappeared. We searched everywhere and found him in the woods dying. We think it was from old age because there weren't any apparent injuries or disease. It was a sad loss because he had certainly become a big part of our family. But the inevitable loss of a pet is part of the process of life, and I think it is valuable for children to experience through their family pets both the joy and sadness that they bring.

Parenting As the Kids Start Reaching Maturity

Ken and I drove to North Carolina for a week the summer of 1974 when he was sixteen, just after he had finished his junior year of high school. We played a number of different golf courses, and Ken did some of the driving. That autumn he applied to three universities: St. Lawrence in Canton, New York. (mainly because he liked skiing), William and Mary in Williamsburg, and Duke, in Durham North Carolina.

I had encouraged him to go to Duke, but he said he didn't want to go to the same school as his father. As it turned out Duke was the only one of the three schools that accepted him and that was on a legacy basis, which meant he would have to start in January for the second semester, when spots had opened up from first semester students flunking out. So he went to George Mason that fall and then he was able to transfer his credits to Duke when he started there in January. Ken even chose accounting as his major, the same as mine. If he hadn't done this we probably wouldn't have started our company together years later. Angels at work—again—I think.

I've always been very proud of all my kids, but I don't think I gave Kathy credit for being as special and unique as she really was. She was very beautiful and also proactive. She was a class officer and captain of the baton corps. At one time she thought she wanted to become an actress, and when she was 14 she went to a summer acting school in Vermont. She was offered the leading role in *Gypsy*, but in the end she didn't get the part because she didn't sing very well. After taking singing lessons for the next two years, she got a job at a dinner theater in nearby Arlington, Virginia. She co-starred in *Can-Can*, earned over $200 a week, and with that money bought herself a car. That's pretty good for a sixteen-year-old—making that kind of money while going to high school and getting top grades.

But with the demands of that sort of schedule, most of the time Kathy didn't get home until two a.m. That led her to decide that she didn't really take to the acting world, and she would rather have a career as a news correspondent. She talked the local television station into letting her produce a weekly program of about ten minutes. The show was about what's happening in the teen world, and it was a big success.

The following fall when she was seventeen, Kathy followed in the footsteps of her parents and her brother, enrolling at Duke University, where she eventually majored in English and minored in political science. She also took some courses in communications at the University of North Carolina. Throughout her college years she did volunteer work at the local CBS station, which gave her the inside track to get a news casting job in Durham after she graduated.

Our younger son David had a somewhat different path towards growing up. Unlike his siblings, as he went through his school years, David cut up a lot in class and gave his teachers a hard time. One time when he was in the fifth grade his teacher said, "David, sit down or go to the principal's office." David picked up his books and started to walk out of the room. The teacher said, "Where do you think you're going."

David replied, "To the principal's office." Of course all the class laughed. David always wanted to entertain his classmates at the teachers' expense.

While in the sixth grade, David got involved with some tough kids down the street, one of whom was very big and who bullied the other kids. I figured David was smoking pot because he wasn't quite himself, and he started falling asleep in class. Finally he even got suspended from school, and the school administration wanted David to get therapy and to include Nancy and me in the sessions. After several consultations, I was very unimpressed with these people, so I decided to send David to boarding school. Therefore, one weekend we drove around Virginia looking into various possibilities, and it turned out that David didn't want to go to any of the boarding schools he saw. I really didn't want him to go either because I remembered all the fun times we had had together, and I knew I would miss him.

In the midst of this crisis period, one evening David started going out the door, and I asked him where he was going. He said some of the guys were camping in the woods. But because I knew he was smoking pot, I told him he couldn't go. He said he was going anyway, and we actually got into a fist fight. It ended up with me telling David that he obviously didn't want me to be his father, so he would have to get out of the house. I gave him $100 and told him to leave, which he did.

The first thing the next morning I went to the meditation ashram where I frequently went to meditate. I simply prayed, meditated, and wept that morning. When I returned home Nancy told me that she had just learned about what had gone on with David that night. He had gone around the neighborhood looking for a place to sleep—to no avail—and he finally spent the night in our basement.

That afternoon David and I had a nice talk. He agreed to change his ways and promised to stop hanging around that big guy down the street. I told him how much I loved him and hoped that he would show more love and respect for me. The following week, when David was home alone in the afternoon, the big guy and a friend start banging on the back door, demanding that David let them in, or else they would break the glass. David let them in and they grabbed all the liquor they could find and left.

When I got home, David told me all about it, and I called the police. A very nice police woman came over, and David told her that he had frequently been threatened by this big kid. She gave him her private phone number, and told David that if it ever happened again, he should give her a call. After interrogation by the police officer later, the one boy confessed, but the mother of the big kid lied and said her son could not have been involved because he was with her all afternoon. I heard many years later that this big kid had spent many years in jail.

The joyful days of David's earlier childhood returned, and we lived happily together from then on. I didn't try to control him as much, and I gave him whatever he wanted. I must admit that his requests were moderate, such as clothing and video games. And I loaned him the money to buy a small, motorized bike, and he paid me back by regularly mowing our three-acre lawn.

That motorized bike ended up playing a big role in an interesting episode in parenting for me. David normally rode it on paths in the woods with a friend, but one day he rode it on our dead end street. He stopped at the end of the street and saw a police car about 100 yards away with its lights flashing. He turned around to come home and discovered that the police car was chasing him. He got scared, drove the motor bike into an empty lot, and turned over. The policeman grabbed him, brought him up to our door, and told us what happened. He left David with us and said we would hear from the police department within twenty-four hours.

Sure enough, we heard from the police department, and before we knew it we were all in traffic court, with David charged with eluding a police officer, which normally had a penalty of having one's driver's license revoked for one year. Not actually having a license yet, that effectively meant that he would not be able to get a driver's license until he was 17. I told the court that I wanted to appeal the case, and they gave me a lot of papers to fill out. As I was filling out the papers, I noticed a card which asked whether we wanted a trial by jury. Without even thinking about it, I checked "yes."

That night I began planning David's legal defense, and I was actually looking forward to the court hearing with jury. I had a law degree, but had never conducted a case in court. The next morning the clerk of the court called to tell me that if I lost the case, I would have to pay the cost of the jury which would be at least $1,000. I told her that that was no problem.

That very afternoon an assistant district attorney called and said, "Mr. de Laski, would you help me out? There's no jury that would ever find your son guilty of evading a police officer. Would you accept a three month delay on David getting his driver's license, and I will drop the felony charge?" I agreed and that was the end of that.

I found out later that a lawyer would never have asked for a jury trial because it is frowned upon by the court system and it would damage his reputation. Courts are used to spending about ten minutes on each of these kinds of cases. But I had had nothing to lose. I think it was angels at work again.

And as he moved into his high school years, David's unique talents and interests were blossoming. He had lots of friends, and he got along well with his teachers. In many ways, he had an ideal set up. His bedroom and a large social area were on the basement level, which opened out into the yard. His friends would come in and out at random without any advance notice. Sometimes I would be reading the paper and suddenly realize that a party was going on downstairs.

David spent a lot of time playing the guitar and took lessons from two different people. He also created several short episodes on video tape and started creating music from his computer. When he went off to college at the University of Colorado he majored in film and became the music director for the college radio station. After college he moved to Los Angeles and worked with a few bands—later starting his own company developing synthesized music with computers. He also stayed connected to his video skills, and in 1992 he flew home and created an outstanding video for our company—Deltek—which we then used widely for promotional purposes.

Many years later when I was 75, David gave Nancy and me a beautiful compliment. He said, "I really like the way you guys brought me up."

I am very grateful to my children for the enjoyment they gave me. Even though we sometimes disagreed on things, I always felt a great deal of respect towards them even when they were young. Most of this is due to my belief in reincarnation as taught by Edgar Cayce. He said that some souls were more evolved than others, and he indicated that each soul, as it prepares to come into physical life again, selects parents and situations which will provide the greatest opportunity for further growth. Therefore I always felt that it was very possible that any or all of my children might well be more evolved than I. My role as a parent was to share with my children whatever I could, but not judge them in any way. I also have felt that they were also helping me along my own spiritual path. For this reason I try not to get upset when they give me advice. In giving advice, mutual respect is very important in maintaining a good relationship.

Mom and Dad During My Adult Years

In many people's life story, there comes a time when one's parents, in a sense, become the children. Usually that happens as the parents get elderly. I guess I could say that the shift in roles came earlier in life for me than it optimally would have. In fact, even as a teenager it often felt like I was the most grown up one in the family. But surely by the time I had graduated from college, had married, and was getting ready to start my own family, my relationship with my own parents had shifted. They were wounded people—my father deeply disappointed in how his life and career had never flourished; and my mother, so often angry, frustrated, and depressed. I still loved them very much, but it would be me that would need to nurture them, rather than to expect it to be the other way around.

In the fall of 1954—as I was graduating from college and getting ready to start life and career as an adult and married man— my father got another government assignment, this time in Addis Ababa, Ethiopia. My mother got a job teaching nutrition to a group of girls in the palace of the emperor, Haile Selassie. My father's assignment lasted two years and was followed by another two years in Phnom Penh, Cambodia. While they lived there, my father took many pictures of the ruins at Angkor Wat, a world heritage site that is thousands of years old. In 1958 they returned to their home in Takoma Park, Washington, D.C.

My mother became depressed for the next five years. My father met me several times for lunch in D.C. to talk about it. She had led a very busy life with three foreign assignments and ran the egg business, but now there was nothing for her to do. Money was a little scarce, but adequate. My brother and I would get together with our families as much as possible, but she was always worried about us. Worrying had always been her way of demonstrating love. Finally in 1965 they moved near us in Fairfax. And it proved to be very helpful to her when we all became active in the Providence Presbyterian Church and later the Unity Church.

For about a year my father did part-time telephone solicitation for an insurance agent. He hated it, but my mother kept encouraging him. He actually did pretty well. Later he got a part-time job doing research at the local public library which he really enjoyed.

For the next five years our families were very close. We were also near Nancy's parents, and they were also included in some of our activities. Both sets of parents started going to Florida for several months each winter, and they each bought year-round houses there around 1971. My brother and I would visit our parents several times a year, sometimes with our families and other times on business.

In 1969 my father became very ill and was bedridden for several months. At this time I was into spiritual healing, and I prayed frequently for him and sent him healing letters. This meant a lot to him, and he showed them with great pride to some of his friends. He finally recovered, but from that time on he had Parkinson 's disease. In 1976 he passed away at the age of 83. We had a simple funeral service in Florida for their friends, and then we had the body shipped to Fairfax where we had a nice memorial service and graveside ceremony.

Only a year earlier, Nancy's father had passed away. While Aram was lingering in the hospital during 1974, I visited him almost every day. Quite a few times I took David with me. It was a healing time for my father–in–law and me. Even though he had been opposed to our marriage, he declared on his deathbed that I had been a good son–in–law.

Aram and my father's deaths were my first experiences with the loss of an immediate family member. I was somewhat concerned because I didn't feel much sadness over my father's death. But I think that this was partly due to the fact that I have always viewed death and the death–experience as very positive events, due to my belief in reincarnation and the evolution of the soul.

I believe another reason I didn't feel much pain at my father's death was because I always loved him and had no outstanding issues with him. Loving others is the purpose of life, and if we have a problem with someone, they should be forgiven and not judged. In contrast to my own reaction at my father's funeral, I was once at the funeral for my father–in–law's brother. As they were lowering the casket into his grave, one of his daughters flung herself on the grave and wept uncontrollably. Her father had been an alcoholic and had mistreated her mother, and she had never forgiven him.

My father's death was, of course, a huge transition point for my mother. For the previous twenty years she had taken good care of my father, and at the same time she had become very active socially. After he died she continued that activity. She moved into an apartment–style condominium in Florida that provided meals and social functions.

In 1989 I experienced another family loss—the early death of my brother Ed, who died at the age of 59 of a liver disease. In many ways, he had had a difficult life. When he was 47 in 1977, he had fallen in love with a woman named Eloise, a divorcee in her early thirties who was raising two children. Ed thought he was only having an affair, but Eloise insisted on marriage; and since Ed was really smitten, he divorced Nancy Lou and married her.

For about five years they seemed to get along pretty well, and Eloise was a good partner in Ed's real estate development business. The biggest problem was that Eloise didn't want to have anything to do with Ed's family. She wanted to get away from Nancy Lou and the six kids, so they moved to Ormand Beach in Florida, where Eloise's parents lived.

While living in Florida, Ed could at least once a month visit our mother who was living not far away. However, I realized how much he missed everyone when we all started receiving Christmas and birthday presents from him. And, even though his business was doing poorly in Florida, he was still very responsible in providing support for Nancy Lou and the children, including college expenses. I think a lot of people underestimate the pain they will experience from leaving their family for another spouse.

We all went down to Florida for his funeral, and it was a very sad affair.

As I reflected on my brother's life, I could see that Ed had always been rebellious, even up to the time he dropped out of the University of Arizona. Several times he ran away from home; he frequently got mad at our parents, and he refused to do any household chores. I always felt sorry for everyone and did the best I could to keep matters running smoothly. Ed's problem might have been due to the fact that he was neglected in his early childhood and, therefore, was crying out for attention. My mother was always looking after me because she was worried about my asthma, and she figured that Ed didn't need her. I can still remember her saying, "At least I don't have to worry about Edgar." In spite of this neglect, Ed never got mad at me, and he always was trying to get me to do things with him such as getting on the baseball field or playing tennis.

The unfoldment of Ed's life reminded me a lot of what I had once read in a book titled *The Uranus Effect*. It says that our lives have three phases. Phase 1 is up to age 20 and is the growing-up period. Phase 2 is from 20 to 40 years old, and it covers the period of career development and starting a family. Phase 3 is over the age of 40, and its focal point is the search for meaning—that is, the search to find God and becoming spiritual. In that same spirit, some sects in India practice celibacy after age 40, and husbands and wives move into separate bedrooms.

In my opinion, that period around age 40 is a very dangerous time for most men, particularly if they have married early in life and have had limited experience with women. I also think that many men fall in love again because they are afraid of growing old. I was very lucky because when I was 40, I was following Guru Maharaji and studying Edgar Cayce's philosophy.

As I mentioned earlier, I was never able to cry after I was about four years old, and this was also the case after Ed's death. I felt very sad for a number of months, so I went to see my psychiatrist friend Dr. James Gordon. He put me into a hypnotic trance, and I was able to visit Ed and tell him how much I loved him and say goodbye. This closure felt so good, and I cried profusely.

Mother's Final Years

My mother and Nancy Lou had always had a very loving relationship with each other, even after Ed divorced her. This was partly due to the fact that Nancy Lou's mother had died when she was in her late thirties, and so she had naturally formed a bond with her mother-in-law. My mother came up to Fairfax each summer for a month and stayed with us and with Nancy Lou, and we all visited her after Christmas annually. Finally when Mom was 93 some friends of hers in Florida told us that she really shouldn't be living by herself, so Nancy Lou invited her to come live with her in Baltimore. My mother thought that was a good idea because, as she said, "Nancy Lou is all alone up there and she needs somebody to be with." Mother never wanted anyone to think that she couldn't take care of herself.

The end of my mother's life came suddenly. In the summer of 1998, Nancy and I were near the end of a cruise around the North Sea. When we were in Estonia, we got a call from Ken saying that grandma had been moved into the hospital and wasn't expected to live very long. The next day she passed away at the age of 99, and we returned home three days later. Ken and Kathy had taken care of all the arrangements. At the funeral service I said a few words. I pointed out that my mother had spent most of her life looking after and worrying about other people. It wasn't until she was 93 years old and being looked after by Nancy Lou that she realized that she needed others. From that time on, whenever she saw me, she would tell me how much she loved me. This was a new experience for both of us. We've always known that we learn how to love by helping others, but we can also learn how to love by letting others help us. Many incapacitated people feel sorry for themselves instead of feeling love for the people who are helping them. Surely that's a missed opportunity.

Don at the time he began his accounting firm

The home on Gresham St. which was also the first
home for the accounting practice

Chapter 10

Building a Business Through Service

In spite of the way it is sometimes portrayed as greedy or unethical, the essence of business is potentially spiritual. Not only is it working directly with spiritual energy that is symbolized by money—even more important, business is based on the principle of service. When we effectively serve the needs of our customers or clients, then our business has a chance to thrive. We even find this modeled for us in the lives of some of the great spiritual leaders, whether it's the years that Jesus worked in his father's business as a carpenter, or Gandhi working for years as a lawyer. Business is the "marketplace" where we have unique opportunities to use our talents to do a good work in the service of human needs.

Don's life story illustrates many talents, and they include accounting, systematic thinking, and good judgment about the financial aspects of life. He built his professional life around these skills, and he did it in a way that was not only ethical and honest but also dedicated to helping other people be successful. As Don's accounting firm grew, notice the ways that he strove to help other people to develop. It is especially evident in the story of how he would help accountants working at the firms that were his clients. He was intent upon helping those individuals build their own successful career trajectory, and he took pleasure in seeing them succeed and take on bigger jobs.

Just as surely business has the potential for being a spiritual activity because it can follow the principle of mutual support and cooperation. We live in times when cut-throat competition may appear to be the norm, but it doesn't have to be that way for our economy to be prosperous—our personal economy or the national economy. This is so well illustrated even in little examples from how Don ran his accounting firm. He looked for ways to have collegial, mutually helpful relations even with a huge accounting firm that might otherwise have been seen as a competitor with unfair advantage.

Honest service, people-building, and collegiality all bore fruit as Don's accounting firm grew and prospered. It elegantly demonstrates what is possible for business.

❋

In Chapter 8, I described the purchase of an accounting practice and starting to work for myself. It was a challenge and a risk—especially with a family that now included two small children—but Nancy and I believed that the risks were worth taking. It became a team effort because Nancy agreed to do all the typing as long as she could do it from home. The small bedroom in our new house became her office, and I would bring the tax returns and audit reports home for her to type. In the beginning there were about 100 tax returns for her to focus on. In the case of a repeat client, we would write the current numbers on the return next to the prior year's numbers. For new clients, we had to write everything from scratch. Nancy never complained, but the typing was really tough. (About ten years later a company called Computax came along and made everything a lot easier.)

Our practice had a very competent young accountant named Don Lee. He was serving his apprenticeship just like I did when I worked for Ernst & Ernst, and because he was an apprentice, his salary was only the standard $3,900 a year. If it weren't for Don, there probably wouldn't have been any year–round clients. When I bought the practice, he was already doing all the work for these year–round customers, and everyone was very satisfied with his performance. This also made it very easy for me to do the consulting work with Welex Electronics two days a week. It was also my job to look for new clients for our practice. I would never have been able to get through that first tax season without Don. When I worked for Ernst & Ernst, I had done only audit work rather than this kind of tax season work at which he was so good.

Building the Business

In addition to personal tax returns our clientele included a group of five urologists, an insurance agent partnership, a builder, and an armored car services company. In the first full year of practice my net earnings were a marked improvement over when I had been working for others—$17,000. That total, however, included the $9,900 that I received from my former employer Welex for my continuing consulting work for them.

Building up an accounting practice had for many years been difficult to do because of limitations imposed on the profession. Up until this time, a CPA could lose his license if he advertised or solicited for his accounting services, but fortunately advertising became acceptable right after I starting practicing. So, I got a list of small government contractors in the Washington D.C. area and started soliciting their business. Since I had considerable government contract experience with Ernst & Ernst, Welex Electronics, and RCA Service Co.—plus the fact that I had a law degree—I was certainly well-qualified. I got five clients from these solicitations, and my services included closing out the books at the end of each month with the help of the clients' accounting clerks. Seasonally, we would also do their tax returns (which they would type), and in some of these cases we provided audited financial statements.

My clients really appreciated the kind of service I gave them, which would always include my regular meetings with management and accounting personnel. At the beginning I charged them $25 an hour and was able to give them all the accounting services they needed for about $500 a month. What's more, all five of these companies experienced considerable growth, which meant that in each case their chief accountants were taking on more and more responsibilities. None of them had accounting degrees, but they all became highly qualified in government contract accounting and experienced successful careers. I like to think that the kind of services I was providing helped support and build expanded careers for those individuals.

(For the reader who might be interested in a fuller picture of what this kind of government accounting work entails, I have prepared an example which appears as Appendix 1 at the end of the book. It is your tax dollars at work, after all, so it might be interesting to see how much accountability must be recorded for any company getting government grants and contracts. This one example shows a three-year comparative financial statement for a typical small government contractor. These particular statements were computer generated many years later, but this is still the basic information that is required.)

In the summer of 1963, having completed his apprenticeship, Don Lee left the firm to start his own practice, and so I moved the office into our house on Gresham Street. It was a tight squeeze in that little bedroom, but it was much more efficient than driving back and forth to the office. All of my work was performed outside my office anyway. For example, my tax clients appreciated me coming by their home for their annual tax consultations. And my government contract clients—to whose offices I made trips whenever necessary—gave me a very nice year-round practice. I really missed Don Lee during the next tax season, but I got through it by working about seventy hours a week. It was hard work, but now our business was starting to thrive. Since I had very little overhead, I was now making about $35,000 a year—an impressive amount in 1964 and something I was really proud of.

With our financial success came the chance to get a larger home. In the fall of 1965 we bought a new four-bedroom rambler for $35,000 on Laurel Street near the city of Fairfax. We paid $7,000 down payment, and our total monthly payment was $150. The second largest bedroom became our office and the two children each had their own room. The following year we finished off the lower floor which included a very nice office.

This move up for us was possible because we were able to sell our house on Gresham St. for $19,500, which netted us enough for the down payment on the new home. In 2006, I drove by the Gresham Street house and saw a man mowing his lawn in the neighborhood. I told him I used to live across the street and asked if he knew what a house like mine was currently selling for. He said he was in the real estate business. Those houses used to sell for $450,000, but because of the recent soft market, they had come down to $420,000. Since that visit I have frequently thought about what a great investment it would have been to hold onto our Gresham St. home—even to have found a way to buy several new residential houses and rent them out for fifty years. My house had increased twenty times in value, and the rental income also would have increased substantially.

A Health Crisis

The following April I had a very severe pain in my lower back. It was so bad I fell out of my chair and had to crawl to my bed. The pain was excruciating. Nancy took me to the emergency ward at Arlington Hospital where they put me in traction and gave me a lot of tests. I was given a shot for the pain, but the relief didn't last very long. I can still remember having an out-of-body experience. I felt myself rise to the ceiling and was looking down at my body writhing in pain. After a few minutes I returned to my body.

The next day the orthopedic surgeon gave me some strong pain pills and wanted to schedule me for a slipped disc operation the following day. I don't remember how it came about, but that same day I got this news from the surgeon, I was talking on the phone about this health crisis to a nurse who I knew from the Fairfax Country Club. She said I was stupid if I didn't get a second opinion because slipped disc operations were very serious and could cause many problems later. She suggested a Dr. Masterson at the National Orthopedic Hospital in Arlington.

I called Dr. Masterson's office, and because it was an emergency and they knew this nurse, they gave me an appointment the following day. Still there in my room at the Arlington Hospital, I telephoned the office and told them to cancel the surgery because I was checking out in the morning. They said they couldn't release me until they got permission from the doctor, and I told them I was leaving no matter what he said. The doctor came in early the next morning, and he was very mad at me. He said he had done a lot for me by arranging for a room and agreeing to do a major surgery the next day. But I was adamant and left.

After a brief examination, Dr. Masterson said he wanted to treat me for gout. He said it was very likely that the stress from my tax season was a factor. He went on to explain that my uric acid level was only slightly above normal and gout is quite rare in the lower back; however, the same thing happened to him many years ago after he had gone through a very stressful time in medical school. The treatment for gout was to take Colchicine, which is an oral prescriptive medicine made from rose petals. In fact, Colchicine has been used for hundreds of years.

The day after I started taking this drug, I was fine. I've always suspected that the profit motive affected the previous doctor's diagnoses. Thank goodness I had the angels working for me through this nurse. During the rest of my life I have had other gout attacks, but never in the lower back and never with this severity. They have usually occurred in the ankle or elbow after any kind of an injury. But in each instance, after I took Colchicine, I was all right. Doctors generally don't prescribe it because its patent has run out, and it is available inexpensively. And so the drug company representatives don't put it in their advertisements to doctors, and it is easily forgotten. My experience tells me that gout isn't understood or dealt with very well in today's medical world. In fact, the wife of one of my doctor clients told me several years later that most physicians today don't know how to diagnose or treat gout.

Taking a Bigger Role in Government Contract Accounting

The firm grew a little each year, and my billing rate was $50 an hour by 1970. Somehow I got about ten practicing psychiatrists as clients. They must have liked me because they kept referring me to their professional friends. Several of them were really financially screwed up. I talked to one of them a lot about money problems, particularly how to divide money between husband and wife. Although this psychiatrist wasn't doing very well with his own money problems, he said that in his clinical experience, the second biggest problem in marriage—second only to sex—was money. Nancy and I never had any money problems.

In 1971 I was asked to attend a luncheon meeting of The Young Presidents' Club and to be part of a three-man panel to discuss government contracting. The other two panelists were partners in Big Eight accounting firms. For much of the 1970s and 1980s, these Big Eight public accounting firms dominated the corporate accounting world—Arthur Andersen, Coopers and Lybrand, Deloitte Haskins and Sells, Ernst and Whinney, Peat Marwick Mitchell, Price Waterhouse, Touche Ross, and Arthur Young.

Nevertheless, that day on the panel, I was the big star of the program because I was the only one who could relate to the various problems which were discussed. After the luncheon, Ron Easley, president of Systems Planning Corporation (SPC), invited me to visit his company and handle his corporate tax work. In a matter of several years this company grew to over $50,000,000 in sales and became my largest client. Because of their size, they eventually wanted their audits done by a national firm, so I introduced them to Arthur Andersen, the firm with which I had worked in my years at Welex Corporation.

Even though I lost that particular audit job, I still did a lot of consulting for SPC and was in charge of their Employment Stock Ownership Plan (ESOP). I sent Arthur Andersen several more of my clients and also used them to help me solve difficult problems. It was a mutually supportive business arrangement between my small company and this large one. Andersen sent me some of their clients for special projects relating to governments contracts, partly due to my unique experience and also due to my lower fees.

One client that came as a referral from Arthur Andersen was Aiken Industries. The Defense Contract Audit Agency (DCAA) had disallowed millions of dollars in submitted costs at three of the company's divisions—ones located in nearby Fairfax, on Long Island, and in Jackson, Michigan. The main problem was that the company had not given the auditors adequate documentation. By working with the Aiken staff, I was able to find what was needed.

It turned out that my law degree was very helpful in getting certain assignments like these, and then being successful at completing them.

On several occasions one of my clients would ask me to carefully check the financial health of a company they were considering for purchase. This was standard practice. Generally an acquiring company has their CPA firm conduct what is known as a "due diligence audit." This is usually done in a very formal, structured way, but I preferred a different and non-traditional style—a more informal approach that involves a lot of walking around and talking to employees.

One instance of doing this stands out in my memory. In this particular situation, the CEO gave me a hard time and wouldn't let me talk to anyone except him. I got very suspicious when I noticed that all the incoming mail was sent through him. Even more alarming was what I inadvertently discovered. The desk where I was working for a few days during this investigation happened to be the very place where the previous Chief Financial Officer (CFO) had worked. In the drawers I found evidence that millions of dollars in company receivables were uncollectible. The company had exceeded the contract values on numerous occasions without any approval from the contracting officer. Altogether, I performed seven of these types of reviews for my various clients who were thinking about acquiring other businesses. Since I found major problems in all of them, none of the deals ever went through. More help from my angels, I suspect.

Making Adjustments to My Firm

In November of 1973, I decided I would make more money and lead a better life if I had a full time accountant working with me. And so I hired a young woman named Gale Reid, who had recently earned her CPA certificate. I think I would have been more successful earlier in my career if I were not so reluctant to spend money for needed staff. The following tax season was a breeze compared to previous years. Not only did I have Gale, this was also the first year we used a computerized system called Computax. We would only have to fill in various boxes on a preprinted form and deliver it to a processing center. A few days later we would get back the completed tax returns ready for filing.

The following fall we decided it was time to move the office out of our home. Nancy was tired of being my secretary, and it was kind of awkward having Gale working in our house. I found a nice place nearby with two offices and a reception area. The night before I was to sign the lease, we were having dinner at a Chinese restaurant and my fortune cookie said, "Reconsider a decision you have recently made." I was very open to the possibility that this might be meaningful synchronicity, and so I thought about any and all decisions I was on the verge of making—especially the one about the lease agreement. But what were the options?

One alternative came to mind. I had heard about an office condo near our house, but had not considered it because it was larger and more expensive than I wanted. But the next morning I went to see it for myself, and before long I had bought it for $60,000—my first and only investment in commercial real estate.

The new space was just right for my growing company. My front office was large enough for a table by the window where I could talk to clients. And to the right of my office was a reception area with room for two desks. Going down the hall there were rest rooms on the left, a library/work room on the right, and in the back were two nice–sized offices.

It was actually more space than I needed, and so I rented out one of the offices to a young attorney, and in turn I agreed to share with him the new secretary I had hired. Making things even more affordable for us, the condominium association for our building also gave us $2,000 a year to handle their paperwork. This decision turned out to be an advantageous move, and I am really thankful for the help from the angels that came through the fortune cookie.

Nancy even ended up joining us there. About a year after the condo office purchase, the new secretary had to leave when her husband was transferred out of town. Nancy decided she wanted to come back to work with me at the accounting firm. We were back as a team in the firm, and it made lots of sense for several reasons. We had been paying the secretary more than Nancy was making as a furniture adjuster at Bloomingdale's, a twenty-five minute drive from home. In sharp contrast, the condo office was only five minutes away, and this allowed her to get back to the house around 3:30 p.m. to be with the children as they got home from school.

Professionally, this new set-up at the office condo was a turning point for me. During the four years I was in this office, my annual income increased from $60,000 to $100,000. It felt very significant for me to have a prestigious office and employees. It's too bad I waited until I was over forty years old.

The Carters

One of my favorite government contracting clients was Delex Electronics. The new CEO, Frank Carter, was a graduate of the U.S. Naval Academy and had completed a career as a naval officer. He and Mary had recently married, and she became the assistant to the CFO at Delex. As my clients, I met with them several days a week and trained them in government contract accounting. Mary caught on very quickly, and soon became the CFO of Delex, and then later CFO for another government contractor.

To this day the Carters have been our favorite friends. We have frequently visited them at their second home in Great Barrington, Massachusetts, and we both eventually bought time-shares and then winter homes in Palm Desert, California. But even more memorable, it was through their friendship that Nancy and I found ourselves with a new home. In 1977 the Carters had just bought a new house in Great Falls, Virginia for $225,000. In a social setting soon thereafter, we were talking about mortgages and taxes. Mary asked me what our mortgage was on our current home, and she was flabbergasted when I told her it was $20,000. She said that was ridiculous for a man of my position, and she told me about a beautiful lot—only two doors down from them—which had just come on the market. I called the developer, and we went to see the property and the architectural plans that he had for construction. That evening Nancy and I signed a contract to buy a three-story English Tudor for $262,000.

The house had been designed by the developer with intentions for it to serve as the signature house of the neighborhood. I found out later that he lost money on the deal because we didn't make any changes from his original design, and he had been counting on any buyer wanting to make expensive changes.

It was extraordinary to watch our new home take shape over the coming months of construction. It sat up on a hill on a partially wooded two-and-a-half acre lot with three hundred feet of road frontage. Behind the house there was nothing but woods. The living room had a twenty-five foot ceiling with a balcony, which had bookshelves and a reading area. The first floor also had a nice TV room, kitchen, and living room. The second floor had four bedrooms, and the basement level was unfinished.

By selling our previous house for $89,950, our office condo for $90,000, and cashing in our savings, we were able to realize just enough cash for our down payment of $100,000. Having now sold the office condo, we had to find a new location for the accounting firm, and so we rented space in Vienna, Virginia, only ten minutes away. However, selling our previous home for some of the down payment meant that there would be a four-month period without a place to live while the new construction progressed. Nancy and David moved into my mother-in-law's one bedroom apartment in nearby Tyson's Corner, and I moved in with some friends. (By this time Ken and Kathleen were at Duke University.)

I only wish that Nancy's father would have been able to see this new home. He would have been proud of us and all the hard work that made it possible. Houses meant a lot to him, and he would have been very pleased. Nancy's mother Mary certainly loved the house. She was always coming over to take pictures of it.

Of course, moving into this spacious new home also meant some sacrifices with the accounting firm's set-up. The new office was considerably smaller than the old one. There was a small reception area and a small office, plus a large office with room for a conference table. Gale had recently left the firm, and I found a young CPA to take her place. Nancy continued to be the secretary for another year, and then she left to start her own career as a real estate agent. But in spite of close quarters for awhile, I was feeling very, very grateful. Over the previous five years the accounting firm and my own spiritual development had prospered significantly—thanks in large part to the Holy Spirit and his army of angels. But there was no way that I could have envisioned what lay ahead.

Chapter 11

The Blessings of Asthma

Everyone's life journey invariably involves facing obstacles, and often those obstacles are related to physical health. Much of the character of a person is seen in how he or she meets those challenges and difficulties of the body. Physical limitations, illnesses, or accidents are all proving grounds for the soul. Potentially they can make us better as individuals.

In Don's life one such chronic challenge has been his asthma. It has been like a thread that runs through his biography—sometimes seeming to limit or block his opportunities, but just as often serving to steer his life in a direction that he was able to meet creatively and make into a blessing.

A health challenge can also present us with a riddle. Where did this come from? Why do I have this difficulty? The depth and sincerity with which a person searches for answers is a measuring rod for that individual. In Don's case, he was able to discover multiple causes and reasons for his asthma, and each of those causes took him deeper into understanding how his asthma really could be seen as a gift.

What's more, the physical difficulties faced by an individual provide another sort of test. Like a fork in the road, one can turn down the path of bitterness and self-pity. Or the individual can humbly learn from the challenges and then lovingly share the fruits of understanding with others who face a similar challenge. Don's life story beautifully illustrates how he has taken that second choice, especially in finding ways to help others deal with the same health difficulties that he has had. That kind of loving service truly is the capstone in turning his asthma into a blessing—to himself and others.

❋

I have been told that I had asthma from the time I was three years old. I was so used to it that I never gave it much thought. I certainly never worried about it. I do remember being rushed to the hospital on several occasions for a shot of adrenalin. The most frequent remedy I can remember for alleviating an asthma attack was for me to breathe in the smoke from what we called "leaves." This was a tobacco–like substance which was placed in a dish beside my bed. I would frequently take this at night so I could get a good night's sleep. I was never quite sure what "leaves" were, but many years later—around 1975—I was at the beach with my brother and several of his kids. In the evening when my brother wasn't around, one of my nieces encouraged me to try a little pot. I didn't like it all that much, but the smell and feeling from that marihuana was just like the leaves I had when I was a child.

Fortunately, "leaves" were not the only remedy available to me as a child. When I was about eight years old, a doctor gave me an atomizer which relieved my asthma attacks immediately. This changed my life because I could carry this with me and could take it whenever I felt an attack coming on. Of course, this was all a bit awkward because in 1940 atomizers were very bulky. They had a long rubber bulb that was attached to a glass receptacle—nothing like the compact ones today that are pocket–size, plastic, and have a small vial with the actual medication.

From age eight onward the use of my atomizer really did change my life because the threat of an oncoming asthma attack did not have to be my constant worry. But it was not the entire answer since the atomizer spray did not help my asthma very much when I also had a bad cold. In these cases the doctor prescribed something stronger: prednisone, which made me feel great. In fact, I used prednisone sporadically until I entered Duke University in 1950. Then I learned that maybe this was not such a good idea after all.

I have related in Chapter 7 my experiences at the Duke University Hospital when I was suffering with mononucleosis and asthma. The first thing I had to do after graduating from Duke in

1954 was to report for induction into the Armed Services. In those days you had to join the army when you were eighteen, but you were deferred until you finished college. After a thorough medical exam, the doctor declared that I was 4–F due to my asthma, and I was given a permanent deferment. Ed had gotten deferred about the same time, but in his case he made it into the army and then later came down with an asthma attack from the cigarette smoke in the barracks. I considered my deferment to be a major blessing of my asthma, because I had always been a very peaceful person and could never fight anyone, let alone kill them. This nature of mine was later confirmed in a life reading which said that in a previous lifetime I was a monk in India.

Asthma, Allergies, and Acupuncture

There are two kinds of asthma, one caused by my allergies and the other caused by lung infections, such as a bad cold. I was a very allergic child. When I was 16 an allergist tested me for over 300 different potential allergens, and I showed sensitivity to every one! On a scale of one to five, some of the allergens were only a one or a two for my test, but there were many fours and fives, such as nuts, mold spores, dust, animals, etc. I had a major reaction to the tests right there at the doctor's office, and I had to have an injection of adrenalin.

Knowing that my asthma was usually allergy–triggered, I have searched over the years for innovative methods to deal with those allergies. In 1998 I met an acupuncturist who gave me a special kind of treatment. I had frequently tried acupuncture, but her approach was totally different. It was a method that used muscle testing—what's referred to as applied kinesiology, although it was certainly new to me. She had about 300 little capsules, each one of which contained a different allergen. I would stretch out my arm and hold a capsule in my hand. She would try to push my arm down. It was really amazing because for those items to which I was allergic my arm would go down with her push, no matter how hard I tried to keep it up. If I was not allergic to what was in a capsule, there was no way she could overcome my resistance and push my arm down. One–by–one, as an allergy was determined, she would give me an acupuncture treatment while I held the allergen in my hand.

One allergy she treated me for was cotton, an allergy I never knew I had. But after this treatment I slept much better at night since it was my sleeping habit to always bury my head in my pillow with a cotton pillowcase. I think she got rid of all my allergies except for nuts. That one continues to this day. When I eat a nut I immediately get a kind of burning on the tongue and shivers. If I have just a small taste of the nut, the reaction will go away in about ten minutes, and I'm fine. But if I eat too much, I will vomit and have an asthma attack.

That means that every time I go to a restaurant, I ask about nuts. It's important for me to check because sometimes they put nuts where you least expect it. Once I was traveling by air and found nuts in my pancakes. And airlines generally serve some kind of nuts with the drinks they offer. These days if I tell them I'm allergic to nuts, they'll run and get me something else. In fact, I've been told that if you call up and tell them in advance that you're allergic to nuts, they aren't allowed to serve nuts to anyone. I'll have to try that sometime.

Some places outside of the United States are more sensitive and accommodating to people like me who have this sort of health limitation. For example, I was so impressed one time when I was visiting in England. Going through the line in a cafeteria, I saw that there were signs indicating each item that contained nuts. I wish they would do that in this country, too. Packaged foods in the United States show ingredients, but not restaurants. Sometimes there is more awareness about the problem in public schools. There are even some schools in which children are not allowed to bring peanut butter sandwiches; or in other schools, children who bring nuts, peanuts, or peanut butter have to sit at a separate table. That's a far cry from the way things were sixty years ago when nut allergies were uncommon and the need for caution was not recognized nor honored. I can remember complaining in vain when a cafeteria cook would make my sandwich with the same knife that was used to make a peanut butter sandwich.

As I have gotten older I have become less allergic to nuts. This is both good and bad. It is good in the sense that I can eat a little bit with no reaction, and it is bad in the sense that I can't always tell if I'm eating nuts and therefore might end up with a major reaction. For example, several years ago when we were staying at our country club home in Indian Wells, California, I ate an almond and had no reaction to it and it really tasted good. Since I thought I was no longer allergic to almonds, I began eating them on a regular basis. Two weeks later we were at a bridge party at the clubhouse, and I felt a little asthma coming on. So I started to take a little of my prescription spray. That's the last thing I remember until I woke up in the hospital the next day.

My wife told me that I had passed out and started turning blue. While waiting for the ambulance, several guys had come in from the kitchen, and one started giving me artificial respiration. He was pushed aside by the other guy who said I needed oxygen, and he gave me mouth-to-mouth resuscitation, which proved to be a life-saver. The ambulance arrived, and they gave me some oxygen, but as they carried me out I was still very blue. The people who were with us at the club that night told me later that they were very surprised that I had survived because they had never seen anyone turn so blue. Some of the people were members of my wife's prayer group, and they told me that they had prayed for me.

A few days later the club sent out a notice to all the members. It told everyone about my nut allergy and the details of what had happened. Later I thanked the man who gave me mouth-to-mouth resuscitation and gave him $2,000 as a token of my appreciation for saving my life.

And so, except for this nut-allergy-triggered asthma, I have been largely asthma-free for most of my adult life as long as I maintain my prescription medicines. However, I developed emphysema when I was about 65, and I have been told that this is a result of my asthma. The fact that I smoked from age 18 to 40 may also be a contributing factor. With emphysema, breathing once again became the challenging issue, especially when exercising and when at higher altitudes. For example, for many years when I played golf, I had to take an oxygen tank with me. I didn't use it when I was taking a swing, but I took a whiff of oxygen after I raked a sand trap or walked up a hill. Things have improved in recent years, as I will describe in the final chapter. I even needed for awhile to sleep with oxygen (because one doesn't breathe as deeply while asleep) but that is no longer required. I have, however, continued to need oxygen when I travel by air, so I need to make special arrangements with the airline ahead of time. The airlines typically charge me $100 for each leg of travel.

Searching for Reasons for My Asthma

Through the years I have frequently asked myself why I had all these problems. I often found myself blaming my mother. At the age of three, I was in the hospital with rickets because I couldn't keep food down and had a major protein deficiency. My mother was going through a nervous breakdown and was very mad most of the time, due primarily to financial problems. She was always worried about me, and so she restricted my activities. On top of that, I was always very sensitive towards my mother, and I can remember often feeling sorry for her. Admittedly, she certainly did a lot for me, but there were also deep tensions between us that must have had an impact on my health. In fact, I enjoyed my best health when I went away from home and was going to college. Even taking into consideration my bout with mononucleosis, my college years at Duke University were overall the best period of health for me.

Getting some space from my mother might not have been the only factor in overcoming some of my health challenges such as asthma and allergies. There may have been physical, emotional, and *metaphysical* factors at work, too. When I started studying the Edgar Cayce readings, I began to wonder if my condition might be karmic. In the Cayce readings about reincarnation, he describes several cases of asthmatics who, in a previous lifetime, had "squeezed the life out of others."

Intuitively this made sense for me about my own condition. I even got some personal evidence that something of this sort might have been going on with me. Around the age of 50, I started going to Santa Fe, New Mexico for past life regression work. In one past life that surfaced during a regression session, I saw myself as a jailer more than a century ago who mistreated many of the inmates. Although there is no way to prove that such a past life scenario has historical accuracy, it was a very meaningful experience for me. It led me to the conclusion that there might well be some deep, unconscious issues within my soul that were playing a role in my health challenges throughout this lifetime.

Equally significant was another experience that came on a later visit to Santa Fe. I attended a special seminar concerning a wide variety of psychic phenomenon. As a part of that seminar, I had a private session with a German psychic woman who was trying to pick up impressions about me by poking around on my arms and legs. Suddenly she said, "Oh, I see that you are an asthmatic. It looks to me like it started when you were a 3-year-old."

I was shocked because this lady knew nothing about me. I proceeded to tell her all about my asthma and my mother. She then asked, "Donald, do you like who you are?" I assured her that I most definitely did. Then she replied, "Do you realize that if it weren't for the mother you had and your history of asthma, you would be a totally different person?" I was speechless, and I walked out of there in a daze. I immediately looked back over my life and realized what a positive impact my mother and my asthmatic condition had had on my life. Today I consider my mother and asthma to be blessings because they helped me become a very sensitive person.

Serving Others with Asthma

I have always felt that a leading cause of asthma might be stress and trauma in early childhood, otherwise known as post-traumatic stress disorder (PTSD). I certainly experienced a lot of trauma at age three with my sickness and my mother screaming at my father all the time. And I have seen statistics that asthma is much more prevalent in the inner city among low–income families. For example, a child who has a very young, unmarried mother and no live–in father is surely under a tremendous amount of stress.

My own struggles with asthma made me want to help others facing similar difficulties. In 1999 Nancy and I played a major role in founding a free clinic for asthmatic children at Howard University in Washington, D.C. This all got started because my good friend Reggie Brown (also an asthmatic) discovered the opportunity when he met Floyd Malveaux, M.D., the Dean of the College of Medicine at Howard University. Previously, Reggie had been a high–ranking presidential appointee at the Office of Management and Budget under the first President George Bush. With the advent of the Clinton administration in 1993, Reggie had lost his job, and now Reggie was working for me for $25,000 a year on a variety of projects.

Through Dr. Malveaux, Reggie learned that Howard University had just completed an asthma research program; and as an application of the research findings, Dr. Malveaux wanted to start a clinic to help needy children deal with their asthma. The basic plan was that the clinic would provide all the medical costs relating to the asthma and provide ongoing counseling. The biggest single expense of the clinic was going to be a full time asthma counselor who would meet with the patients on a regular basis and teach them how to manage their condition. The counselor would also go around the city educating people about the program and urging them to participate. Dr. Malveaux already had a counselor in mind who was available, but Reggie and I didn't think she was the right person for the job, so we put an ad in the paper and found Ellie Thornton, who had dedicated her life to dealing with asthmatics. She was a nurse who had asthma herself, and she had even adopted a son with asthma.

Nancy and I starting making an annual donation to the clinic of $90,000, and the clinic quickly became a big success, with more than seventy–five active participants most of the time. In 2005 Dr. Malveaux left Howard University and went to work for a non–

profit affiliate of the pharmaceutical Merck & Company. The program was called the Merck Childhood Asthma Network. They conducted research for asthmatics in places which had a high incidence of asthma, such as Puerto Rico, and later in the areas impacted by Hurricane Katrina. Meanwhile, after years of being the spearhead of the Howard University asthma clinic, Ellie also left Howard University to work for yet another asthma charity. With both of these two key figures gone, the clinic that we had founded at Howard University died off—in large part because the federal government started a program to provide free medical services to disadvantaged children. Nevertheless, the clinic at Howard University had served a very valuable purpose and had helped thousands of people.

But that wasn't the end of the story about Nancy's and my commitment to help asthmatics. In 2006, Dr. Malveaux called me and said he wanted to hire Ellie for his program, but Merck wouldn't put it in the budget. So we shifted our same annual charitable contribution to Dr. Malveaux's program, and Ellie had a new phase in her life's work, now involved with children who are part of innovative asthma research programs.

In 2007, I was at Dr Malveaux's house to have dinner and negotiate our contract for the coming year. Ellie was there, too, and as the evening progressed I had a chance to chat with her. I asked how her son was doing, and she said that his asthma was well under control. There was also good news that he was doing very well with his university education in Florida. Then I said to her, "Ellie, you and your son were very blessed to have asthma. If you hadn't had asthma you wouldn't have known Dr. Malveaux or me and you wouldn't have your current job. And you've told me a number of times that you adopted the child you did because he had asthma."

Ellie was blown away by this. It was the same feeling of astonishment, surprise, and appreciation that I had had years ago when the psychic in Santa Fe had made me look at my "handicap" with asthma in a whole new way.

Guru Maharaji

Maharaji as a young man

Don with portrait of Edgar Cayce's son, Hugh Lynn

Don and portrait of Edgar Cayce,
with Cayce's grandson, Charles Thomas

Chapter 12

Spiritual Development

The depth and quality of one's life is largely shaped by how we deal with questions about values and purpose and meaning. Those are the questions of spirituality. Time and again, Don's life has demonstrated his willingness to explore spiritually beyond the limits of traditional religion. Although he has often worked and served within a church, he was called to a deeper examination of some of the more mysterious parts of the Bible (such as Revelations*), to the meaning of healing and how he might be a healer himself, and to tools for personal spirituality such as dream interpretation and meditation.*

This part of his story challenges us all to consider how adventurous we are willing to be as we think about questions of the meaning of life or our own role in the larger scheme of things. We are sure to be impressed—and inspired—by the frequent times when Don was willing to push the edges of his own understanding.

❀

When we lived in Maryland and Washington, D.C., we attended the Takoma Park Presbyterian Church on a fairly regular basis. My father was somewhat religious and taught Sunday school, whereas my mother went along with the church because it was the thing to do. I was a Cub Scout and later a Boy Scout at this church, and so in most ways my strongest connection to that church was because of what I was getting out of scouting and not because of any religious connection.

But as often happens to a young person, the dynamics of family life played a big role in religious practice, and so when I was sixteen I agreed to join the church in order to make my father happy. Young people who wanted to join the church would attend a six-week study program on church doctrine called the communicant's class. This wasn't easy for me because this class was not really teaching me to think for myself and make my own faith decisions. For example, each of us was expected to believe in the Apostle's Creed in order to become a member. But I questioned many parts of the Creed in the class, and the answer was always the same, "It's in the Bible." I later discovered that the Apostle's Creed itself is not in the Bible. Its origins are somewhat mysterious but surely well after the New Testament was written; and, in fact, the earliest appearance of the present version dates back only to the eighth century.

Even as a teenager, this dispute about the Apostle's Creed brought into focus for me one central issue that has always bothered me about Christianity. The Creed—and for that matter, most of Christianity—asserts that Jesus is the *only* begotten son of God, and *only* through him can one find the kingdom of heaven. Other great religious teachers have accepted Jesus as a great spiritual leader but not to the exclusion of other great masters. As I understand spirituality, it makes a lot of sense for Jesus to tell his disciples that only through him can they find God. But if other people or cultures want to follow other spiritual leaders, isn't that fine? In fact, Jesus says throughout the New Testament, "Judge not, lest ye be judged." There's no question in my mind that if Christians had been more respectful of other religions, there would be much more peace in the world today.

When I went to Duke University, I attended church only during my first semester. Thereafter church attendance was rare because the active fraternity life and all–night card games made it difficult to get up in the morning. But in 1960, as my wife Nancy and I had recently started our family, we decided we should start going to church again. Because we had been brought up as church members, we felt we wanted our children baptized. We joined a Methodist church near our home on Gresham Street. We were never very active in this church, but we enjoyed the Sunday services, and they had a nice Sunday school for our young son Kenny and provided babysitting for Kathy.

After my parents returned in 1958 from my father's job assignment in Cambodia, they first moved back into their Takoma Park house. But in 1965, they bought a house near where we were going to live, and they joined a new Presbyterian church that was being built next door to them. When we moved into our new house, my parents were already charter members of this church, and so we decided to join also. In many ways it was fun going to the same church, except for the fact that I was once again faced with my father's expectations. Whenever I missed church, my father always wanted to know where I was.

Nevertheless, his concerns were short-lived because Nancy and I soon became very active in the Providence Presbyterian Church. Nancy was active in the ladies' group and taught Sunday school; I was a scoutmaster, deacon, elder, youth leader and involved in several Bible study groups.

A Broadening Vision of Spirituality

During this period I was not only very active in church life, I was also beginning to study extensively the broader ranges of spirituality. I was reading about other religions, reincarnation, and extra-sensory perception (ESP). And when I was in my mid-thirties, I ran across a biography about Edgar Cayce called *The Sleeping Prophet* by Jess Stearn. I was deeply inspired by the story of this man Cayce. As a very young man at the turn of the 20th century, Cayce discovered that he had the psychic ability to give health readings. These clairvoyant discourses, given in order to diagnose and recommend natural healing methods, were obviously from a higher source. The information was of a very technical nature, and the case reports showed considerable success in healing people for whom mainstream medicine of the times had given up. Cayce even discovered that he could give readings for people who were thousands of miles away without the use of a telephone. A typed report of the verbatim, stenographic transcript was mailed to the recipient. (All those reports are now available to the general public in an electronic form for individual study and research.)

But it wasn't just this pioneering work in holistic medicine that intrigued me. Later in his life—in fact, after he had been giving exclusively medical readings for more than twenty years—Cayce found that he could give information on a much wider variety of topics, even about spiritual growth. From a very early age, Cayce was a very religious person. He taught Sunday school at a Presbyterian church, and he read the whole Bible once for every year of his life. One day he found himself giving a reading for a man, and unexpectedly he started giving information about that man's previous lifetime hundreds of years ago. This bothered Cayce a great deal because his church didn't believe in reincarnation. Many more readings like this followed in the years to come, but it took Cayce himself quite a while to personally accept a broader view of spirituality and the soul than he had learned (or taught in his Sunday school class) in the Presbyterian church.

This philosophy from the Cayce readings was certainly a challenge and a great opportunity for me, too. I discovered that Cayce eventually gave readings on such topics as Atlantis, man's creation, the birth and life of Jesus, an interpretation of the *Book of Genesis* and the *Book of Revelations*, as well as making many predictions about the future. Many of his prophecies dealt with earth changes and world peace, and he said the biggest problem would be in the Middle East around the turn of the century.

All of Cayce's readings were recorded and sorted by subject and are available today in many publications. They are even available in their entirety as a database for computer access and research. After giving nearly 15,000 readings, Cayce died in 1945 at the age of 67, but his work is carried on today at the Virginia Beach, Virginia headquarters of the Association for Research and Enlightenment (A.R.E.).

Getting More Deeply into the Cayce Material

Just reading about Cayce's philosophy was not going to be enough for me. Nancy and I wanted to see the organization he had founded in Virginia Beach. During one of our first visits to the

A.R.E., I went to their library and studied what Cayce had to say about asthma. I discovered that from 1921 to 1944, Cayce gave 166 readings for 107 different individuals who had asthma. Many of those readings mentioned that when certain spinal vertebrae were out of alignment it could cause bodily influences to aggravate the asthma. In those cases, Cayce usually recommended chiropractic or osteopathic adjustments. The readings also recommended breathing the fumes of apple brandy from a charred-oak keg— hardly the kind of treatment I had ever heard about from my doctor, but one that sounded interesting as a natural, home remedy. He also recommended to many asthmatics the use of an energy medicine device called a wet cell appliance. The main medicine he recommended was atomidine—a special preparation of iodine that was to be used sparingly (just a few drops in a glass of water).

I tried all of these remedies, including more than a year of regular chiropractic adjustments. I think they may have helped, but I had to keep in mind that most asthma treatments used today were not available when Cayce was giving his readings. For his recommendations he had to work with what was available in the 1920s or 1930s.

Most recently I discovered how easy and convenient it is to do research in the Cayce material with computerized searches, and I've placed some of my favorite passages about Cayce's spiritual philosophy in Appendix 2 at the end of this book. In some readings given to asthmatics, Cayce indicated an influence from reincarnation—that is, in a previous lifetime the individual had "squeezed the life out of others" and in doing so had created a kind of soul-memory that now had to be met and overcome in the current lifetime. Perhaps something similar is true for me. In those Cayce readings, the emphasis was upon how the purpose for this current lifetime with asthma was to be more loving and considerate of others—that is, the very *opposite* of "squeezing the life out of others." In fact, I have tried in many ways to make my life one of love and consideration. So, in a way, I'm glad I have had asthma since it has made me a better person.

One of my favorite groups of Cayce readings is about the creation of humanity. There are hints about this in the Bible, but Cayce went into elaborate detail about how the soul came into being. My favorite Cayce-based publications were written by Eula Allen, a woman who knew and worked with Cayce. Her series of books was written in the 1960s and entitled *The Trilogy*. Each of the three books (*Before the Beginning*, *The River of Time*, and *You Are Forever*) dealt with some aspect of the creation of the world and of man. In brief, Allen described Cayce's philosophy as saying that in the beginning all souls were with God, but they wanted to leave God and take on experiencing the physical world, especially bodies—where, at first, only the bodies of animals were available. This separation from God is symbolized in the Bible by the eating of the forbidden fruit in the Garden of Eden, as well as by the Parable of the Prodigal Son. In Cayce's story, as presented by Eula Allen, the human body was eventually prepared for us as the best vehicle through which we could experience the material world and have a chance to reconnect to the spiritual truth of who we are. Although the Cayce readings indicate that our purpose is to return to God, there is much work and time involved. But when the human soul does return, each soul will be much more realized than when leaving eons ago.

The Book of Revelation indicates that no one will return to God until everyone returns. For this reason many great masters choose to return to earth in a physical body to help others. This broad view of spirituality spoke deeply to me. But it makes me sad to see how some religions embrace the belief in how a great spiritual being can come back to help us, but they interpret this in a very limited and self-serving way. For example, the Seventh Day Adventists are strong believers in The Second Coming, but the problem is that they believe Christ will save *only* the Adventists.

The Book of Revelation has long held a fascination for me, and Cayce gave twenty-four readings specifically to interpret it. Those interpretations have been studied carefully by Cayce scholars and by groups over the years, and one group in particular has impressed me with the wisdom they were able to derive. This group of seven people working together for seven years in New York City was led by an artist named Shane Miller. Subsequently, they published a book about their results of studying Cayce's deciphering of *The Revelation*, as well as a thirty-minute video program featuring Shane Miller's beautiful artwork to illustrate the Cayce interpretations.

I had the chance to hear Shane Miller and see the video program at a five-day seminar which I attended. That really made the material come alive for me. As he described it, the first half of *The Book of Revelation* deals with the development of *individual* man; and, the second half deals with *collective* man—all of us as humanity. The seven churches mentioned by John are symbolic of the seven endocrine glands and the seven spiritual centers (or "chakras" as they are called in Eastern religions). Those seven endocrine glands are:

- The pituitary gland, which can reflect divine love, harmony and balance, but also indecision;

- The pineal gland, which is related to soul-memory;

- The thyroid gland, which is the center of self-expression and free will;

- The thymus gland, which is linked to our immune system, as well as our efforts to be loving at a personal level;

- The adrenal glands, which have control of issues related to anger, fear, and determination;

- The cells of leydig, which are related to our imaginative capacity; and,

- The gonads, which relate to sexual reproduction, physical security, and sometime our self indulgence.

The second half of *The Revelation* indicates that 144,000 perfect souls will lead mankind to 1,000 years of peace which is called the first redemption. Then the animal nature of man will arise again before the second redemption brings permanent peace.

As intriguing as I found the Cayce interpretation of *The Revelation* to be, I also wanted to explore other aspects of his spiritual teachings, and to do so in a small group seemed like a good discipline. In 1966, I began participating in a "Search for God" study group which met weekly near my home. The first such group was started by twelve people in Virginia Beach who met regularly to discuss and practice reaching a higher attunement with God based upon the Cayce readings. Cayce himself was a member of that first group, and he gave general readings for this group about the aspects of soul growth.

When I started attending a group, there were about 1,500 *Search for God* groups throughout the United States and Canada. How blessed I was by the angels to have such an outstanding group which met close to my house. The group was led by a lady named Esther Ham who was a long time student of the Edgar Cayce material and a very respected leader at A.R.E. The basis of study was a small book entitled *A Search for God* with chapter headings that seemed to focus on the spiritual growth aspects of Cayce's work and not the sensationalistic, psychic side of his life that attracted many people. The chapter topics we studied were meditation; cooperation; know thyself; ideals; faith; virtue and understanding; fellowship; patience; the open door; in his presence; the cross and the crown; the lord thy god is one; and, love.

Meditation and Dreams

Each *Search for God* meeting would start with a group meditation followed by discussions, insights, and personal experiences. Sometimes we would spend a whole evening on just one page of the *Search for God* book. Even though a Book II with further lessons was developed and published, we never finished Book I. I think it was meant to be this way because if we finished Book I we might have thought we were fully evolved.

Meditation was the key element of the Cayce recommendations. I had been doing a progressive meditation that I had read about in some books on Eastern religions. In this technique the meditator first concentrates on his feet and then slowly, over the course of about thirty minutes, moves up his body to the top of his head. Cayce does not insist on any particular meditation technique, but he has suggested starting out with alternate nostril breathing. You breathe in through the right nostril and exhale through the mouth, three repetitions. Then breathe in through the left nostril and exhale through the right nostril, three repetitions. The next step is to recite aloud or silently to yourself an affirmation, which may be very brief, such as, "Be still and know that I am God." The affirmation could also be the Lord's Prayer or any spiritual statement which means something to you. Each chapter in the *Search for God* book also has an affirmation. The next step is to try to let go of all your thoughts, but when your mind wanders, return to the affirmation. This meditation can be done sitting or lying down for about twenty minutes, twice a day, at approximately the same times daily.

Cayce also recommended that we pay attention to our dreams. In order to remember your dreams, it's a good idea to keep a notebook next to your bed so you can make some notes as soon as you awaken. Some people are very good at interpreting dreams, and there are also books which set forth universal symbols. Some examples are blue means truth (as in, "true blue"); water means spirituality (such as with baptism); and green means supply or health (just as the color of our money, and the color of surgeons' gowns).

Cayce's ideas about dream interpretation led me to another important man who lived at about the same time as Cayce, the psychiatrist Carl Jung. His writings about dream psychology are extensive, and he also believed that many of our dream symbols are universal ones—what he called archetypes. For example, he wrote that wings indicate death. To illustrate this, I had a very good friend who was in our church study group who kept having a recurring dream in which she had very large wings. A minister at a local Unity church said it meant she would die soon. Since she was in perfect health she laughed it off, but she asked her husband to take her to Hawaii, because she wanted to go there before she died. While in Hawaii she died in her sleep. Her husband was never very clear as to her cause of death. I felt bad about her passing but it seems that maybe this was her destiny, and her dream had foreshadowed it.

Nancy and I attended a seminar on dreams conducted by Elsie Sechrist and Hugh Lynn Cayce, Edgar Cayce's son who pretty much ran A.R.E. after his father died in 1945. Elsie had written a book about dream interpretation and universal symbols, *Dream, Your Magic Mirror*. Attending seminars like this one was an important part of my learning how to work with my own dreams.

Another seminar that was especially memorable was on the topic of the soul's purpose and evolution. Psychologist and Cayce scholar Herb Puryear gave a fascinating lecture in which he presented ideas about how *The Wizard of Oz* could be symbolically interpreted to tell us about the soul's spiritual journey. For example, he said that Dorothy's dog Toto represented the Spirit of Rebellion. He was black which symbolizes evil; but he was just a small dog, which might mean he was just a kind of mischief. In fact, in the story, Toto was always getting Dorothy into trouble. For example, when the tornado came, Dorothy had to get Toto, and she didn't make it into the storm cellar. If it weren't for Toto, Dorothy would never have made the trip to Oz. This is just like the biblical story of Adam; if he hadn't eaten the forbidden apple, he would never have left the Garden of Eden. According to Puryear, Adam and all mankind are trying to return home to God—just as Dorothy was always trying to return home to Kansas. What's especially important is that Dorothy was much more advanced in her wisdom and understanding when she returned home, just as mankind will be more advanced when we return to God, compared to when we left.

This lecture by Herbert Puryear deeply stimulated my interest. Afterwards, I made an in-depth study of *The Wizard of Oz* and its author L. Frank Baum. He was a photographer and theosophist. *The Wizard of Oz* was his first book. Something about that story has captured the imagination of millions of people over the decades, and the Hollywood movie is what most people think of first when they hear the words "Wizard of Oz." But there are some very significant differences between the way Baum wrote the original story and what became the Hollywood screenplay. For example, in the Hollywood version, the whole story in the Land of Oz is depicted as a dream that Dorothy had after being knocked unconscious from the tornado. But the book treats everything that happens in the whole story as the same reality. And in the end, Dorothy doesn't just wake up from a dream and find herself back in Kansas, like we see in the movie. Instead, she is sent home by the Wizard, and as she is traveling through the sky, her red slippers fall off. This symbolizes that she no longer needs her spiritual leader, who was Glenda, the good witch of the North. She has connected to her *own* spiritual power and authority.

There have been several very successful Broadway shows based on the story, and Baum also wrote other stories about the characters in Oz. But the fascinating thing I learned from my studies was that the first book was written very quickly. I feel that *The Wizard of Oz* was divinely inspired, and it reminds me of how quickly Lincoln wrote the Gettysburg Address, something else that I believe must have been written with divine inspiration.

Cayce and Youth Groups

I was asked to lead a young people's group at the Providence Church on Sunday evenings, and so on one of our visits to Virginia Beach I decided to ask Hugh Lynn Cayce what he thought I should teach. He asked me how my meditation was doing, and I admitted that I was being somewhat negligent along those lines. He then told me that if I would focus on my own spiritual development, I would *know* what to teach. I thought that was great advice, and I recommitted myself to meditation so that I could connect to my own intuitive wisdom about what to teach the group.

There were about twelve teenagers in our study group, half of whom were hippies and the other half were born-again Christians. The hippies really trusted me and considered me to be one of them. One time the whole group went on a campout, and one young couple (from among the hippie side of the group) was setting up their tent as if they were planning to sleep together. They were surprised when I said they couldn't do that. I explained that I would get in trouble with the church if word got out that boys and girls were sleeping together.

Although we didn't have any more campouts, we did go to the Amish country in Lancaster, Pennsylvania, and stayed on a Mennonite farm. We went to their church the next morning and met with the young Mennonites afterwards. Both sets of kids really enjoyed getting to know each other. I felt that this kind of a trip really helped the members of my group broaden their understanding of religion, spirituality, and the different kinds of faith that are right here in America. And I included other activities like this for the group, including a memorable visit to a black Baptist church in Washington, D.C.

I also felt intuitively inspired to introduce to these teenagers some of the more esoteric ideas I had been learning. We spent about six weeks studying *The Wizard of Oz*, and then we went through the creation story according to Edgar Cayce. The kids also put on a Christmas pageant which was very successful. The congregation really appreciated the production. It's the only time I ever directed any kind of a production, and I think I did a pretty good job. I actually wrote an original production for this event which I think was divinely inspired, but I never had the nerve to show it to anyone, except Nancy, who typed it. We ended up using a script for the production which seemed like it would be less controversial.

Right after this I was asked by our pastor to represent our church in running a group foster home for teenage boys that was being established in Fairfax County. The county provided a child psychologist, and we hired a couple to be foster parents. Each of three churches sent a representative to serve on a committee which was the governing body of the home. The group had about eight boys who for various reasons did not live with their parents. I became quite close to some of the boys, and once we went out to

Bagley's Farm for a campout (the same farm where we had occasional Boy Scout campouts, as I described earlier). After about a year the home was closed because relatives showed up, and the foster parents ended up adopting two of the boys. The entire experience, however, was a wonderful example of how people in church communities can get together and do something of service that really demonstrates their beliefs.

Healing and Group Work

Once when Nancy and I were at the A.R.E. we met a Presbyterian minister and his wife, Sid and Mary Counsel Crane, from a nearby church. They were leading a course on spiritual healing which we liked a lot. Later they came to northern Virginia and conducted another course which we also attended.

Soon after having attended these healing courses with Sid and Mary Counsel, we learned that they were planning to move from Virginia Beach and would be living not far from us. Sid was leaving the ministry and taking a position as a personnel director for an organization in northern Virginia. Mary Counsel called me one day and announced, "Guess what? We joined *your church.*" This couple became very popular with all of our friends at the church. We started a special group of about twelve people who met every Monday evening and worked on spiritual development. The rest of the congregation referred to us as the Monday Night Group.

We studied material that wouldn't be considered mainstream for a church affiliated group. One example was *The Aquarian Gospel*, by Leo (Levi) H. Dowling. He was born in 1844, at Belleville, Ohio, and began preaching when he was 16. When he was 18 he became a pastor at a small church and was a chaplain in the Civil War. The flyleaf of the book says it was transcribed by Levi from the Akashic Records. I immediately remembered that Edgar Cayce claimed that the information that came through him was also from the Akashic Records—an ancient Sanskrit term referring to a repository of all knowledge and all events of human history.

The words in *The Aquarian Gospel* flow so beautifully. The early part of the book describes the early training and studies of Jesus and John the Baptist. Levi's inspired visions showed them receiving schooling in many Eastern religions to supplement their training in Judaism. When Jesus was a young man he traveled throughout India and Egypt, both studying and preaching. He frequently proclaimed that all men were sons of God. I found that *The Aquarian Gospel* included just about everything that is in the New Testament; however, there are many things in *The Aquarian Gospel* which are not in the New Testament, such as the early life of Jesus and his travels to the East.

In our group study of *The Aquarian Gospel* I was finding answers to some deep religious questions that had long concerned me. For example, the doctrine that Jesus was the son of God had always bothered me. But in Chapter 139 of *The Aquarian Gospel*, Jesus clarified this. He said that, "All men are sons of God by birth . . . but all are not the sons of God by faith. He who attains the victory over self is son of God by faith . . . He who believes and does the will of God is son of God by faith." I had also been troubled with the idea as reported in the Bible that Jesus had come to just a few people in a small corner of the world; but, *The Aquarian Gospel* makes the history of Jesus' work sound more global. It claims that when Jesus was resurrected, he appeared to people all over the world.

The Monday Night Group practiced a lot of meditation and healing. One member of our group was healed from multiple sclerosis. It was a truly powerful group to be a part of. What's more, my own experiences of healing were not confined to just the Monday Night Group. I had experiences of my own with remarkable healings.

During the time when I was a scoutmaster I often conducted campouts. On one such occasion, one of the boys was hit on the head with a rock, and his head got a lump the size of a tennis ball. He was passing out and I took him to his tent, placed my hand on his head, and prayed. After this short period of prayer and laying-on-of-hands, I then went to his father, who was also one of our leaders, and I told him to come quickly because his son was severely injured. But at that moment, his son then came running by, seemingly just fine again, and called out to us, "Hi, Mr. D." When I checked his head, there was no lump. I never said anything about what I had done.

Since the mid–1930s, the A.R.E. has had a prayer and healing group called "The Glad Helpers" which does healing by the laying–on–of–hands for anyone who shows up, as well as distance–healing for anyone who requests it. I attended these Wednesday morning group healing sessions whenever I was at the A.R.E., and I definitely feel that these sessions helped my asthmatic condition.

In 1972, Charles Thomas Cayce, grandson of Edgar Cayce, sponsored a healing session conducted by Chief Rolling Thunder. Volunteers from the audience at the conference came up on the stage, and before each session began each volunteer was asked why he wanted to be healed. Chief Rolling Thunder said that spiritual healing is much enhanced if its purpose is to help others to carry out God's will. This is a principle of healing that I have taken to heart, and I believe it's one of the most important factors for us to keep in mind anytime we are searching for a healing.

Probably one of the most remarkable healing stories I have experienced started with the arrival one night at the Monday Night Group of a strange little German lady named Syria. She said the "little people" told her something was going on here, and she wanted to check it out. These "little people" were dwarf–like creatures which only certain people could see. Syria met with our group from time to time, and I began taking reflexology treatments from her. Meanwhile, a very good friend of mine at the church, Jack Williamson, was at Walter Reed Hospital suffering from brain cancer. I went to visit him, and we discussed some of the healing activities of the group. He asked for a healing, and this asking was an important part of what followed. I put my hands on his head and began praying and meditating. Afterwards, there was a very high energy feeling in the room, along with a light, playful spirit. We even joked around with each other and with another friend who was also there. Jack said he couldn't wait till the doctor came in the next day, because he thought he had been healed.

The next morning, at 4:00 a.m., my phone rang and it was Syria.

She said, "Oh, Donald, I just saw the most beautiful death. Jack Williamson just died. Jesus was there with many angels. Everything was brightly colored and the music was magnificent." I turned over and went back to sleep thinking that Syria was crazy because Jack had been healed. When I got up for the day, I called Jack's wife at mid-morning and asked how he was doing. She said, "It's strange that you should call. I just learned that Jack passed away this morning at 4:00 a.m."

I was saddened by Jack's passing, and at first I was also very disappointed at his death because I thought that I had become a great healer. But later I came to realize that it was probably God's will that Jack died at that time, and maybe the healing assisted him in crossing over to the other side. There may well have been a spiritual healing, even if his physical body was not able to survive and continue living. But what was also important was the fact that this experience proved to me that we need not be afraid of death because it can be a beautiful experience. Syria's verifiable psychic experience of what it was probably like for Jack to pass over was a powerful reminder. And since then there have even been cases in which I have related this story to someone who is facing death and it seems to make a big difference for that person, too.

This story was also important for me because of my own brush with death in 1982. At the time, because of my asthma, I was seeing a man who was trained in both iridology and macrobiotics. Iridology is an alternative medicine practice in which patterns, colors, and other characteristics of the iris are examined for information about a patient's systemic health. Macrobiotics emphasizes locally grown food. That means organically grown whole grain cereals, legumes, vegetables, fruit, seaweed and fermented soy products combined into meals according to the principle of balance (known as yin and yang).

One day I suddenly started having a severe pain in my side. This alternative health practitioner looked into my ears and eyes. He said that I was having a gall bladder problem, and he would try to fix it. In the meantime, he recommended that I stay away from meats and sweets. The remedies he tried with me did not fix my gall bladder problem, and after a few weeks he told me he couldn't really help, and I should have my gall bladder removed.

A few days after getting this news and advice from him, I was having a nice dessert and the pain became unbearable, so I asked Nancy to take me to the hospital. On the way there I threw up several times. In the emergency ward they asked what the trouble was, and I told them that I had a bad gall bladder that needed to be removed. They looked at me strangely, then asked who my doctor was. I said my only doctor was a macrobiotics expert. They immediately gave me lots of tests, and soon thereafter the chief emergency physician came in to me to announce that my gall bladder was splattered all over my ribs. Even more alarming, he then said that I had an advanced case of pancreatitis. He said he was glad I didn't have my own doctor because it allowed him to order a surgeon immediately without having to check with another doctor. He then came even closer and said softly, "It's quite possible that you won't pull through." As shocking as a statement like that can be, nevertheless, I immediately thought of Syria and her vision of Jack's beautiful death. Although I didn't want to die, I had absolutely no fear of doing so.

Fortunately, the surgery went well, and the surgeon was amazed at how quickly I recovered. I had a very long scar on my stomach, and the surgeon said I could take a pain pill every three hours. But a total of one pill is all I ever needed.

Moving on to the Next Phase of My Spiritual Journey

Things in our lives have their own timing and seasons, and in 1972 our Monday Night Group was breaking up, and many of us decided to leave Providence Church. Some of us, including my parents, found our way to Unity of Fairfax. We all felt that the sermons were much more inspiring than we had been used to at Providence Church. All of the other great religions were given considerable respect at Unity. In fact, Unity's most forceful affirmation and its favorite invocation is, "There is but one Presence and one Power in the universe, God the Good and Omnipotent." I felt like I had found the right new home for my continuing spiritual journey.

But at the same time, there was something in my soul that wanted something more. My life was feeling a little empty. Of course, I had a nice accounting practice, but it was somewhat boring because I had been doing it for fifteen years. Fortunately I had three wonderful children and a loving wife to keep me occupied. But I didn't want to be active in the new Unity church in the same way as I had been at Providence Church. There was a sense that I had "been there, and done that."

I entertained the idea of taking courses and classes through Unity. They had an extensive study program with courses that could be taken at Unity Village, Missouri and/or with home-study. These courses could lead to becoming an assistant pastor at the Unity church, and at the same time you could keep your regular job. It could even lead later to becoming a full minister and starting your own Unity church. I was on the verge of signing up for this training when Guru Maharaji came into my life. He would give me just what I wanted for the next twenty years.

Chapter 13

The Guru Finds Me

Along his or her life's journey, a seeker will be fortunate enough to experience pivotal moments that make possible new levels of understanding and purposefulness in life. Don's life has been blessed with several such episodes, including his discovery of the Cayce teachings. But none was more powerful and influential than finding a personal spiritual teacher, Maharaji.

To meet a teacher or guru means to have the opportunity to make commitments of service and devotion, putting aside one's own ego and personal agenda. It means to make a commitment to something bigger than oneself—even to work in a spiritual community for common purposes. But perhaps what is most important, a personal Master can lead the seeker to a deeper understanding and experience of meditation—coming to know an inner peace that allows him or her to "be in the world but not of it"—to work hard but not be attached to the results, and simply allow things to unfold as they are meant to do.

❊

In 1973 I attended a lecture sponsored by the Association for Research and Enlightenment (A.R.E.) at which the principal speaker was a fascinating man, Dr. Raynor Johnson. He was born in England and educated at Oxford and London Universities, earning a Ph.D. in physics, the field in which he then taught in Belfast, Northern Ireland and in Melbourne, Australia, for many decades. After his retirement he began to write books about spirituality—books that wove together the practical scientist in him, along with the mystical side of himself that he had discovered.

The topic of his talk the night I heard him speak was having a spiritual teacher or guru as an indispensable part of a personal spiritual quest. My *Webster's Dictionary* defines "guru" as a personal spiritual teacher, but Johnson and millions of others from Hindu-ism and other Eastern religions have a somewhat different point of view. They see the guru as a perfect spiritual being sent to you by God.

In his book *The Spiritual Path*, Raynor Johnson makes even more explicit what he was talking about that night. Anyone who hopes to truly experience Enlightenment *must* have a guru or Master.

> It is true that through earnest seeking and aspiration in many lives, individuals find their way to the foothills of the mountain of God. Those who arrive there know that it is quite impossible to climb this great mountain without a Guide who knows the path. Whatever his other tasks may be, a Master's chief task appears to be calling souls to Him who are ready to make the climb . . . (pp. 78-79)

What was most memorable for me in that evening's lecture was Johnson's answer to a question posed to him: "How do you *find* this guru?" He replied, *"The guru will find you."*

My Introductions to the Teachings of Maharaji

A few weeks later I was reading an article in my *Duke Alumni Register* by a Duke Medical School graduate, Dr. John Horton. He explained how he had been following Guru Maharaji for a num-ber of years and had been practicing his meditation techniques. Horton went on to enumerate some of the benefits of meditation, and he wrote that he had found that *asthmatics* received consider-able relief from meditation. He then mentioned that he had just opened an office in Bethesda, Maryland, which was about a half hour's drive from my house.

The next week I was in Dr. Horton's office. But rather than dis-cussing my asthma, we ended up talking about Maharaji, who was just sixteen years old and had been preaching in India since he was three. His father had been a guru in India, and Maharaji was the youngest of four boys. Maharaji had been in the United

States for several years now, and he was being sponsored by an organization called Divine Light Mission. I found this to be somewhat synchronistic because when Hugh Lynn Cayce was asked how long one should meditate he replied "until you see the light."

Maharaji went all over the world giving programs, and Dr. Horton told me that the next event would be in Toronto in a couple of weeks. Naturally I went. I figured the guru had found me.

There were about 7,000 people at the conference center in Toronto. The first thing I noticed upon entering the hall was that almost everyone was in their mid–twenties or younger. The air was full of incense, and there were hundreds of devotees—known as "premies"—sitting on the floor in a lotus position with sheets over their heads, meditating. Maharaji's mother, Mata–ji, was on the stage along with one of his brothers, Raja–ji. Another brother was directing the orchestra. None of these relatives made a presentation to the group, but there were several speakers who were referred to as mahatmas, each presenting some spiritual teachings in preparation for Maharaji's arrival on stage.

After a couple of hours Maharaji came out on the stage and gave "satsang" for about an hour. Satsang is a Hindu word meaning "speaking from within." Maharaji's main message was the importance of going inside of ourselves and being able to live in the present moment. He was a very inspirational speaker who would always look straight out at the audience and speak without any notes. In Maharaji's teachings, as I heard them here at my first program, the most important discipline is what he calls the practice of Knowledge (with a capital K), and it has three basic elements: Satsang, Service, and Meditation.

Satsang is the listening to or speaking about the joys and benefits of practicing Knowledge and going within. It is always given without notes or advance planning, and there is very little religious dogma involved. For example, whenever Maharaji was asked about reincarnation, he would typically reply, "Don't worry about your past life or your next life, but focus on *this* life." He never compared any religions, although he sometimes quoted from the sayings of Krishna in the *Bhagavad-Gita*, as well as passages from the *Bible*. In the early years that I was involved with Maharaji, any premie could give satsang, whether it was at a major program or to small groups. About twenty years ago, however, Maharaji decided that the premies were confusing each other, and so he decided that he would be the only one to give satsang—in person, on audiotape, or on video.

Service is the giving of one's time and/or resources to help Maharaji do his work in propagating Knowledge. Each program required a lot of volunteer help for ushering, food service, planning, etc. In addition to giving of our time in this way, all of us were also encouraged to make donations to The Divine Light Mission. Tithing was recommended, and several times Maharaji quoted from the *Bible* and from Krishna, saying, "For every bag of rice you give me for my work, I will give you back ten fold." My annual income at that time was about $60,000, so I donated about $6,000 a year. In the years that followed, I certainly ended up getting a lot more than ten times that back.

Meditation is the third element of Knowledge, and the meditation techniques which Maharaji gave were to be kept secret. An aspirant would go to satsang programs in his or her community for three or four months, and then receive the meditation techniques by Maharaji directly (or, in later years, by a visiting mahatma). The recommended time for doing meditation was one hour daily, preferably in the early morning.

Making Deeper Commitments to Maharaji

My introduction to Maharaji in Toronto was just the start of many trips to attend his presentations. In the late 1970's I went to Maharaji programs in Florida, New York, Philadelphia, Toronto, Montreal, Kansas City, Los Angeles, Australia, England, and Italy. Many people went to India from time to time, but I didn't go because I had heard how often Americans would get sick while they were in India. The programs I attended with Maharaji were very exciting and invigorating experiences. I found that it was a good idea while at a program to first meditate in the morning, even though we would also be meditating with Maharaji at the program in what was called a "Knowledge Session." Generally, at a program Maharaji would give satsang in the morning and then in the early evening. We would receive the rite of "darshan" which involved walking by Maharaji while he was meditating, and kissing his feet. There was also a wonderful playful side of Maharaji, and occasionally he would put on his Krishna outfit and dance on the stage while we all sang. The music at these programs was fabulous, and we always had an outstanding orchestra with singers.

Several programs especially stand out in my memory because of their celebratory flavor. In Ocala, Florida, the program was outside and it lasted until two o'clock in the morning. It coincided with an annual celebration of Maharaji's father's birthday, and the ceremony was called "Holi." Maharaji would squirt water over everyone with huge fire hoses. Another year we had a Holi festival at the Polo Grounds in New York City, and *Life Magazine* did a big article on it with a double page picture. One thing was sure to happen when attending *any* of these programs—whether it was a Holi festival or not. Any problems which you thought you had when you arrived would disappear, and life would become beautiful in every way. It wasn't an intellectual thing—*it was an experience*. In fact, when trying to tell people afterwards about a program, it was frequently difficult to remember exactly what Maharaji had said. The impact of being with him at the program was *the way it took us inside of ourselves*, not how we mulled over his words.

During the 70's and early 80's many premies lived in ashrams in a communal fashion and shared all of their income. In the Chevy Chase, Maryland suburb of Washington, D.C. there was a men's ashram and a women's ashram. Sometimes the men would share some money with the women, and the women might help out with some of the cooking for the men. I would go to the ashram several evenings a week to listen to or give satsang.

Service to Maharaji

Around 1980 I went to see one of the mahatmas, a man named

Randy Proudy, and asked him how I could become more dedicated to Maharaji's work. I was really hooked on this work, and I wanted to do more things to serve Maharaji. Randy put me in touch with Jim Emerson, who would become my mentor for quite a few years. Jim said that Maharaji needed an accountant for various businesses, some of which were providing him with part of his personal support, since Maharaji never received a salary from Divine Light Mission for any of his services. He thought it was important for him to have his own ways of supporting himself.

My first assignment was to do a certified audit for a company in Miami named Decca that was, among other things, refurbishing an old Boeing 707 to be used by Maharaji. I was provided with several accountants from a local ashram to help out. One of these accountants was a good tax man named Larry Thomas.

After the Miami audit had been completed, I asked Larry to come to Washington, live at my house, and help me during tax season. I needed help, since the CPA I had hired previously had quit suddenly over religious objections. It turned out that he was a "Born Again Christian" and didn't want to work for someone who was chasing after a guru. But with Larry on board at my accounting firm, it turned out to be my easiest tax season ever, and it was so wonderful having a premie living with me. While practicing Knowledge it seemed that problems like being short-staffed at the accounting firm always worked themselves out.

Finding good people to work at my firm continued to happen through connections with other premies. I met one named Fletcher Drake, who was a masseur at Dr. Horton's office. One day while he was giving me a massage, we were talking about my accounting practice, and he indicated that he was a part-time bookkeeper and would like to become my employee. I said I would give it a try, and it worked out exceedingly well.

Then, I met a woman at satsang one night named Mary Moore, and she wanted to become my secretary and office manager. After I had hired her, I started to occasionally give her some accounting work to do at her desk in her spare time. This kind of accounting write-up work grew very fast, and she did such a good job that I had to hire someone else to be my secretary. Both Fletcher and Mary were very dedicated and learned very quickly, and they ended up working for me for many years. Another premie, an experienced accountant named Midge O'Mahoney, showed up one day and she focused on working with some of my government contractors. She had a lot of executive talent, and after about two years she went to work for one of my clients. From 1978 to 1982 my full time staff (including myself) went from two to five. All of my new employees were premies and, except for Midge, all of them lived in the ashram. It was out of this core group—plus my son Ken—that a new company, Deltek, emerged in 1983. But that's another story, and it's told in Chapter 14.

Even though all the premies were very dedicated to their work, a Maharaji program would always take priority. One year a big program was scheduled for mid–April, right in the middle of tax season. I naturally said that some of us would have to skip the program, but against my better judgment, other plans were made. We told all our tax clients that if their tax information was not in by April 5th, we would file for an extension. None of our clients seemed to mind. We turned all of our tax returns over to Computax on April 9th, and off we went. When we returned on April 12th, we discovered that Computax had had a big delay in processing the returns for all their clients, but we weren't affected because we had gotten ours in early. Here was another example of how, by practicing Knowledge, problems seemed to work themselves out.

It's a good thing I had a larger staff because I was doing quite a bit of traveling—both for Maharaji-related accounting work and also for my other clientele. I frequently met with Maharaji's lawyer in New York and was also privileged to meet with Maharaji on several occasions. Many people get very nervous when they first meet Maharaji, and they find it difficult to speak. I had this problem for a couple of minutes at my first meeting, but I soon got over it. Altogether I met Maharaji on five occasions—two of which involved me giving a status report on business matters. Maharaji was very easy to talk to and always put me at ease. I think that when Maharaji is on–stage giving satsang he is experiencing a high level of spiritual energy, which is not present when he is at a social or business meeting.

One Maharaji–owned business I spent a lot of time on was a wholesale natural foods company in Denver. Maharaji also had three retail food stores in Seattle, Kansas City, and Denver. I flew out to the headquarters in Denver about once every six weeks, but there were problems with what was going on there. Other people were in charge, and I didn't agree with what was being done. The business was almost bankrupt yet no one seemed to be taking things seriously.

In 1984 I finally let Maharaji know how bad things were, and I said that I would lend the company $300,000 if he would let me take over. He personally called me a few days later and told me to go ahead. I was president for a few months, and then I noticed a premie named David Cohen who was keeping me up to date on all the payables and how to keep all the unpaid vendors happy. Soon I appointed David president, and I became the Chairman of the Board. Under this new management team, the company grew considerably, and we bought a new building which added quite a bit to our efficiency. But eventually we realized that competition in the wholesale food business was getting pretty fierce, and so we sold the company in 1988 for ten million dollars. This was like the shrimp boat business in the "Forest Gump" story. I was just watch-ing things play out. In retrospect I see how being a regular medi-tator helped me to stay unattached to what was going on. I certainly cared about the business and I was working hard to make it succeed, but meditation was helping me get myself out of the way and to just let things happen.

My Family and Maharaji

My deep involvement with Maharaji's work certainly had an impact on my family. Of all my family members, it was our son Kenneth who eventually became as committed as I have been to Maharaji. Ken graduated from Duke University in 1979 with a major in accounting. First he took a job for the large accounting firm Arthur Andersen for three years. But when I gave each of our children $3,000, Ken quit his job and took a three month–trip to Europe, with my encouragement.

Right after he returned from Europe, he showed up at the ashram during satsang with his girlfriend, Tena. The leader asked if anyone was interested in receiving Knowledge, and Ken raised his hand. And a few months later he, in fact, did receive Knowledge. He moved to Seattle and worked as a clerk at the retail health food store that was part of the Maharaji business that was based in Denver. For a while Ken lived in the ashram in Seattle and spent a lot of time having satsang with several mahatmas. Later he bought a little house of his own there.

Our younger son David also had some direct contact with Maharaji, going to many Maharaji programs with me, including a Holi festival. He always loved music, and while I was at satsang, he would take guitar lessons from one of the premies. He got to know many of the premies quite well. They were a good influence on him because many of them were ex–potheads, and they would tell him about how screwed up they used to be. When David was about sixteen, he received Knowledge, and he enjoyed attending satsang which we were having on a regular basis at our house.

Eventually Ken married Tena, who received Knowledge; and, David's wife Syd also received Knowledge. Although Nancy enjoyed going to formal satsang with me and got along well with all my premie friends, she was never interested in meditation or receiving Knowledge. She would always say that she didn't need it. Our daughter Kathleen was very busy with her career, and she was definitely very different from the typical premie.

Things Change within the Community

In the mid–eighties things were changing in the premie community. Maharaji had married and was starting a family. Premies were moving out of the ashrams, getting married, and pursuing careers. Since there were not many new people receiving Knowledge anymore, Maharaji decided to make the practice of Knowledge less oriented toward Indian culture. Accordingly, the leaders became known as instructors instead of mahatmas; Divine Light Mission became Elan Vital; and the ceremonies of darshan and Holi were no longer done in North America. During this period of transition, Maharaji was starting to spend a great deal of his time in India. In fact, nowadays there are very few programs in North America, and most of those are only a one-hour appearance by Maharaji.

Although many of my old premie friends have become less involved, there is still a significant group who have regular meetings and watch videos of Maharaji. In 2004, Maharaji started a new program called "The Keys"—a series of DVD instructional videos with Maharaji giving satsang for over twenty hours. These Keys can be used for receiving Knowledge, or for someone like me, to get re-inspired.

Maharaji did a great deal for me, uppermost being to help me find a sense of purposefulness, peace, and ultimately prosperity. Whereas I had learned about meditation from the Cayce material and even tried to practice meditation as regularly as possible, once I became a dedicated follower of Maharaji, my devotion to meditation became much deeper. I also found in Maharaji's work a feeling of community that I had never experienced before in my spiritual studies. As Maharaji began to focus his efforts more and more on other places in the world and come to the United States much less frequently, much of that sense of community began to fade for me. And yet, looking back, I have a renewed feeling for just how important those two decades were for my spiritual growth, and I have decided in the process of reviewing this part of my life that I want to watch all of the Keys so that I can remember his inspirational messages. A few samples of his teachings—not from "The Keys" themselves, but from other of his published satsang sessions—are included in Appendix 3 at the end of this book.

Chapter 14

Building a Company
By Going with the Flow

Creating a business organization is as much an art as it is a
science. An entrepreneur can follow a model or system, but ulti-
mately the art of building an organization from the ground up takes
courage, intuition, and faith. The remarkable story of Deltek's
inception, steady growth, and fabulous success is a mixture of many
crucial ingredients and principles—elements that Don had already
been nurturing in himself since he was a youngster finding creative
ways as a boy to make money for his family.

As you read the account of how Deltek came into being and thrived,
be sure to read between the lines and see the heart of what was going
on. This was not a matter of luck. Nor was it solely from dedicated
hard work, although there was plenty of that, too.

First of all, the story shows how Don's career has always been able
to **flow with what comes naturally** for him. He has not tried to be
something that he is not. He knows where his strengths lie, and he
patiently allows things to unfold around those strengths. This capacity to flow naturally also means "using what is at hand," being grateful
for whatever resources are available and working creatively with
them.

Second, there is a commitment to really **serving clients and
customers**. Prosperity will be the likely result if service is the prime
intention. Related to service is a third ingredient—to dedicate one's
endeavors to **something bigger than oneself**. In this case, Don and
his son Ken were spiritually devoted to their teacher and guru
Maharaji, and they dedicated the new business to him. Simply with
that intention the company itself was impacted. This commitment
was heightened by the way in which other people who shared this
spiritual dedication were given key spots in the organization. Others
who had "received Knowledge" from Maharaji—that is, "premies"—
were a vital part of the leadership of Deltek.

*A fourth principle about building a vital business organization is **generosity**. Don wanted his key employees to feel a sense of ownership in what they were helping to create. He knew that this really was a team effort, and he found a way to share the abundance that manifested.*

Most of us will never create a business as big and as successful as Deltek. But these four principles of business life—illustrated so well in Don's story—are meaningful on any scale as we use our talents in the work world.

❁

The story of our very successful business—Deltek Systems—really begins with my experiences much earlier in adult life with making money. As I already described in Chapter 5, I have always been adventurous and entrepreneurial when it comes to finances and abundance. That chapter concluded with my experiences in college, but the story of making money had many more key events through my early married life and into the mature years of my professional life, including the stories that are told in Chapter 10.

But the quantum leap in my business success was made possible by some fortunate investments I made—even ones that I made when I was a young father wanting to find a way to be prosperous and support my wife and baby son.

Stocks and Investments That Set the Stage for Bigger Things

Back when I was just twenty-six, I was a new father and intent on finding creative ways to make a good living for my new family. The stock market seemed like a place where I could make money using careful research, hard work, and my intuition; so I started exploring how the whole thing worked. It was 1958, and while working at the American Psychological Association (APA), I would usually walk over to Merrill Lynch at lunchtime and watch the stock tape with Rod Baer, the vice-president of APA. At this time I didn't have more than several thousand dollars to invest, but I was hooked for life. I always felt that it was a lot better to gamble on Wall Street than at the casinos because only on Wall Street were the percentages in your favor. I think that if more young people were introduced to the stock market at an early age, there would be a lot fewer people in casinos.

Rod had given me a book entitled *The Battle for Investment Survival* by Carl M. Loeb. Mr. Loeb recommended that your stock portfolio should be a basket of not more than five stocks which you think have a good chance of doubling within eighteen months. He also said that you should sell a stock whenever you have a twenty percent loss, but you should always let your profits run.

My most successful investment was Fairchild Camera and Instrument Co. This company was the forerunner of computer chips and video cameras. I spent a lot of time researching this stock. I went to an annual meeting, and I read *Electronic News* every week. In 1964 I bought this stock for $30 a share and got out 18 months later at $150 a share for a $50,000 profit. Other stocks I did well on were Kent cigarettes (the first non–mentholated filtered cigarette) and Coleco (video games and Cabbage Patch dolls). I don't remember my bad investments, but of course, I never lost more than 20% on any one stock because I followed Loeb's rule.

In the early 1970s I made two financial investments not connected with the stock market. The first one involved one of my government contractors named Adaptronics. This company was owned by three individuals, one of whom wanted to sell all his shares. I ended up buying thirty percent of the company for $50,000, payable over five years. The other investment was through a lady I met at my "Search for God" study group in Fairfax, Virginia. She was a realtor, and she told me that there was a 120–acre piece of property for sale about one mile south of Leesburg, Virginia. The property included two old houses, and a sixty–five–year–old widow owned it. She was asking $2,000 an acre and was willing to take back a $140,000 seventeen–year mortgage with a six percent interest rate.

It sounded like a good investment to me, and to cover the down payment, I divided the investment into fifteen units and sold thirteen units to my tax clients for $8,500 each. I kept the other two units as my management and finder's fee. I was able to lease the houses and the land for enough to cover the mortgage and taxes. My brother Ed was so impressed with this arrangement that he formed many similar partnerships with clients from his insurance business. Soon thereafter he stopped selling insurance and devoted all of his time to land development. Every year I would prepare tax returns for each of his partnerships.

In 1982 Adaptronics was acquired by another company, and my share of the purchase price was $650,000. In 1988 my land in Leesburg was sold for $25,000-an-acre which netted me $350,000. These lucrative investments provided the funds for two important things—significant upgrades to our home on Hidden Creek Dr., and even more importantly, the capital that I would need for Deltek Systems—our very successful company. But the other key ingredient for Deltek—something every bit as important as the financial resources to create the company—was our son Ken coming back to Virginia to join me and work together.

Ken and the Birth of Deltek Systems

In January of 1983, Ken called me from Seattle and said he would like to join my accounting firm. This made me very happy, and since we had never discussed it, I was flabbergasted. I considered this to be another gift from the angels (or maybe from Guru Maharaji since Ken was now a premie). I could think of no better way for the company to grow than to have Ken, a CPA, join us. I thought we might change the name of the company to "de Laski & de Laski," or to "de Laski and Son."

Ken showed up for work in early February, just in time for another busy tax season. I had often thought that there was a need for a book about government contract accounting which would include all the relevant financial statements. I always knew that Ken was a good writer, and we decided to do it together. For several months we sat up in the loft of the living room, and I dictated everything I knew about government contract accounting and showed how it related to the various financial statements. The main statement called the "contract data sheet" would list each contract with columns for contract value, direct labor, overhead, general administrative (G&A), profit, revenue, billed receivables, and unbilled receivables. Since there were often many categories for each item, this sheet could easily need more than forty–eight columns. I first learned about this statement when I worked for Ernst & Ernst in 1954, and of course, I refined it over the next thirty years in my accounting practice. (See Appendix 1.) Unbeknownst to me, those conversations with Ken in our loft would become the start of something much bigger than I ever could have imagined. Computers would be the extra ingredient.

During the previous year we had spent a lot of time trying to find a computer system that we could recommend to our government contract clients. A few systems were available which ran on mini–computers, but they cost about $50,000, not including the software. This was too expensive for most of our clients, and none of these systems provided the statements that we wanted anyway.

Several of us were sitting around the office one day, and we decided that we would *develop* a system for government contractors—a system that would run on a micro–computer, the sort of desktop personal computer that is so commonplace here in the 21st century. In 1983 these computers had been on the market a very short time and were used primarily for computer games and general purpose accounting. This venture would not have happened if I didn't have over half a million dollars in my pocket from the recent sale of my stock in Adaptronics.

Our plan to develop software for a micro–computer obviously meant that we needed to find programmers, and a very special young man came into our lives through our relationship to Maharaji. In 1974 I had received Knowledge at the same time as a couple by the name of Reggie and Emmy Brown. Reggie had graduated second in his class at West Point and had served in Vietnam as a major under General Norman Schwarzkopf.

When I met Reggie he had a major government job with the

Office of Management and Budget in Washington, D.C. But a few years later, in 1979, he and his family moved to Florida to work for Maharaji's company called Decca. When their son Eric was sixteen, he received Knowledge and went to work for Decca as somewhat of a prodigy, developing their computer software. I soon heard about this remarkable boy. In Florida myself, working on the audit, I was told by Decca employees that Eric was a real genius. It was a statement I took in and luckily filed away mentally.

In 1983 the Brown family, including Eric, moved back to Maryland, and soon thereafter I invited Eric to join our company. If he was the computer genius I had heard him to be, then it would be a perfect fit. Ken and I had new ideas about creating government accounting software for micro-computers, and we needed someone just like Eric.

In response to my offer, Eric said he would love to, but his parents were planning on him going to college in the fall. I would have to make my case to Reggie and Emmy. And after I told them how much we needed Eric and that our company's success would benefit Maharaji, they agreed that it would be all right for his college education to be delayed by a couple of years. In 2010, Eric was still working for the computer company that evolved—as one of the vice-presidents now—and he never did go to college.

We also hired another premie, Peter Novak, who had several years of programming experience and graduated from the University of Maryland with a degree in computer science. Peter's formal education and Eric's imagination and genius were very critical in the success of our software development.

That summer our son David started programming for us, too, and he continued for three years while he went to high school. In November of 1983 we incorporated the business, and David came up with the name "Deltek"—"Del" coming from the first three letters of de Laski, and "tek" coming from technologies. In January, 1984, we delivered the payroll, accounts payable, and general ledger module to one of my clients, Cost Engineering Research (CER) who had agreed to pay us $5,000 after delivery of the complete system. In those days our micro-computers cost about $8,000 and it was felt that a software package should not exceed the computer cost. The last of the basic modules were delivered to CER in September, 1984, and we now had our new product up and fully working.

We were also working with a number of other government contractors, one of which was Frank Carter's company called Defense Systems, Inc. We would sell a single-user system for about $8,000, plus 10% per year for telephone support and regular upgrades to the software. We then also provided on-site consulting services for the same billing rate we used in the accounting practice, which in 1984 was about $100 an hour. Both the support fee and the consulting fee would increase from time to time. In a few years we were able to provide multi-user systems so that many people at one company could be using our software, and we would charge about $13,000 for up to five work stations, $20,000 for six to ten work stations, and so on.

Our goal was to be very service-oriented to our customers and their needs. In some instances a client would ask us to provide some new program, and we would usually charge him for it—unless it was something that every customer was likely to need, in which case we would develop that new feature for everyone. By 1990 we had developed a number of additional modules, such as inventory and travel, which a customer could buy as optional aspects of their Deltek system.

Deltek Begins to Grow

Deltek was starting to get so big that it needed my full attention. And so, in 1985 I sold my accounting practice to another firm on the same terms as I had bought it—twenty percent of gross receipts over seven years. I did, however, continue to do some consulting for Maharaji's companies because that work of service was an important part of my commitment to my guru.

About this time I divided up the Deltek stock. I kept 42%, gave 40% to Ken, and the rest was divided among key employees. At this time the stock had a very low appraised value so the tax consequences of these transfers were very nominal. I wanted those key employees to have a sense of ownership in the company. It was really a team effort that was making Deltek successful, and this gift to the key employees was in the spirit of generosity and prosperity that I wanted for Deltek. Fletcher Drake got 3% of the stock and gave 2% to Maharaji. Ken and I each gave Maharaji 4%, so he received a total of 10%.

Prosperity and growth continued for us, oftentimes because of word-of-mouth, but sometimes because we made some good decisions about advertising. John Sanders started a weekly newspaper for the Washington D.C. area that focused on local technology companies, most of which were government contractors. We advertised in this newspaper and attended conferences created by Mr. Sanders. In fact, he would frequently ask us to lead a conference on government contract accounting; and, of course, we would talk about our software. By attending all the conferences we got to know the leaders of virtually all the government contractors in the Washington, D.C. area, and by the early 1990s we had sold our software to about three hundred of them.

Another person who was invaluable to us in this period of expansion was Bob Strauss, who gave courses throughout the country on government contract accounting and management. He told countless people about our software. What's more, many people who were already users of our system went to Bob's courses, and they would tell their fellow course attendees how great our system was.

It was very easy to get listings of government contractors throughout the United States. Our mailings would include miniature financial statements (including the contract data sheet). We would follow up the mailing with a telephone call to these prospects, and the accounting manager was always very happy to talk to us. We could even promise a free site visit to help a prospect decide whether to buy a Deltek system. By this time we had hired several sales people who would visit these prospects on a sales tour in order to give demonstrations. Sometimes I would go on these trips myself. I vividly remember a sales tour I took with Denny Barrow, who had worked at one of Maharaji's companies before coming to work for us. The tour started in Denver and ended up in California. We visited twelve companies and within one year they all became our clients.

By 1992 we had about 160 employees of which about one third were programmers who were busy with new modules, annual upgrades, and special requests from clients. We had also started developing a new system called Cost–Point which was more state of the art and was needed by larger clients. When Cost–Point was completed in 1995, many of our existing clients converted to it and paid an additional fee.

Our success in the United States made us feel ready to expand overseas. Dzien Do was one of our key software engineers, and he was in charge of the programming of the basic package. He was now given a new assignment—to set up a facility overseas. Most software companies were going to India, but we chose the Philippines because it had more of an American culture and we felt that better English was spoken there. Dzien and I spent many hours over several months at the Philippine Embassy in Washington, D.C., to get everything arranged. We started with twenty–five employees in Makati, which is a suburb of Manila. It has grown considerably since then and now has more than 200 Deltek employees at that facility.

As another way to grow, we were constantly thinking about acquiring other companies, and I conducted two due diligence studies, one of which was a company that specialized in law firms. We ended up turning them both down, which was the same thing that had happened when I did this kind of work for my clients through my accounting practice. But we finally found one company that looked right for us, although on this one I had nothing to do with the due diligence review because Nancy and I had been in California for our winter residency in Palm Desert when all of this was going on. The deal was arranged by Ken, and in 1992 Deltek acquired the software company Harper & Shuman, located in Cambridge, Massachusetts, which specialized in architectural and engineering (A&E) firms. This was a good fit with Deltek because the accounting requirements of A&E firms were somewhat similar to government contractors. We paid about twelve million dollars in stock, and it turned out to be a very successful merger. When I returned from my usual winter stay in Palm Desert, Ken took me to Cambridge and introduced me to all of our new employees.

The company was truly blossoming under Ken's leadership. He had effectively been the CEO from about 1990, but he did not officially receive that title until February, 1996. From the beginning Ken and I worked well together, but after the first five years Ken just naturally started taking charge. I let go of the reins because I knew I would be retiring soon and because I knew very little about computers. In fact, I largely focused on hiring good people. I continued to spend most of my time in recruiting new employees and overseeing employee benefits. This work in choosing the right people may well have been my most important contribution to the success of Deltek. I have a knack for reading people—call it intuition, common sense, or my openness to having the angels bring me the right people. It's probably a combination of all three.

Going Public

At the end of 1995 Deltek's annual sales were $27 million and net earnings before Federal income taxes were about $10 million. This was a very profitable company and it would surely be attractive to investors. I had always dreamed of Deltek becoming a publicly owned company, and so we decided in early 1996 that this was the time. We thought it would be good for the employees because it would enable us to give out stock options to them, and we would be able to use the stock for future acquisitions we might want to make. Another good reason for offering stock to the public was that we had worked very hard for over ten years, and we wanted to sell some of our ownership of the company.

Going public is not as easy as it may sound. You have to have the assistance of professionals who know how this is done. After a considerable amount of research and visitations, we finally settled on Montgomery Securities and William Blair and Company as our underwriters. And since we were about to become a public company, we were required to increase the size of our board of directors. Up to this time our board consisted of just three—our attorney for many years Bob Gregg, Ken, and myself. Now we added three outside board members who had considerable experience with government contractors. We also hired a high level CFO named Alan Stewart who had spent a number years with the Securities and Exchange Commission (SEC).

After Ken and Alan made numerous presentations throughout the country, we began trading on the NASDAQ exchange at $11 a share in January, 1997. I can still remember how excited I was to watch Deltek trade on TV from my hotel room in Palm Desert. Since we now had about 16 million shares outstanding, this put a value on the company of about $176 million. Ken and I each sold about $5 million of our stock, but we each still owned about 30% of the company after the public sale.

Going Private Again

Deltek grew very rapidly over the next several years, and its stock went as high as $20 a share. However, in 1999 the entire software industry stopped growing, due in part to what was called "the Y2K problem." Most software programs referred to the year with two digits, such as 98, 99, etc. and therefore, with the year 2000 coming up, a lot of software had to be changed because computers would assume that 00 meant the year 1900. The stock market also fell, particularly for high-tech companies, and Deltek stock fell as low as $5 a share and stayed there.

In the meantime, Deltek's sales had increased to about $95 million for the year, but its earnings had dropped due to heavy development expenses. In spite of reduced earnings, we began to feel that the share price did not properly reflect the value of the company. So Ken and I decided to find a way to re-purchase shares. In

2002 we made the decision to "go private," which meant that we would buy the publicly owned shares and not be listed on the stock exchange anymore. It was virtually the opposite of what we had done five years earlier. But being successful in business requires a willingness to be flexible and even reverse course when it seems prudent.

Our independent board members engaged a brokerage firm to conduct an appraisal, and a price of $7.33 was set as a fair price at which to buy the shares at an approximate cost of $20 million dollars, some of which was borrowed from the Sun Trust Company. From 2002 through 2004 Deltek did very well as a private company with annual sales increasing from $110 million to $150 million. It was not surprising that we now began to look very attractive once again to investors. During this time a number of equity companies offered to buy us out, but Ken turned them all down.

Finally, however, in 2005 a company named New Mountain Financial bought Deltek at a value of $35 a share, with the stipulation that the existing shareholders would retain 25% of the company. If it had been left up to me, I would have accepted far less, and I am very much indebted to Ken for his management of the sale of Deltek. Mountain View has done a wonderful job managing Deltek, and I'm sure glad that we kept a one-fourth share of the company.

Looking Back at the Deltek Experience

In retrospect I can see that starting Deltek was another example of going with the flow. In 1983 all of the necessary ingredients were in place. We had a small nucleus of dedicated people; we had an understanding of what we wanted to accomplish; the technology was in place; many potential customers were available; and we even had plenty of money. In looking back, one would think that it would have been totally stupid not to start Deltek, but a lot of things can get in the way of not doing what's obvious, such as negative thoughts and people problems.

When asked how I came to start Deltek, I have told people I was like Forrest Gump. He saved lives, started a company, and worked with U.S. Presidents just by doing what came naturally.

Don and Ken pictured in a Baltimore Sun article about Deltek

Don and Nancy going to a gala in 1994

Chapter 15

Homes, Grandchildren, and Travel

Two of the great images of human life are home and adventuring.
They are like roots and wings. The two form a dynamic polarity that
enriches life. The first is a place of safety and familiarity. Home is
where we come back to ourselves and where we relax into the mutual
support of spouse, children, and grandchildren.

But just as important is the theme of adventuring away from
home—to go out into the world of the unknown and discover new
places, maybe even discover new things about oneself by getting
away from what is familiar.

Each of us experiences in different ways this universal rhythm of
moving back and forth between "nesting" and "exploring." Each has
his or her own story of the homes they have lived in and all that went
into finding, securing, and shaping that home space. And symboli-
cally those homes relate to the deeper issue of "coming home to
ourselves"—that is, finding the inner spiritual home.

And just as surely each of us has stories of going out into the world.
Trips, excursions, adventures. Something in us potentially opens up
and starts seeing life in a new way because of exposure to different
cultures and geography. But even those travels can be seen in a
deeper and metaphorical way. It's the journey to find ourselves. Of
course, we don't have to go on death-defying explorations such as
Odysseus in the Greek myth. Every trip into unfamiliar lands can help
us to expand ourselves—even beginning to feel ourselves to be global
citizens.

In Don's life story we find lovely examples of these two themes—
home and travel. In earlier chapters there have already been many
references to his homes over the years. And now in this chapter we
get the final parts of the story. Each home has been a special place,
helping him to shape his identity. The same thing has happened to
each of us over the years in our own series of homes. As you read

about this final sequence of homes in Don's life—especially the stories about how he found each home and what new opportunities it created in his life—think about what the universal theme of "home" has meant to your own life journey.

In the same way, Don's story here in this chapter and in Appendix 4 includes many examples of trips and adventures to unknown places. Each trip has provided an opening in his awareness of the world and his place in it. Let those accounts stimulate you to consider how travel and adventuring has impacted your own biography. How has going into the unknown changed you? In this ancient and archetypal "dance" back-and-forth between home and travel, our sense of who we are is shaped.

✸

My life has largely revolved around three central themes: my spiritual life, my family, and my work. In recent chapters I have reflected on the stages of my spiritual development; and in the previous chapter I described the incredible success in the latter years of my working career—success that allows me now to find a new expression of my work through the De Laski Family Foundation. (More about that in the next chapter.)

But here in this chapter of my life story, it is fitting to return to home and family, and what they have meant to me. And one of the first things that comes to my mind when I think of family is the *fun* we have had together. It has happened in so many ways, and one way that has been very special to me is our vacation times—even the wonderful opportunity to have a vacation home.

Vacation Spots and a Home for the Family

In the mid-1970s, when David was seven and when Ken and Kathy were in their teens, the family started to ski. We would frequently go to a ski lodge in western Maryland named Wisp. I loved the beginner's slope there called "Possum Run," which was a very gentle slope that went on for about two miles. I was actually not very skilled as a skier, and Nancy didn't ski much at this time in our lives, but Ken was amazing. Very quickly he developed fantastic skills. Before long he could even do somersaults while going down the slopes. But there were also awkward moments for Ken with his dad.

For example, one time he and I were going up a ski lift. When we reached the top, Ken dropped gracefully off of his ski lift chair, but I fell out clumsily. Several people rushed over to help me get up as I lay sprawled out in the snow. Ken was so embarrassed that he just gazed out over the mountain, as if he didn't know me. I don't remember telling anyone about this moment because I didn't want to embarrass Ken. I suspect that most families have accounts of teenagers who aren't always sure they want to be affiliated with their parents—especially in awkward moments.

Western Maryland wasn't the only place we traveled for family skiing vacations. One time we all went to Mt. Snow in southern Vermont. We had planned to stay for a week. However, it rained a lot, and the snow was mostly slush. And so we left after just two days and drove north for about one hundred miles to Killington, where there was colder weather. A huge snow storm arrived just after we got there, and we ended up staying several extra days to enjoy the skiing. It was a wonderful and memorable family time.

Skiing in Killington stands out in my memory for another episode. Kathleen's high school class went on a ski trip there, and I went along as one of the chaperones for a busload of the students. It was another case of my teenager being embarrassed by me. Kathleen felt like I was trying too hard to just be one of the kids—especially being a little too friendly with the girls on the bus.

In the mid 1980s Ken encouraged us to take a long weekend trip to Canaan Valley, a ski and golf resort in West Virginia, about two hundred miles from our home. Ken had discovered this place when his high school German class visited a German community nearby. Canaan Valley is more than 3,200 feet above sea level, and has an annual snowfall of 145 inches, about the same as our favorite places in Vermont. Ken and I ended up buying a three-bedroom chalet at Timberline ski slope for about $85,000. Many guests came up to visit us—my mother, nephews and nieces, Ken's in-laws, Frank and Mary Carter, and Reggie and Emmy Brown, and we even had a Deltek staff retreat there.

Nancy and I especially enjoyed cross-country skiing together at our Canaan Valley home, but it wasn't just skiing that made Canaan Valley a special family vacation spot for us. We used this home year-round. The golf course was beautiful and challenging, and we enjoyed boating, fishing, and hiking. We could even ride the ski lift to the top of the mountain in the summer, and then hike downhill, picking blueberries along the way. And we also had ample animal friends there, with deer and Canadian geese particularly memorable.

However, times and family rhythms change, and by the 1990s we found ourselves rarely making it to Canaan Valley, and so we sold this vacation home that had so many wonderful family memories. Skiing didn't end for some of us, though. For Ken and his family skiing now became a Rocky Mountains event. Most experienced skiers say that they like to go West because the snow is powdery in comparison to the East's wetter and icier snow. Nancy and I weren't skiing much more anyway at this point in our lives, and we were starting to spend more and more of our winters in Palm Desert, California. It was a natural evolution to have said good-bye to our West Virginia vacation home which we had enjoyed for ten years. And there were other adventures to come, some of which involved international travel, as I will discuss later in this chapter.

The Family Home

A person's home is such an important place. The longing that we all feel to have a safe and lovely home is probably a reflection of something spiritual. That is, each of us has a spiritual home, whether we remember it or not.

My life has been blessed by having a series of beautiful and comfortable homes over the years. I have always felt deeply grateful for how I have been blessed in this way, and each home has been a special place that I have tried to respect and take care of the best way I know how.

In Chapter 10 about building my accounting practice, I told the story of how the Carters helped us find a lovely new home on Hidden Creek Drive in Great Falls, Virginia. To continue that story, around 1980 we started upgrading that home. We wanted to make it fit our family even better. We finished off our basement and created a large rec room, a bedroom, a full bath, and a kitchenette. This downstairs space became David's abode. It was also spacious enough for large meetings, and for about two years, we would hold satsang meetings of Guru Maharaji premies—often as many as twenty-five of us. (David also enjoyed this because he had recently received Knowledge from a leader in Maharaji's organization).

In 1986 we made even more changes—building a large sunroom off of the kitchen, which became our family eating room and next to it, an outdoor swimming pool and hot tub. We also built stone steps going up to a patio under a stately 150-year-old oak tree. That upper patio extended down to the lower level and another patio in front of "David's abode" and then on out toward the street.

In 1988, after Kathleen was married, we combined what had been her bedroom with our own bedroom to make a more spacious master bedroom suite, including an enlarged and modernized bathroom and more closet place. As time passed we always needed more closet space since Nancy loved to shop.

We were really blessed to be able to make so many of these customized improvements to our home on Hidden Creek Drive and make it into just the sort of place where family, friends, and work colleagues would feel welcome. One of the reasons we made these changes was that for the first time in our married lives Nancy and I had extra money—the funds that had come from the sale of the Adaptronics stock that I mentioned in a previous chapter. However, even though we got considerably more money in years thereafter, these improvements to our home on Hidden Creek Drive were the last major construction changes to any of our homes. Both of us were tired of what's involved, and we just didn't want to ever have to go through that again.

The Family Expands: Marriages and Grandchildren

On May 14, 1986, Ken got engaged to his longtime girlfriend Tena Renken, and they set a wedding date of August 30. They had dated off-and-on for many years. Ken admitted to me that the main reason he had come back to Virginia was that he wanted to be with Tena again. (Thank you, Tena, because I also got my accounting business partner from his return—plus Nancy and I were able to see him far more often than when he was on the West Coast.)

Ken, Tena, and our families decided that the wedding ceremony should be at our newly remodeled home. The pool and the resurfacing of the driveway were both finished just the day before the wedding. And what a beautiful wedding ceremony it was. I can still so vividly remember Tena and Ken descending the stone steps to the lower patio to take their wedding vows. We even had two ministers. Tena was Catholic, and priests were allowed to give the wedding vows only in church. However, the priest said that he could do other parts of the ceremony there at our home. Ken got a minister from the local Unity Church to give the wedding vows. Later, that evening at the reception, David (who was the best man) gave a beautiful toast. And, of course, the angels made sure that we had perfect weather for the occasion.

Just thinking back to this very special event—the first wedding among our children—I am also struck with the synchronicity of it all. Sometimes it is only in retrospect that we see the profound patterns that are playing out in our lives. In this case, I suddenly saw the many coincidences, and for me they feel like they have the hand of destiny in them. Just like me, Ken had ended up going to Duke University, where he majored in accounting, just as I had done. He became a follower of Guru Maharaji, even as I had, too. He came back to Virginia where we worked together to create a software company. And what's more, we both had two ministers of different churches officiating at our respective weddings.

It wasn't too much later until Kathleen also married. About a year after Ken's wedding, in July of 1987, Kathleen's boyfriend Edward Grubb, asked if he could see me privately next time he was at our home. They had been dating for about two years, and he was in charge of the western hemisphere division of Control Risks, a British security company. The two had first met at his Washington D.C. office when Kathy interviewed him for ABC television regarding issues related to kidnappings overseas. So after dinner when he and Kathleen were with us, Edward and I went into my study, and he asked me for Kathleen's hand in marriage. This was very much in keeping with his English upbringing. I was only a little bit surprised, but I was very pleased and told him that it was fine with me and that I was very much delighted.

Edward and Kathleen were married on January 2, 1988 in a lovely ceremony at Christ's Church, a historic Episcopal church in Alexandria, Virginia, where George Washington worshipped. Edward's parents, two brothers, two sisters, an aunt from Zurich, and many other friends came from England, and we enjoyed four or five days of parties and celebrations.

In 1993 my younger son David started to date a girl named Syd, and three years later they moved in together in a house that David bought in Los Angeles. He had started his own recording company, and Syd worked for an advertising company. During these early years as a couple, David frequently said that after five years going together they would either break up or get married.

One evening after about four years, Nancy and I were having dinner with the two of them, along with Syd's parents, Stan and Rosemary Stuhlbarg. When David and Syd were away from the table, I said to Stan and Rosemary, "How are we ever going to get these kids married?" We discussed this a few minutes, and it was evident that they shared my sentiments 100%. They seemed very happy that I would speak up and say how I felt. I had clearly hit on common ground with my statement, and Rosemary's face lit up with delight because she and Stan were also married young, and the Stuhlbargs shared along with the de Laskis' a commitment to very strong family values. In fact, years later David commented about how shared family values were a major reason why he and Syd had been drawn to each other. As Syd put it, "We were cut from the same cloth."

In keeping his often repeated pledge, David and Syd did make a big change at the five-year mark of their relationship. They announced their engagement about a year after that dinner with the Stuhlbargs. They were married in November, 1998, at a beautiful estate they had rented for the day on a mountaintop in Santa Barbara, California. Our whole family was there, and we had a wonderful time. At the wedding reception I gave the following toast, "May the children of David and Syd give them as much pleasure as my children have given me." David liked this toast so much that he included it in a write-up about the wedding sent to all of his friends.

Although I didn't tell David at the time, I had had some reservations about giving this particular toast because I didn't know whether they were planning on having children. I was concerned that maybe this sounded a bit presumptuous of me, but it certainly hasn't turned out that way. Parenting has become a huge part of Syd and David's lives. In 2000 the first of their two sons, Zevin, arrived, followed three years later by his brother, Dexter.

Those two grandsons were a blessed addition to an already lovely group of four granddaughters. Ken and Tena's daughters Daphne and Dana were born in 1991 and 1992. And their cousins Catherine and Amelia were born to Kathleen and Edward in 1991 and 1994. Nancy and I are so proud of each one of our talented and beautiful grandchildren. Nothing gives us more pleasure than big family gatherings with the whole de Laski clan, which initially occurred at Rehoboth Beach in Delaware. Since then the reunion site has shifted. In 1991 Ken and Tena bought a beautiful summer home in Saint Michaels, Maryland, and ten years later Kathleen and Edward bought a similar home nearby. Since both houses are on the water, family reunions have included a lot of boating and fishing. What's more, this has become the spot where we have celebrated Thanksgiving annually. Everyone's friends and relatives generally add up to more than thirty people.

A Virginia Home for Just Nancy and Me

One day in June, 1992, Nancy and I were having dinner in Great Falls, and she suggested we drive around the corner to see a house which had been on–and–off the market for about three years. She said that the asking price was well over two million dollars—more expensive than we had considered for us—but she wanted me to see it anyway. It was a beautiful four-story house on a three–acre lot; and what's more there was a vacant lot next door that was also on the market.

After driving by and seeing the house from the outside, I told Nancy I would like to tour the house, and so she made an appointment with the agent for the next day. I just happened to call Ken that night, and he said he had just gotten a flyer in the mail announcing that that very house had just been reduced to $1,800,000. The next day it took all morning to complete the tour of the house because it was so large. The ground floor had an indoor swimming pool with a hot tub, Jacuzzi, sauna, and steam room with shower. Next to that was a billiard room and long bar. Then came a double room with a sitting area and fireplace, a separate TV room, and a wine cellar. Still on that lowest floor and going toward the front of the house was an exercise room, another bathroom, and an office with a fireplace.

The main floor just above was even more impressive. Walking in the front door of the main level, we entered a large foyer with a formal living room on the right and a dining room on the left. Walking back through the foyer we stepped down into a Great Room with large windows and a twenty-four foot ceiling and a beautiful bar in the corner. To the right of this room was a library; and beyond that, the master bedroom and bath. To the left of the Great Room was the kitchen and family dining area and beyond that, a laundry room and entrance to a three–car garage.

Continuing to explore, we found on the next floor up a series of four bedrooms and three full baths plus a large playroom which looked like it would be perfect for art and music (such as Nancy's dulcimer) or having a hideaway to wrap gift packages.

And there was even another floor on the very top which had a living room, small kitchen and dining room, a bedroom, and two bathrooms. All totaled, the house had nine bathrooms, five fireplaces, one elevator, and was almost 15,000 square feet of living space.

It was far more space than we were used to, and there was a big question about what the house was really worth and what kind of price the builder would be willing to accept. We found out that he had gotten an offer on the house three years ago for $3,300,000, but that contract had fallen through. Since then a number of other contracts had also been written, and they had also fallen through. And so the house had never been lived in. Just as Ken had told us the night before, the builder was willing to take $1,800,000 for the house if the contract would close by June 30. That date was important to him because it was the end of the fiscal year for his construction business, and he wanted to write off his loss in his current tax year.

For both Nancy and me, this house seemed like it was meant for us. This was just our first time to see it, but it felt right to make an offer. In fact, since 1959—a span of 33 years—this would be just the fourth time that we would be buying a home, and in three out of four cases we made an offer from just that initial visit. And so, we told the agent we could offer $1,750,000 for the house, but that I would have to call my bank in the morning to see if they could quickly lend me a million dollars. The bank reps came out the next day, and after seeing the house for themselves, they said they would waive the appraisal and there would be no problem to settle in a few weeks. With this new home purchase coming together so smoothly, we decided it would be a great investment to go ahead and secure the vacant lot next door, which we bought for $250,000. Nancy still had her real estate license so she received commissions of $50,000 on this deal and $20,000 on the sale of the old house some months later. These were the last transactions she was involved in during her real estate career.

We put our old house on the market and sold it seven months later for $600,000, creating a net gain of $225,000. A few years earlier that home on Hidden Creek Drive had been worth about $900,000, but we were currently in a very soft real estate market—but the soft market was in our favor with the purchase of our new home.

Taking care of this new home on Deerfield Pond Court was not going to be easy. And so we also put an ad in a local newspaper for house servants. A wonderful Serbian couple by the name of Vlastimir and Borka Milosavljevic showed up. I could never remember, pronounce, or spell their last name, but it didn't matter because they quickly became a part of our family, and I called them by their first names.

We reached an agreement with them that was good for all four of us. In addition to their salary, we agreed to provide for health insurance, their automobile expenses, and yearly contributions to their retirement savings. The contract also called for us to provide room and board for them. And so, the fourth floor of our new house became their year-round home, even during the four-and-a-half months a year when Nancy and I were in California—allowing Vlastimir and Borka to come and go as they liked from the Deerfield Pond Court home for that part of each year.

The contract called for Borka to have duties as housekeeper and cook. Vlastimir had responsibilities related to household repairs, yard work and landscaping, shopping, and even occasional butler duties.

And so, in September of 1992, the four of us took up residence in our new home. Borka and Vlastimir literally waited on us hand-and-foot, and they were much more to us than just servants. We truly considered them as part of our family. Borka was such a great cook that I preferred not to go out for dinner. And she was a born caregiver. I sometimes commented to friends who visited us, "She makes me feel like I am Guru Maharaji."

As I mentioned, the employment contract called for the two of them to have lots of free time when Nancy and I went away to Palm Desert for the winter. Borka and Vlastimir were required to do very little during those four-and-a-half months, and I naturally thought that they would look forward to this period of time.

But when we returned each year in early May, Borka always wept and hugged us because she had missed us, and she was so happy that we were home.

Another lovely fact about Borka and Vlastimir was that they were very compatible and never argued with each other. I think this had a positive effect on the relationship I had with Nancy. I would feel embarrassed if they saw me arguing and fussing with Nancy.

Having this large, new home in Great Falls affected our lives in many others ways, as well. We had quite a few overnight guests— my mother and sister-in-law, Nancy Lou; David and his family; other friends and business associates. Four or five times a year we would have some kind of an event ranging from Deltek parties and fund raisers to board meetings and spiritual seminars.

Another aspect of this home that was particularly fun for me was the wine cellar. Both my son Ken and my son-in-law Edward are wine connoisseurs, and I too started to collect wine. In fact, I made this into quite a hobby and project for myself. I invested about $70,000 in wine, collecting nearly 1,300 bottles—most of which were high quality Bordeaux wines and cabernets. I became a student of Robert Walker and his famous point system for rating wines, and I made my investment purchases from a list he published of the top 100 Bordeaux wines from vintages of 1982 to 1990. I paid from $45 to $112 a bottle—except in one instance I bought a case of 1990 Petrus for $500 a bottle, with the intention to serve it in 2005 when Nancy and I celebrated our 50th wedding anniversary.

I discovered that these purchases really were good investments. A dozen years later, most of these wines were worth over $400 a bottle—and the Petrus had a retail value of $6,000 a bottle. We didn't serve it at the 50th anniversary celebration. It was just too hard to imagine going through a case of wine in one afternoon that was worth $72,000. But Nancy and I did enjoy a bottle of it the next day with my wine merchant. And it was really good. Nancy thought it was the best she ever had, but certainly not worth $6,000.

Frankly, I still find it very difficult to spend more than $100 for a bottle of wine. My favorite wine is pinot noir—a red wine that needs only about two years to age, and my favorites cost from $30 to $60 a bottle. Since becoming a wine connoisseur I rarely drink a highball, but I do drink too much wine.

Travel Adventures

As the kids grew up and left home to start lives of their own, it created space for Nancy and me to start seeing vacation times in a new way, and we wanted to try some overseas travel. I had, of course, spent a year living in Japan with my folks when I was sixteen. And I had had some international travel experience focused on a very specific purpose: to attend Guru Maharaji programs in Australia and other countries. But this would now be something new and expansive for my vision of what the world is all about.

We decided to start taking trips as a couple—to Europe, in particular. And it seemed like a great opportunity to get this started would be to visit with Kathleen and her new husband Edward in his homeland of England. In May, 1988, just six months after they had married, Nancy and I met Kathleen and Edward at Heathrow Airport, and they drove us to Cambridge University, Edward's alma mater. After touring the campus, we went punting on the Cam River and then drove to York to see the monument to the Allied air crews who served in World War II. We also got to renew our acquaintances with Edward's parents and many brothers and sisters, all of whom we had met at the wedding.

I learned in an embarrassing way that the English are not as inclined to have ice for their beverages as we are in the United States. While the rest of my group was out visiting some beautiful old houses, I was waiting in the garden by myself when the butler brought out some beverage choices along with a container of ice. When he left, I took a look and found that there were only about half a dozen very small cubes. I went ahead and put them all in my glass and poured myself a drink. When the butler re-appeared, he was extremely upset to find that just one person had consumed all the ice cubes they had in the household. I had far exceeded my quota, and our host had to go to a neighbor's house to get more ice cubes for the others.

I also learned something about fashion on that trip. It was now into June, and it was unusually hot (in the 90's) so Edward and I went shopping for shorts and sandals. We changed right into them, and then headed out to a pub for some beer. The pub wasn't air-conditioned, and so our casual clothing felt really good, but everyone else in the pub was dressed in dark, heavy suits with ties. Edward and I really stood out. All the customers in the pub looked at us and our strange outfits, but it seemed to me that we were the only ones dressed for the occasion!

The trip to England was a very special one for us because we were getting to know the homeland of our new son-in-law and experience so many aspects of history. But it was some time before we ventured outside the United States again. In 1997 we had brief trips first to Bermuda and then later to Nova Scotia and a drive all the way into Prince Edward's Island. And then in 1998 we made a commitment for what proved to be one of our most memorable international excursions—an extensive Baltic Sea cruise with the Carters and three other couples who were Naval Academy friends of theirs.

It all started with a call from Mary Carter, who made this trip sound so spectacular that we just had to go. We even agreed to Mary's proposal that Nancy and I secure the most lavish accommodations on the cruise ship—a fantastic suite, with a large area for gatherings, a bar, and even a piano. It was very expensive—$25,000—and I complained to Mary about that. She replied, "Oh, come on, Don. You can afford it." The suite provided a perfect gathering place nightly for Nancy and me to be with the Carters and the other three couples who became very close friends for many years thereafter.

The trip began by our flying to London, and from there we took a two-hour train ride west to Somerset. There we spent three days with Edward's parents, including a trip to the beautiful old city of

Bath. I enjoyed soaking in the historic mineral waters of Bath, which were originally used by the occupying Romans about 1500 years ago.

We then took a three-hour train ride to Harwich on the east coast of England to begin our cruise. City by city, the cruise liner visited the great capitals of Scandinavia—first Oslo, then Stockholm, and on to Helsinki. I was especially impressed with a visit to the home of composer Jean Sibelius in the Finnish capital city. The following day, as we were pulling out of the Helsinki harbor, I played "Finlandia" on the piano which I had practiced before leaving home. (The group was very moved, and one lady even mentioned it to me eight years later.)

Our next port-of-call was St. Petersburg, Russia. I was struck by the poverty. The day we were there, the financial situation in Russia had grown even more dire with the value of the ruble dropping to almost nothing against other world currencies. Teenage girls came up to us begging for money, and some of them carried a doll wrapped in a blanket in hopes that we would mistake it for a real baby. The contrasts were so stark because we had toured the opulent palaces of the Czars and visited the spectacularly beautiful opera house.

After St. Petersburg we continued on to Estonia, and it was there that I received a call from Ken saying that my 99-year-old mother was failing quickly and would probably die very soon. He agreed that there was little that I could do, and since the cruise was nearly over, he said that he and Kathleen could take care of anything that would happen until we got home. The cruise moved on to Copenhagen, and then back to our starting point in Harwich, England. During our last night in London another call came from Ken with the news that my mom had passed over. It was sad not to be able to be there with her in the end, but she had had a very long and rich life, and the two of us had been able to form a deeper bond in her later years—especially as she began to discover that she couldn't exclusively *give* to others—she needed to *receive* also. Nancy and I were able to get back to Virginia just in time for her funeral, which I described earlier in Chapter 9.

All these travels I have just described—plus many others that are included in Appendix 4—have had an important impact on me in several ways. They have given me a broader picture of how people live; and they have deepened my appreciation for the United States as well as an appreciation for other nations and their history. The trips have also been a way that Nancy and I deepened our marriage relationship. In the busy-ness of daily life, we both routinely ended up with so many daily activities that are not done together. And with these educational and vacation trips we had the chance to be together throughout the day.

A Final Home

In Chapter 6, I described a sequence of three homes we have bought at the Vintage Club in Indian Wells, California from 1997 to 2003. Nancy and I formed a plan to keep our current home there as a winter residence for as long as we could. However, after many wonderful years in our large home in Great Falls, Virginia, it became evident that we would want to find something smaller and more convenient for us as a final home. And so, in the summer of 2006 we began making arrangements for our new residence. We had received an appealing advertisement in the mail about a soon-to-be-constructed assisted-living facility about fifteen minutes away in Bethesda, Maryland. Once again we made a decision and made a purchase on our first visit—without even having to look anywhere else!

The new complex is part of Sunrise Senior Living and is called Fox Hill. Residents purchase a unit, and then assisted living is available whenever it is needed. We chose three units which we put together at a cost of about $2,600,000. Our units look out over the Burning Tree Country Club, and we have two bedrooms, an office, TV room and a combination kitchenette and eating area. We also have several sun rooms and a balcony. The general facilities include four dining rooms, social rooms, library, indoor swimming pool and spa, and outdoor walking areas.

We hoped to move into this facility by December of 2008, and our return from California in the spring of 2008 was challenging because we needed to sell our home and prepare to downsize from 15,000 to 3,700 square feet. At our age we knew we really needed to make a change while we were in reasonably good health, but the main problem in such a move was that we were sure to really miss Borka and Vlastimir. Little did we realize what unexpected and sad events were just around the corner as we got ready to make this big move. More about that in Chapter 18.

Cutting the ribbon for the new practice studios
at George Mason University, with university president Alan Merten

Don at 60

Chapter 16

Giving Money Away

Although the title and content of this chapter is primarily about money, its meaning runs much deeper. Money is simply an external representation of a life-long quality of Don's soul. Throughout his life, giving and sharing have been essential aspects of his way of being in the world.

In fact, Don's life bespeaks generosity and giving. Of course, "giving" is a much broader topic than simply donating money to good causes. Generosity flows from a giving attitude. It requires a frame of mind that believes in the abundance of the universe. And that a giving attitude spills over into many forms of sharing and service.

If we look back to patterns from early in Don's life, we see that this giving attitude has always been with him. It didn't suddenly appear when he became financially wealthy and wanted to share his money with good causes. Consider how, as a teenager—with trust and compassion—he would loan money to customers who needed eggs but couldn't afford them. Or, remember how as a young man he devoted countless hours of volunteer time to the Boy Scouts. These are but two of many examples of this giving attitude.

As we read these pages about Don and Nancy's philanthropy, we are sure to be touched by how many lives they have been able to impact with their generous financial support. And we may find ourselves wondering if we would be as generous ourselves if life blessed us with tremendous monetary resources. But the deeper question that this chapter raises for us all is not about money. Instead we are challenged to see ways in which we are already blessed in our own ways, and to ask ourselves about the extent to which we maintain a "giving attitude" and share of our personal "wealth" in whatever form that may take—creativity, time, energy, knowledge, or maybe even money, too.

❀

In recent years I have had lots of money, but I never wanted to waste any of it. I feel that it is God's gift, and it is something that I have tried to share. Some rich people I know seem to have a very different point of view. They spend a lot of money on multiple homes—even four or five—private jets for only occasional travel, art collections, and multiple golf memberships which are rarely used. I could never do this. To my mind, this money has a higher purpose, and I have many times felt guided to find the people and organizations. And in addition to charities, I give and save money for my family—including nephews and nieces. I feel very good about including Ed's children this way, and I can see how it is related to my love for my brother.

The stories of finding a higher purpose for God's money begins with my connections to a very remarkable doctor. I did not go out looking for him and his organization. In a sense, he found me.

The Center for Mind-Body Medicine

In 1990 a premie friend of mine introduced me to Dr. James Gordon, the founder and executive director of the Center for Mind-Body Medicine (CMBM) located in Washington, D.C. Jim is a psychiatrist and graduate of Harvard Medical School, and he specializes in alternative medicine. From the first time we met, I have always enjoyed being with Jim because we think so much alike. We both meditate, and he was acquainted with Guru Maharaji—in fact, when I met Jim he had just written a book about yet another guru. I discovered that Jim was a practicing Buddhist and, of course, I have always respected Asian religions. And I was very pleased to learn that Jim always started each Board meeting of CMBM with a meditation.

At my request Jim created and then managed a research study for asthmatic children. The services in this research project were coordinated through elementary school nurses in the Washington, D.C., area. At this time the staff of CMBM consisted of only Jim and a secretary. I donated $50,000 to help him expand his work and have increased it over the years. For several years he taught a class without pay at Georgetown University on nutrition, although he practiced psychiatry on a part time basis. For many years CMBM has also given a five–day annual seminar called, "Food for Medicine" which doctors and other care givers from all over the country attend. This is very important because most medical schools in this country do not teach nutrition. CMBM also has a program called Cancer Guides in which the participants learn all the various alternative remedies for cancer. The graduates of this program are listed on the CMBM web site (www.cmbm.org) and can be contacted by anyone who has been diagnosed with cancer.

During the Kosovo outbreak in 1998, Jim turned his attention to helping large groups of people deal with post–traumatic stress disorder (PTSD). This program was so successful that it was later carried out in Israel, Gaza, post–9/11 New York City, and post–Katrina New Orleans. Jim and his teachers trained hundreds of caregivers, who in turn helped tens of thousands of people. The program was truly holistic and involved meditation, dancing, exercising and psychological counseling.

Over the years since I met him, I have provided periodic accounting and administrative assistance to Jim, and I helped him streamline his staff which by 2006 had grown to twelve employees with a total budget of about $2,500,000. One example of how I was able to help administratively was in early 2003 while I was at our winter home in Indian Wells, California. Jim called me about a problem that had been going on for almost a year and half. It began in September, 2001. CMBM had scheduled several conferences that had to be cancelled due to the 9/11 attacks, and many conference attendees were unable to get flights to the conferences. They had to cancel conference reservations at three separate hotels. After many months of extensive negotiations with conference hotel facilities, the outstanding charges were still $200,000. There looked to be no way that it could be paid.

Jim told me in the phone call that since he had done all he could at this point, he just wasn't going to worry about it any further, but I felt differently. I called the three hotels that were involved. I told managers at the three hotels that CMBM was bankrupt, but I was donating half the outstanding debt for any hotel that was willing to reduce their obligation by half. All three hotels accepted immediately. Needless to say, Jim and all the staff were extremely grateful.

The Center for Mind–Body Medicine has had several other milestones which continue to make me very proud of this organization. In 2006 the organization received a two–year grant of $1,500,000 for its work in foreign countries. The grant came from Chuck Feeney whose biography entitled *The Billionaire Who Wasn't* was published in 2007. This fascinating book explains how Mr. Feeny is trying to give all of his assets away (estimated at four billion dollars) within the next ten years.

In 2007 Jim Gordon received the Bravewell Award, a gift of $25,000 given to each of five awardees. This award is given by a group of philanthropists who are committed to making integrative medicine the standard of care for all medicine. The awards event included a seminar given by each recipient during the day, with further comments given at a black tie dinner in the evening. Jim described the work of the Center, told stories, showed pictures, and even mentioned my name. The response to his presentation was overwhelming and many people were moved to tears.

In April of 2010 Jim wanted to start a program in Haiti. After the huge earthquake, millions of people were suffering from PTSD due to lack of food and housing. He had no funding so the de Laski Foundation gave him $200,000 so he could get started. He made wonderful progress setting up a training staff and making contacts. It seems that major charities such as the Red Cross had received millions of dollars in donations for Haiti, but they were not letting go of the money. So my foundation gave him an additional $400,000 to carry him through 2010, and pledged another $600,000 for 2011. He hopes to get 6 to 9 million dollars for this program if money is released from the Red Cross.

Music

After we had moved to Deerfield Pond Court, Nancy became involved in 1993 with a local group of women called Friends of the Great Falls Concert Series. In the early 1980s Tim Rowe—a highly respected musician and lecturer for the Smithsonian—had started the Great Falls Concert Series with five musical programs a year, all performed at local churches in Great Falls. For two of those annual concerts Tim would organize a full orchestra of about thirty-five musicians (with himself as conductor), and the other three annual productions were operatic performances, as well as chamber music groups, and piano and instrumental soloists.

Nancy and I got very involved in this work. We have a long-standing commitment to supporting the arts, and this was a wonderful initiative taken by Tim Rowe right there in our own town. After each of the five annual concerts, the audience of about 60 people would gather at someone's house for refreshments. And for the annual performance near Christmastime, we had the post-performance celebration at our house, which often included youth choirs and other entertainment.

Tim Rowe's work also gave us a very good opportunity to meet young musical artists at the beginning of promising careers. We looked for ways to make a difference in the careers of talented men and women just getting started, and we funded a $2,500 scholarship through Tim's organization—to be given annually to a deserving young artist. The first recipient was a violinist named Janice Martin. Five years later we got to see her again, not in Great Falls, Virginia, but all the way in California when she was a featured performer at a concert hall in Palm Springs, not far from our winter home. We went backstage to see her after the show, and she expressed deep appreciation for how we had been helpful to her. And, of course, we were very proud. There were other successful recipients of our award, one of whom was an opera singer, Jessica Swink. She appeared with the National Symphony Orchestra at the Kennedy Center as the winner of their Young Soloists Competition in 2003. And she has sung twice at the White House.

As I mentioned, Tim was an experienced lecturer for the Smithsonian Institute, and once he even set up a music and culture trip to Strasburg, Austria—one of the home cities of Wolfgang Amadeus Mozart himself. (The organization had changed its name from" Great Falls Concert Series" to "Amadeus Concerts," in large part because we wanted to make it clear that people from all over the Washington D.C. metropolitan area were welcome, not just those in the small town of Great Falls.) In addition to Strasburg, the trip to Austria included a stay on the same estate where the movie *The Sound of Music* had been filmed.

Tim's activities through Amadeus Concerts also included outreach into the local community. He conducted rehearsals at local schools so that children would be exposed to this fabulous music and always held a number of lecture series. He even gave piano lessons, and I was one of his many pupils. I had taken piano lessons for four years when I was a boy, but as an adult I had only occasionally kept up with playing. It was a delight to get these lessons from Tim. I suspect he looked forward to it, too. He would come over to our home; we'd have my lesson; and then I would open a good bottle of wine; and we would have dinner.

In the fall of 2004 Amadeus Concerts was having some financial problems, so we gave them a $20,000 matching gift. Tim was very appreciative; but that winter, when I was in Palm Desert, I got a very shocking phone call. Tim had been found dead in his car on the side of the road in western Virginia. He had committed suicide by stabbing himself in the chest. For a while the police thought that he had been murdered, but later a note was found stating that he did this to protest the state of all the poor people in our country. I personally felt that he did it because of extreme depression, and his self-described protest was just a mask for his deep personal pain. Tim generally seemed happy, but he was a very private person, and he lived by himself. In retrospect we know that no one really knew what was going on inside him.

I was president of Amadeus at the time of Tim's death, and here I was nearly 3,000 miles away and not due back to Virginia for a couple of months. Thank goodness that the previous president,

Bill Chadwick, was there to fill in for me.

With the founder's death, there was a lot of talk about closing Amadeus, but a group of us wanted to try another year, partly because there were financial resources at hand and an audience of people who looked forward to the start of a new season of concerts. In fact, we now had about $30,000 in the bank, and so we hired Scott Wood on a part-time basis to be the executive director and conductor, and we set up a number of committees to coordinate things that Tim used to do. The first year without Tim was tough, but things worked out. Amadeus began to find new life, and by the last program of 2007 there was a sell-out crowd—a first for us.

But Tim is not forgotten, and so often when I drive through Great Falls, I think of him and miss him so much. I feel that if I had known him better, maybe I could have helped him. He brought so much happiness to others and was loved by so many people. I think we could help our friends so much more if we would let them know how much we love them.

Other Arts Organizations

Nancy and I have had a long interest in operas, concerts, plays, and art museums; and we have frequently made donations of several thousand dollars to them. In May, 1997, we were invited to a dinner at the home of Rusty Powell, the director of The National Gallery of Art. I hardly knew Rusty, and I assumed that this was just another run of the mill fund raiser. It turned out to be a very small, intimate dinner. Nancy was seated next to Rusty, and I sat next to the Chairman of Development. Near the end of the dinner I asked her why my wife and I were invited to this event, and without answering the question she congratulated me on the recent public offering of Deltek Systems. I helped her out by asking about the needs and programs of the museum. And by the end of the dinner Nancy and I had agreed to support a special program for local school children. Throughout the year, they would be transported to the National Gallery from their schools and given special tours and other activities. We have continued to support various programs at the museum, and we have attended many social functions which always include some special art exhibition, one of which was attended by Bill and Hillary Clinton.

A few months later Duke University found out about us the same way. They are always alert to identify alumni who may be in a position to be philanthropists to the school. We ended up giving them a $100,000 endowment for undergraduate drama majors. Ten years later this endowment has grown to $226,000, but the disbursements to the students have gone up only from $5,000 to $8,000 per year. Of course tuition for the students has gone up at a considerably faster pace. I'm in the process of trying to get Duke to pay out more, but I don't think I will succeed. It has taught me to be careful about endowments, and I don't plan to create any more scholarship endowments. I think a better way to help out is to pay a portion of the student's tuition each year.

The Family Foundation and George Mason University

In 1996 Nancy and I set up a 501(c) 3 non-profit corporation that we named The Alliance for Medical Care. It was to carry out a program at Howard University for asthmatic children, a program that I described in Chapter 11. That program was very successful but short-lived, and in 1998 we terminated the Alliance for Medical Care due to various tax requirements and established the Donald and Nancy L. De Laski Foundation. We had decided that we wanted to do most of our major giving under one roof and not have a separate charity for health care. Five years later we changed the foundation name to The De Laski Family Foundation in order to encourage other family members to participate.

The Family Foundation has been a benefactor to many organizations, large and small. We find them—or we find each other—in a variety of ways, oftentimes having nothing to do with philanthropy at first. For example, In the mid-1990s George Mason University (G.M.U.) invited Deltek Systems Inc. to give regular classes to professionals on government contract accounting. Deltek instructors were paid a teaching honorarium, and the university and Deltek split the profits. Not only did we make money, but it was great publicity for our software. But this was only the beginning of our relationship with G.M.U. First we gave a $50,000 scholarship endowment designating students from Washington D.C. who were majoring in the performing arts. But G.M.U. couldn't find anyone from D.C., so they had to open it up to other geographic areas. One of these scholarship students has become a fantastic dancer and has a very promising career.

We soon became acquainted with the Dean of the College of Performing and Visual Arts, Bill Reeder. One day I said to Bill, "I think George Mason should start a summer music camp for high school students, and I'll put in $100,000 to get it off the ground. To go to music camp kids have to go far away to places like Interlocken Center for the Arts in Michigan, and we've got facilities and teachers right here." Bill liked the idea, and the Potomac Music Camp was born. Over three hundred students attended the first year, and in subsequent years it grew to six hundred. Each summer there are eight different camp sessions lasting one or two weeks each, and each one specializes in different forms of music such as strings, woodwinds, jazz, and brass.

The Family Foundation gave the initial seed money, and then another equal gift the second year. But thereafter the Potomac Music Camp became self-sufficient. Soon thereafter another need came into focus. The College of Visual and Performing Arts at G.M.U. was sadly lacking in practice facilities, so The De Laski Family Foundation donated one million dollars for construction of fifteen practice rooms next to their main building. When it was completed, we had a big celebration with President Merten (a picture of the ceremony is on the first page of this chapter). And the expansion of facilities continued since the College of Visual and Performing Arts was growing so fast that additional facilities were essential. Our Foundation subsequently donated four million dollars toward the construction of a new building for the College. The Foundation's gift has been matched by the State of Virginia to make this new building possible, and we look forward to its completion by the end of 2010.

Our connections with George Mason University have deepened over the years. I have served on the G.M.U. Foundation Board for about five years, and Nancy has served on the Board of the College of Visual and Performing Arts. In 2006 our daughter Kathleen began to serve on the Board of Visitors—the supervising Board for the entire University—but this appointment was on her own merits and has nothing to do with us. They had been courting her for many years because of her outstanding professional accomplishments. In fact, she had been invited to join the Board before Nancy and I ever got involved with G.M.U., but her boss at Sallie Mae (the nation's leading provider of student loans) would not permit it at first. It was only when she switched to part-time work at Sallie Mae that Kathleen was able to finally accept the invitation to join the Board of Visitors. (She has had a very impressive career, but I won't go into it because this book is about me.)

The Sitar Center and Mount Vernon

In 2002 I participated in a panel discussion sponsored by George Mason University. It was given for the benefit of non-profit organizations. The other two speakers were grant writers, and I was the only one there who was a donor. I told the audience that one central focus of the De Laski Family Foundation was children in the Washington, D.C., area. What's more, I told the audience that we prefer to have a close relationship with the people who work in the various charitable organizations that we support.

After the program a lady came up to me and told me about the Sitar Center—a facility in downtown D.C. where children of poor families could come after school to learn music, art, and dance. A few days later I visited the Sitar Center for the Arts in the Adams Morgan section of D.C. where I met Rhonda Buckley, the executive director. Rhonda was a very attractive woman in her early forties who had never married and had dedicated her life to helping young people. The facility was very old and run down and far too small for the 100 children who were coming each day after school.

Since the Center was in the process of arranging financing and raising money for a new facility, our foundation donated some money and a new facility was occupied by the Center in 2004. This center includes a two hundred seat auditorium which was named after us and is used for musical programs put on by the children and other organizations in the area. It also includes a Steinway piano which we donated. By 2010 the Sitar Center was working with over 500 children a year.

As little known as the Sitar Center is likely to be to most people living outside of Washington, D.C., another organization we have supported is one of the most famous and historic. Since 1998 Nancy has served on one of the Boards at Mount Vernon. This one is called The Life Guard, and it meets twice yearly to help support fund-raising efforts and other various projects. I usually attended with her because it is almost an hour's drive from our home in Great Falls, and there is always a nice dinner and event after each meeting.

We became involved in and gave financial support to the renovation of many small projects there on the grounds at Mount Vernon. We made a lot of friends there and enjoyed all the activities, such as dinners on the veranda of George Washington's historic home, live shows, and lectures. One lecturer is especially memorable for me: David McCullough, the biographer of John Adams and Harry Truman, as well as the author of an outstanding book about George Washington and the founding fathers entitled *1776*. He is widely referred to as the master of the art of narrative history, and I found his lecture about George Washington to be particularly engrossing. This lecture and others from the series were given for a limited group of officers and major donors, and the small group setting really gave us a chance to get to know these extraordinary speakers.

For some time, Mount Vernon had been making plans and raising money for a major new education and museum facility which cost $125,000,000. The project was successfully completed in 2006. In order to preserve the beautiful grounds this entire new facility was built underground with farm animals grazing above it. The main lobby has some very realistic statues of Washington's family and there are several theaters and museums. As part of this major capital project by Mount Vernon, we donated $100,000 for the development and publication of a complete museum catalog, which now sells in the gift shop for $60.

One day Jim Reese, the Mount Vernon C.E.O, showed us the plans for an exhibit in the museum which displayed Washington's false teeth and also provided information about dentistry in his time. We thought it would be a very unique museum room, and we were happy to donate its cost of $500,000. But that was not the final way that we helped with this expansion of visitors facilities. They were planning to have a 20-minute, Hollywood–produced movie about George Washington, but time was running out and they had not yet secured a pledge to cover the estimated cost of $4,000,000. I found out about this problem at a lecture given by one of Mount Vernon's governing regents; and so, after checking with Nancy, I agreed that our foundation would pay half the cost. We got to watch some of the filming and were encouraged to make suggestions which resulted in some changes that cost us an additional $300,000. Many of our friends who have visited Mount Vernon tell us how much they enjoyed the movie, especially the beginning which says, "This movie was made possible by the generous support of Donald and Nancy de Laski and the Ford Foundation."

One of the reasons that Nancy and I feel so good about supporting Mount Vernon is the message and lessons of our first President which are being preserved there. In these times very little is taught in the schools about George Washington and early American history. Mount Vernon provides teaching materials throughout the United States for the schools, and they give special seminars for teachers.

In 2007 when I was attending one of Nancy's Life Guard meetings, Jim Reese said he wanted to get a university involved in the education program, and I volunteered to contact George Mason University. I called Alan Merten, the G.M.U. president, and he gave me some e-mail addresses of people who should be part of such a collaboration. I got to work on setting up some meetings to explore what might be done between these two institutions that we are so much a part of.

The first meeting was held there at Mount Vernon among half a dozen people I had contacted; and then we had a follow–up meeting on campus at George Mason University. In 2008 and 2009 the De Laski Family Foundation donated $250,000 so that G.M.U. could create a web site about Martha Washington, and two graduate fellowships were provided to work with George Washington's letters.

Other Charitable Organizations

Over the past twenty–five years we have attended about six plays and musicals a year at the Arena Stage in Southeast Washington, D.C. In the last five years these events have all been by American playwrights, and many have been original productions. The Arena Stage also provides a very extensive summer camp for young people to participate in music, dance, and drama. In January, 2008, Arena relocated for two years to Arlington, Virginia, while they did a major, beautifully–designed refurbishment of the existing building. The total estimated cost of these renovations was 140 million dollars. Major donors to this extensive capital project, including the D.C. Government, provided about half the cost. Other donations—big and small—came in to make this important renewal possible for the Arena Stage. Our Foundation was glad to donate 3.2 million dollars toward the project. We also continued to contribute between $25,000 and $50,000 a year to underwrite various shows, and Nancy and I were members of the Board of Trustees. We took great pride in the quality of this theater and what it has brought to the cultural life of the nation's capital.

But not all of our organizations were in the Washington, D.C. area. As I mentioned in Chapter 11, I have occasionally gone to the Deva Foundation in Santa Fe for past life regression work with Rachel Kaufman and her husband Rick. Around the year 2000 Rachael started spending a lot of time going to Israel and Palestine in order to help families deal with their stressful lives. In fact she was doing the same kind of work that Jim Gordon of CMBM was doing. In 2003 Rachael started a camp where she would bring teenage girls to Santa Fe from Israel and Palestine (including Gaza) in order to get to know each other. There were two sessions yearly of this camp program, and each had twelve girls and lasted for two weeks. I attended the camp in the second year and was almost brought to tears when the girls would talk about their experiences. But they also had a lot of fun doing various art and music projects.

The main cost of these camps has been the airfare to bring all the girls to Santa Fe, and we have been happy to make donations to help underwrite those expenses. In recent years Rachel has also gone to the Middle East a number of times each year to conduct follow-up meetings which include the girls' parents. In 2003 the Deva Foundation gave a special name to this aspect of their Foundation: Creativity for Peace. It is a wonderful organization doing a very important grassroots form of peace-building. And we also enjoy our friendship with Rachel and Rick. Since Rick and I loved to play golf together, he and Rachel visited us several times at the Vintage Club. On their visit in 2004, I told them that we would increase our support from $100,000 a year to $250,000 for each of the next four years.

But things continue to be very tough for these girls in the Middle East and for their families. In late 2006, I was in Jim Gordon's office and he told me that things were so bad in Gaza that people were killing each other in the streets for food. I called Rachel and offered to send $50,000 to Gaza if it could be gotten to the people. She set up an arrangement where the money was sent to a dentist's office in Gaza, and some of the girls who had previously been in Rachel's camp helped to distribute it. Over 100 people were helped, and I received lots of notes of appreciation. We sent a proposal to the Gates Foundation to see if they would provide major funding for this program, but they were not interested. They are probably just like we are in that they fund only programs which they bump into on their own. I think a lot of charities waste a lot of time and money sending out grant proposals to people they don't know.

When we are in California each year for about four-and-a-half months, we spend much less time on philanthropy and social activities, but there are a few charities in which we are involved. The Living Desert is a very well known reserve in Palm Desert where you can see the animal and plant life in their beautiful natural habitat. I always like to visit the wart hogs, which are very ugly, and watch the graceful giraffes. Since we are supporters of The Living Desert, they frequently give our grandchildren special behind-the-scenes tours. We also support an organization which gives food and clothing to very poor families in the town of Mecca, which is purported to be the poorest town in the United States. And we support The McCullum Theater in Palm Springs which does Broadway shows and concerts. There are many, many other smaller charities to which we donate money—through our Foundation and personally—and each one is some work that has touched our lives.

All of the charities which we support have just fallen in our laps without any research on our part. They have virtually all been based near our homes and generally involve giving to the arts or helping young people.

I can't imagine how dull our lives would have been if we did not participate in these organizations. But looking back I realize that giving money is not the only way of having this kind of fun. I have come to know many people who also have a lot of fun by volunteering their time to helping others. When I was younger, I enjoyed being a scoutmaster, and Nancy enjoyed being a volunteer usher for twenty-five years. Just maybe, the angels helped me make a lot of money because they knew I would do good things with it.

The Vintage Club

Don with Mark Thurston as they work on editing this book

Chapter 17

Steady Rhythms and New Adventures

"Maturity" is a word that is frequently used in an offhand way, *seeming to connote merely "getting older." However, there is a* *deeper meaning—a kind of "spiritual maturity"—which is exempli-* *fied in Don's life. As is often the case with something spiritual,* *integration is the key. Two qualities that could be seen as opposites* *are instead melded in a skillful and balanced fashion. The integration* *that comes with "spiritual maturity" creates a harmony of 1) steady,* *familiar rhythms, and 2) bold new adventures.*

This chapter starts with some of the steady, familiar rhythms. We *get a snapshot of Don's life in his mid-70s. In these retirement years* *he has found a lovely pattern of family times, recreation, and the arts.*

Next come some of his new adventures, which keep his growing *edges alive. He continues to work with his health using alternative* *and holistic treatments alongside the best of mainstream medicine.* *He is exploring how readings and advice from intuitives can give him* *new insights about his life's purpose. And he is playing a pivotal role* *in the formation of a new center about consciousness at a major* *university. His work is still going strong to help change the world for* *the better.*

❈

I celebrated my 76th birthday on February 1, 2008, at our home at The Vintage Club in Indian Wells, California. As has been the family custom for the last four years, my niece Sally and her husband Paul flew out from Maryland; my nephew Don came from New York; and his son Rob from Los Angeles also got in on some of the reunion and festivities, too. We enjoyed a fancy catered dinner in our home, and the Carters, who have a place nearby, were also in attendance. I really look forward to family celebra–

tions like this—not just because it's my birthday. Some of us played golf, and the kids spent a lot of time on the tennis courts and the club's large swimming pool and Jacuzzi. For that year's celebration and reunion, we also went to a vaudeville show in Palm Springs called "The Follies." In fact, Nancy and I went to this show (which runs from November until May) for many years in a row. It is held in the same theater from which Jack Benny did his radio program in 1932.

But birthday celebration reunions weren't the only time we had visitors. The rhythm of our lives at our winter home included other family and friends. My younger son David, who lived just two hours away in Pasadena, came out three or four times a season, usually with his wife Syd and their two young sons. And our older son Ken and our daughter Kathleen came out with at least part of their families during Easter vacation annually—usually on their way to or from a ski trip.

We generally had several other overnight guests each year such as Bill Reeder, Dean of School for Performing and Visual Arts at George Mason University, and Rick Philips and Rachel Kaufman from Creativity for Peace. Each of our visiting groups had at least one member who was looking forward to playing golf. I had discovered the principle that one will always see more of family and friends with a home that people like to visit.

I was so glad that we bought a home at the Vintage Club. The weather has always been ideal with highs from about 60 to 90 degrees and very little rain. The golf opportunities are wonderful with two 18-hole courses that are never crowded. Even though Nancy didn't play golf, she also looked forward to coming out to Indian Wells each year. She always appreciated nice weather and participated in art courses, Bible classes, exercise work, and several charity boards—including the renowned McCullum Theater, with its concerts, operas, Broadway shows, and ballet. There was no shortage of enjoyable activities which we could do with the Carters and our friends from the Vintage Club.

The Los Angeles area is also very accessible, and in the winter when we were living in California, that made for easy trips to visit

David and his family. For example, in February of 2008 we drove to Los Angeles to see Wagner's opera *Tristan and Isolde*. We had always wanted to see this opera because the main aria is what Nancy and I always listened to when we were dating at Duke University. Tickets and a very nice dinner were arranged and paid for by the development director from the Washington Opera. David and Syd also joined us, even though I warned them that, including the two intermissions, this opera is four-and-a-half-hours long! They hung in there pretty well, but I told David that he might prefer some shorter operas such as *LaBoheme* and *Madam Butterfly*.

The next day at David's house I discovered that Sam, David's dog of almost twelve years, was very sick and had been diagnosed with cancer. That night David woke up and found that Sam was not in the house, but was outside in the far corner of the yard. The next day, after we had left, they had Sam put away. As I related in Chapter 9, in a similar way, our cat Carburetor went off into the woods to die. I think that it's very interesting that many pets prefer to be alone when they pass away. Sam and I loved each other a lot, and I was always petting and scratching her when we were together. I'm so glad I was there to say good-bye to Sam. Maybe that's the real reason we went to the opera.

Renewing My Connections with Mark Thurston

In the 1970s on one of my trips to Virginia Beach and the Association for Research and Enlightenment (A.R.E.) for a conference about spirituality, I met Mark Thurston and heard him lecture. He was a pretty young guy then, just recently out of college. But over the years that followed I had lost touch with him. I had become more and more deeply involved with Guru Maharaji, and the A.R.E. was no longer a central part of my spiritual life.

But all of that changed when Nancy and I got re-involved with the A.R.E. in 2005 by attending a one-week intensive program in Virginia Beach on the topic of "Wellness and Rejuvenation." It was a very comprehensive residential program in which we got to actually live the patterns for health advocated by Edgar Cayce. We did various exercises early each morning after drinking hot water with lemon juice; we worked with our dreams (which Mark specializes in); ate a natural foods diet for all meals; received many massage and spa treatments; had appointments with holistically-oriented doctors; and we even received a "sand pack," getting buried up to our necks at the beach, which is a health practice recommended by Edgar Cayce for sweating out toxins and cleansing the body.

Mark had been working at A.R.E. for well over thirty years at this point, and he was a central part of the Wellness Week with us—conducting our sessions on attitudes, emotions, and meditation. By this time of re-connecting with him, Mark was a published author of nineteen books on various aspects of spirituality, consciousness, and holistic health. At the end of the week, Mark told Nancy and me about small-group courses that he was now doing with his wife, Mary Elizabeth Lynch. He invited us to attend one in Washington, D.C. that was coming up in just two months. The course had been created by a non-profit organization that he and his wife co-founded called the Personal Transformation and Courage Institute (PTCI). They have courses and seminars throughout the country, and it was synchronistic that just a few weeks later their only program that year in our Washington D.C. area was coming up. The synchronicity of all this looked like the work of my angels.

The course had eleven participants for the three days, and it involved some in-depth self-exploration. One exercise was a partner exercise, and because there were an odd number of participants, Mark jumped in to create an even number while Mary Elizabeth led the process. We were randomly assigned partners, and I ended up with Mark as my partner. (Maybe it wasn't really a coincidence.) The exercise was called "Inquiry," and it involved one of us repeatedly asking the other a carefully chosen question, which was announced by Mary Elizabeth. I was the question-asker first, and my job was to pose to Mark the question, "What do you long for?" During that first stretch, one of Mark's answers really touched me. He said that he longed to have more men friends.

And so later that morning, as we were winding up the exercise, I said to Mark that I would love to be one of his male friends. He replied that he would like that, too; and from that exercise our friendship began to blossom.

Nancy and I enjoyed the course so much that over the next two years we hosted courses with Mary Elizabeth and Mark several times at our home in Great Falls. The large Great Room in our home was an even better site for courses in the D.C. area than the church meeting room had been. One of the exercises in the course "Healing the Wounded Heart" was especially memorable for me. It involved reconnecting with our own inner child. Using a guided meditation, Mark and Mary Elizabeth slowly took us back to the age of four or five, and we were invited to re-experience the feelings and thoughts of that child. Then we were taken out of the meditation and asked to write a short letter as if we were still that child—and to do the writing with the opposite hand than we normally write with. The letter would be from the child to the grown-up self. It was rather awkward and vulnerable to do this; but I wrote the following letter left-handed as the little boy Don, writing to the grown-up Don:

> *Dear Big Don:*
> *I am doing the best I can. I want to succeed and make my parents happy. I am happy about everything.*

Then we were asked to put the pencil in the hand we usually write with, take a new piece of paper, and write another letter. This time the letter was to be from the grown-up self back to the little child. I wrote:

> *Dear Inner Child:*
> *I love you. Stay with me. It is so important for me to stay in touch with you. Let us lead each other. You give me the feelings that I need to make me happy, and I give you the power and ideas that you need. But we are oneness. This body will be gone some day, but you will live on forever. This weekend I have*

gotten to know you so much better. I am very lucky. I have the feeling that you are so much older than I, and that you can teach me so much.

We have enjoyed seeing PTCI thrive, and our Foundation has become a significant financial support to this work. In 2008 they conducted 37 courses, seminars and programs and had nearly a thousand people involved in these small group intensives for spiritual growth.

Going back, though, to how the friendship between Mark and me unfolded: We also invited Mark and Mary Elizabeth to come visit us at our Indian Wells, California, home, and they came in the winter of 2006. They frequently traveled to California for their courses and seminars, and it was easy to add on a short visit with us. A big part of the trip was the chance for Mark and me to get to play golf at the Vintage Club. But in the end, the most important result of the trip was my impetus to start writing this autobiography! The project came into being simply because of a question I asked Mark one evening during his and Mary Elizabeth's stay. I told him that I had often thought about writing a book on *The Wizard of Oz*, and I wondered if he thought it was a good idea. He said he would think about it and let me know in the morning.

The next morning he said that he had a different plan in mind for me: I should write a book about my life, and he would do everything he could to help. He even offered to set up his telephone at his office so all I had to do was call-in, and he would record my voice telling my story. He suggested that he could then get it transcribed, and we would work together to edit it. He said he felt that my life story illustrates many important principles about personal transformation, and he would like to use the book as reference material for the participants of the PTCI seminars.

A few weeks later I got started and found that I really enjoyed the writing. I wrote up first drafts on my own, and I never did need to use Mark's telephone recording and transcription option. And he was a big help by giving suggestions, editing, and writing preambles for each chapter. As we got portions of the book into second or third draft form, I would then send e-mails of those pages to members of my family for feedback and comments. It's a remarkable thing to see a book come into being—especially when it is your own life story! And both Mark and I have been surprised to see it turn out to be a manuscript of some 90,000 words.

And what's more, the book is taking a visual form, too. We are creating an accompanying video that will allow parts of my story to be told even more vividly. Mark and Mary Elizabeth's son Michael is our photographer and video editor. He is a 2007 graduate of the University of Virginia, and digital art is one of his areas of expertise. We've made one trip with Michael to all the places we have lived in Virginia, Maryland, and Washington, D.C., and Michael took still photos and video footage for a short program to be produced in parallel to the published book.

I feel so fortunate to have this wonderful opportunity of writing this book. It has given me enjoyment and a purpose over a period of several years. I think the angels had something to do with all this. If I didn't have a home at the Desert, or if I hadn't gone to that health week at A.R.E., I wouldn't have re-connected with Mark and this book would not have happened.

Health Challenges:
Integrating Mainstream and Alternative Medicine

My health at age 76 wasn't great, but it could have been worse. I had to order oxygen when I traveled by air, which made it difficult to take trips. I was somewhat weak in the legs due to Type II diabetes, and that leg condition generally limited my golf to just nine holes.

Ten years earlier my pulmonologist diagnosed me with emphysema which he thought was probably caused by my asthma and/or smoking for twenty years. Such a condition is incurable and is generally treated with steroids—either prednisone, which is in pill form, or Advair and albuterol, which are inhalants. In the past I had used prednisone sparingly—only when I had a lung infection—because it would cause the adrenal glands to atrophy.

When my oxygen exhale level dropped to nineteen (sixty is normal), the doctor put me on oxygen. This means I was plugged into an oxygen machine at night and had an oxygen tank with me on the golf course and when I worked out on a treadmill. When I flew anywhere, I needed to make arrangements in advance for oxygen because of the thinner air at higher altitudes.

In recent years, though, my understanding of what's wrong with my respiratory system changed. It all started in 2005 when an Amish iridologist named Jake Schwartz, who I met at an A.R.E. seminar, told me I did not, after all, have emphysema. (An iridologist is someone who makes diagnoses by examining the eyes.) That sounded like welcome news, but I wasn't sure he was right, since I was yet to have any medical doctor say the same thing. But confirmation soon came. In November, 2006, I changed pulmonologists to a Dr. Lo Russo, who had been recommended to me by a doctor that I met at a nutrition seminar given by The Center for Mind Body Medicine. Dr. Lo Russo confirmed that I did *not* have emphysema but instead bronchiectasis, which is an excess accumulation of mucous in the lungs.

Dr. Lo Russo occasionally wanted me to use prednisone, but my search for a more natural treatment continued, and this time I turned to my daughter-in-law Syd for assistance. She had been studying homeopathy for several years under the guidance of a woman named Nkem Ndefo. Homeopathy is an old form of medicine which was quite popular in the early decades of the 20th century. Remedies are prescribed which increase the troubling symptoms, which in turn stimulates the body's own immune system to cure the problem—somewhat like the process found with an inoculation. In May of 2007, as Nancy and I were about to make our annual move back to Virginia from California, we stopped in Pasadena to see David and Syd, providing an opportunity for me to meet with Nkem. She was glad I was no longer on prednisone because that interferes with the body's immune system, and she prescribed some homeopathic remedies for me. Of course I was still taking Advair and albuterol, but she said I should try to keep them to a minimum.

Three months later I was feeling very good, and was no longer taking Advair. When I visited Dr. Lo Russo in September of 2007, my oxygen exhale level was up to 22. His treatment might have helped too, but I feel that the homeopathic remedies were responsible for my improvement. Although I mentioned them to Dr. Lo Russo, I didn't push the matter because I know from experience that most all medical doctors do not want to give any credit to alternative medicine. Dr. Jim Gordon of the Center for Mind Body Medicine is a rare exception to the rule.

Spiritual Advice: Being An Agent for World Change

In the summer of 2007 Nancy and I attended a seminar at A.R.E. and heard a lecture given by an astrologer named Raye Mathis. I was very impressed and thought it would be a good idea for me to have a reading and maybe even refer to it in my book. Since I have always been someone who is looking for proof in everything, I naturally have a lot of doubts about the validity of astrology; but on the other hand, I always try to keep an open mind. Most astrologers maintain that each of us has free will, and the position of the stars and planets at the time of our birth (the natal chart) indicates tendencies or patterns of our energy.

In the astrological reading I eventually got, Raye described several examples of my innate energy patterns: effectiveness in writing and communication; and working with the less fortunate, especially women and young people. She also said I have a close connection with the feminine, and that my "father energy" is in a weak or depressed condition in my natal chart. This really hit home to me because I never liked to fight, and I much prefer to talk to women rather than men—except for Mark, with whom I often enjoy stimulating discussions.

It was also very interesting that Raye indicated an especially meaningful period of time which could be seen from my "progressed chart"—that is, the current position of the planets in relationship to where they were at the time of my birth. She said that from March, 2007, through March, 2008, Uranus would be passing over the spot where Venus was at my birth and that astrologically this would probably be related to forging relationships which could have a big impact on the world. Mark Thurston and I started working together in early 2006, but the main part of our work was taking place during that very time frame, particularly an initiative with George Mason University on consciousness and transformation, which I will describe later.

This material from Raye Mathis was stimulating, and it made me think that I would like to get further input from an intuitive source. In a previous chapter I referred to some life readings I had in Santa Fe, and now I decided I would like to have a new one. Mark told me about a respected clairvoyant in Virginia Beach named Mary Roach. I made an appointment with her, and after a three-month wait I had the reading by telephone while at the Vintage Club in January of 2008. Before the reading occurred, I sent Mary four questions—one of which asked for insights about a lucid dream I had had about thirty years ago. I gave her the details of this powerful dream, and I asked her to tell me what it meant. In the dream I was with Jesus at the Feeding of the Multitudes. Immediately after this miracle I saw myself follow Jesus, as if he were a friend of mine. I then observed yet another miracle—the healing of the woman at the gate.

To my surprise Mary told me that this was not a dream, but a recollection of something that actually happened. She said that Jesus and his family were good friends of mine, and that he had even healed my son who was suffering from a serious lung disease and was spitting up blood. As Mary saw and described it, I was a Jew and tried to get the other Jews to accept Jesus, but they didn't like him because his teachings were at variance with their current beliefs. For many years thereafter—until I died at the age of ninety—I would tell and retell stories about my experiences with Jesus, even making a written record of them. Mary described how I was very careful to include only what I had actually experienced, and I never embellished my stories with superstitions and exaggerations.

If my lucid dream and Mary's interpretation are accurate, then this might explain why, at a very young age in Sunday school, I took exception to some things in the Bible—such as Jesus being "the *only* son of God" and the resurrection of the body. Mary went on to say that I have many other past life memories of this period with Jesus, and I can potentially remember them. She suggested that regression hypnosis could help these memories surface, and maybe I will explore this method later.

During the clairvoyant reading Mary also said that in another lifetime I had been a very well educated Indian monk who did an extensive amount of meditation. In contrast, she said in this current lifetime in America I am supposed to meditate only about half an hour a day and be actively involved in trying to make this a better world. In other words, she did not see my soul-purpose now to be inordinately long periods of meditation—but instead to have regular, brief periods of meditation, and then to focus on how I can help to make the world a better place. Actually her comments about this were very pointed—it is a part of my mission to help to change the world.

Later in the reading Mary confirmed that angels have been and still are a key influence in my life. She said there were several angels who are often trying to help me, but that the central one is my guardian angel. She characterized this angel as having a feminine vibration and gave her a name—Axena—pronounced "Ah-ZEE-Nah." Axena indicated to Mary that she wished that I would ask her for help more often. "Thank you, Axena for all your help, and I will be in touch every day."

Don the chef at a family gathering making dollar pancakes

Fox Hill in Bethesda, Maryland, Nancy and Don's new home in 2009

Chapter 18

Dealing with Challenges

There is one thing that all of us can be sure of. Unavoidably, we will all face difficult challenges and losses. No matter how blessed we may otherwise be with fortunate life circumstances, there will still be rough times. The measure of a man or woman is in how those hard situations are met.

In previous chapters we have seen how blessed and fortunate Don's life has been. And here in this chapter we see him facing the most difficult time of his life. It required him to find the very best within himself—patience, understanding, service, and love. May we all be able to meet our own deep challenges in this same spirit of grace, and be willing to offer loving support and appreciation to those around us.

On February 1, 2009, I celebrated my seventy-seventh birth-day at our home in Great Falls, Virginia. It was a nice catered affair with about fifteen members of my family along with Mark Thurston, editor of these memoirs and my long-time friend. By this time Mark and I thought that we would be finished with the book, and we had even drafted an epilogue. But then so many things began to happen, and it quickly became evident that more would need to be written.

Financial Upheaval and the Stock Market

The stock market was doing poorly during the first half of 2008, but it really fell out of bed in the second half of that year and into January of 2009. During this time the market averages were off about 40%, and my own investments were off about 30%. I reduced my investments in stocks and became heavy in cash. It made me feel much more relaxed, and I spent much less time fooling around with the stock market. But on the other hand, I also knew that whenever the bear market ended, a lot of these losses would be recovered in a very short time.

For a while I was kind of proud of myself for letting go of the stock market, but I couldn't break a habit that I'd had for fifty years. Consequently, I eventually began to sneak back into the market by buying stocks that I felt had been heavily oversold. Plus, this was a very historic time. The economy was being compared to the Great Depression, and nobody knew where it was going.

Barack Obama

All my life I had voted Republican. Many years ago I even went door-to-door for Goldwater. He was not very popular, and the *Washington Post* even said he would do away with Social Security.

Most of my friends over the years are also people who voted Republican. But in 2008, Nancy and I were at dinner one night with some friends, and I casually mentioned that I was voting for Obama. These friends seemed very surprised.

My intention to vote for Obama was, in part, because I didn't like John McCain. He prided himself on being a maverick and demonstrated it by selecting Sarah Palin as his running mate. I had also heard that he didn't get along with his fellow senators. Both he and Hillary had many management problems in running their campaigns, whereas Obama did an excellent job. I don't remember ever being as interested in a presidential campaign as I was in this one. I felt that Obama was a gift from God, and a black U.S. president might do much to bring peace to the world.

Higher Consciousness and a New University Center

Throughout most of my adult life I have attended many seminars and read a lot of books relating to higher consciousness and extra sensory perception (ESP). My interest in spirituality and consciousness, in fact, goes back to my early college years. As I described in Chapter 7, when I was attending Duke University, I was required to take a religion course, and I elected one on Eastern religions. Whenever I have studied a religion (as a college student or into my later years), I have always looked for the proof of what people believe—that is, I have had a deep curiosity and feeling of inquiry about things spiritual and anything related to an expanded picture of who we really are.

By the time I was celebrating my birthday in February of 2009, that inspiration coming from my days at Duke had fully blossomed into something new. It would be about modern day college students having their consciousness changed, just as it had happened for me 60 years ago. But the story went back to the autumn of 2007 when Mark and his wife Mary Elizabeth were visiting Nancy and me. In the midst of a conversation with Mark, I had a sudden inspiration. I said that I thought it would be nice if the things we had been discussing about consciousness could be taught at a major university. Mark was very enthusiastic, and we immediately began to explore the possibilities, starting with my contacting the president of George Mason University, Dr. Alan Merten. Mark and I worked together to prepare a preliminary proposal about courses that could be developed and taught, and I sent it to a number of key administrators at the university—names that Merten sent to me right after I first contacted him about my idea. We were proposing that the De Laski Family Foundation make a large financial commitment to the university to make some new courses available.

During the winter of 2007–08, while Nancy and I spent our usual four months at our home in Palm Desert, California, I began to get feedback on our ideas. I was amazed at the immediate enthusiasm that resulted from our proposal. When Nancy and I returned to Virginia in the spring of 2008, we attended a meeting of about twenty-five leaders of George Mason University, and we were very impressed by what we heard. We received many thanks from them, and when I was asked to say a few words, I said that my angels were responsible. A lady came up to me later and said that she also believes in angels, and she was so happy that I mentioned them.

The final proposal for the Center for Consciousness and Transformation came from the university to our foundation, and it was for ten million dollars spread over ten years. We received it in July of 2008, and Nancy and I signed it with no revisions. A summary of the document is included as an appendix at the end of the book.

Mark was hired in the important role of Senior Fellow, as described in the proposal, with primary duties for creating courses and developing an undergraduate minor. It called for him to work with the Center's director in allocating research grants to George Mason faculty. Mark was well suited for these duties. For over thirty years he had taught master's degree courses on consciousness at Atlantic University in Virginia Beach, and he had led hundreds of workshops, courses, and seminars. He had also written nineteen books on raising consciousness. Mark really appreciated this opportunity. He had been involved with A.R.E. for a long time, and it was time for him to move on. It made me feel good to be able to help create such a special opportunity for someone like Mark. I definitely feel that his angels were also at work.

There have been other university centers over the years that have made valuable contributions to the understanding of consciousness. When I was at Duke University, Dr. J.B. Rhine's center was doing pioneering experiments with ESP, although his program never had the scope or the broad support of the university the way we are aiming for at George Mason. In a similar way, Dr. Ian Stevenson (author of *Twenty Cases Suggestive of Reincarnation*) received a large endowment to set up a center at the University of Virginia Medical School. Even after his recent passing, this work continues as the Division of Perceptual Studies. However, it does not reach out into student life and academic courses of study in the way we envisioned for the new George Mason activities.

I believe that in today's world there is much more openness to topics such as consciousness and expanded human potentials. And a university setting is perfect because most college students would prefer to use the scientific method to learn about raising consciousness than to rely on religions where a lot of superstition is involved. Mark and other faculty at George Mason will be getting far more support for these programs than was ever given to Rhine or Stevenson at their universities. I think that this program has a huge potential and could help change the world. By the fall semester of 2010, the Center had four fully-subscribed courses about consciousness and mindful living that did not exist at the university 18 months earlier.

More About Borka and Vlastimer

In Chapter 15 I described how in 1992 a wonderful Serbian couple by the name of Borka and Vlastimer came to work for us. Sadly, in 2002 Vlastimer was diagnosed with leukemia. It progressed quite slowly until the middle of 2008, and he became bedridden in September and passed away on November 4th in their apartment on the fourth floor of our home. In those final days I spent a lot of time with Vlastimer and felt sort of transformed when I kissed him goodbye as they were carrying him away. This was a new experience for me because I had never been present when my parents and brother passed away.

Vlastimer never suffered any pain. He went to the hospital only for blood tests, and he never used morphine. One of the reasons for this lack of suffering was that he went to a homeopathist in Washington, D.C. who had been discovered by their daughter. (I started using the same doctor and my health has improved dramatically. I no longer use oxygen at night, and when I awake in the morning my blood-oxygen level is about 92, whereas previously it was around 85. Normal is about 98.)

After his passing, Vlastimer was flown to Sarasota where a small funeral was held, and he was buried in a plot that had been arranged for by their grown children. When Borka returned a few days later, she would go to her room and weep for hours. I gave her a week off in early January which is the Serbian Christmas season, and she went back to Florida to be with her children. When she returned she said her children had given her a small Shih Tzu puppy. To her surprise I told her to bring it home, so the next day she had her shipped to Virginia. The dog's name was Beebee, and I was immediately struck by how cute she was. The companionship of Beebee seemed to help Borka's weeping to diminish.

A Major Problem

In the previous chapter I mentioned that as a result of a fall that Nancy had in the middle of 2007 she seemed to have some difficulty in speaking and eating due to a damaged nerve in her upper lip. This condition continued to worsen. By October of 2008 she couldn't swallow, and her weight over those eight months went from 140 to 108 pounds. She also developed a lot of trouble walking and had to start using first a walker and finally a wheel chair. Her inability to eat became so severe that her doctor sent her to the hospital where a feeding tube was installed in her stomach.

She was then sent to a neurologist where MRIs and other tests were performed. When we met with the doctor after the tests, his first comment was that everything looked fine, and my first reaction was that this was very good. But then he went on to explain that they were quite certain that Nancy had Amyotrophic Lateral Sclerosis, otherwise known as ALS or Lou Gehrig's disease. Since they don't know what causes ALS, they run lots of tests to determine if they can find some other problem. If everything is fine, then it is assumed from her symptoms she must have ALS. All of the doctors were quite certain that her condition was not caused by her fall in 2007. ALS is a progressive, disabling disease. Walking, speaking, eating, swallowing, breathing, and other basic functions become more difficult over time. Lung failure is the most common cause of death among ALS patients, and in most cases death occurs three to five years after symptoms begin, although in some cases people live for over ten years. Since Nancy has had no trouble in breathing, we were hopeful that she would live longer than most people with ALS.

Our New Life

With this dire diagnosis and the feeding tube in place, we began a new life rhythm. Borka fed Nancy around 8:30 a.m. and 4:30 p.m., and I fed her around 10:30 p.m. Each day Nancy would get four eight-ounce cans of a special formula which had over one hundred ingredients and a daily total of about thirteen hundred calories. She also got about twenty-four ounces of water a day. Borka did all the cooking, laundry, cleaning, and grocery shopping, which probably resulted in at least a twelve-hour workday. I don't know what I would have done without Borka. Maybe she is one of my angels in human form.

Although I had a lot of free time during these months, I was constantly thinking about the needs of Nancy. Our friends frequently called to ask how she was doing, and we set times for them to drop by. Fortunately, Ken arranged for her to get a new computer, and she spent many hours daily online, communicating with friends, shopping, and finding menus for Borka to cook. We were having luncheons and dinners at least twice a week for family and friends. In spite of her condition, Nancy was still able to go to a social function about once a week. I drove her wherever she needed to go, but we had nurses who came to the house.

We were not used to the cold weather, and the winter of 2008-09 was the first time in many years that we were not in southern California. But with Nancy's illness we had decided that such a trip was impractical, and we put that home on the market.

Getting Ready for our Final Home

In the last section of Chapter 15, I described our new home in Bethesda, Maryland. Settlement was scheduled for January 13, 2009, and the contract specified that we could cancel without penalty anytime prior to then. Due to Nancy's deteriorating condition, I decided I wanted to cancel and stay in our Great Falls home. Things were going as smoothly as possible in caring for Nancy, and why complicate matters with such a stressful move? Besides, with the bad real estate market, I would much rather own two expensive homes than three.

However, Nancy threw a fit when she heard about my plan because she was looking forward to decorating and living in the new home. My daughter, Kathleen, saw my point of view, but my two sons adamantly felt that I should give Mom whatever she wanted. I finally relented and let Nancy have her way, which is what I've always done during our married life. I must admit that I began to feel a lot better about the decision because of Nancy's positive attitude, and she never complained about anything. But the move and downsizing was a huge undertaking. I was certainly glad that we had added a third unit to our apartment at Fox Hill because Borka agreed to come with us and that would become her personal living space.

Feelings

The last year living at our Great Falls home was certainly the most difficult time of my life. I was frequently depressed and felt very little joy. However, I started to look forward to living at Fox Hill because it would give me a chance to do lots of things with other people. In the meantime, though, it was very painful to see my life's partner fading away. Nevertheless, Nancy's cheerful and appreciative attitude was very helpful. During this time I was very thankful that Nancy's mind was still very sharp, which is not the case when someone's final years are clouded by Alzheimer's disease. In many of those cases the afflicted don't even know who their caregiver is.

I really began to look forward to our many visits with friends and family. David planned a trip out here in early March of 2009. Mark Thurston spent two or three nights a week with us in the last few months of our time in Great Falls, and he would bring Nancy and me up to date on new developments with our Center at George Mason University. Our niece Carol Sue started a new career in spiritual coaching, and her sessions with me were very helpful in talking me through my problems.

I couldn't help but feel that something good for both Nancy and me was coming out of this experience, painful though it was. For the first time, Nancy was totally dependent on others, and she could feel love from many people. After leaving Deltek I had spent very little time in helping others except for giving away money. As wonderful as philanthropy may be, it's not the same as helping people in a direct, physical way. These circumstances brought to my mind something Edgar Cayce said when asked about how one enters the kingdom of heaven. He replied, "By leaning on the arm of someone you have helped."

Don at Mount Vernon with Dr. Alan Merten, President
of George Mason University

Chapter 19

Moving On

Life is always about change and transformation. Don went through some of the biggest changes that any of us can experience, including the passing away of his life partner. But what is it that allows us to truly "move on" and experience what life has in store for us next? Surely it has something to do with deeply appreciating the past so that we can move on in a way that honors all that has come before.

It is inspiring for us to read about how Don found ways to be open to what life would bring him in this next phase. He continued to be curious and open intellectually and spiritually, he was intent on his own health and healing, and he was committed to using his talents in service to the greater good. In this spirit of "Letting Life Happen" we can only wonder what would still be ahead for him.

❀

Nancy and I moved into the Fox Hill retirement community on April 20, 2009. The move was fairly easy. We were permitted to put about thirty boxes across the hall in an empty apartment, and then Borka and I gradually unpacked them over several weeks and brought the contents over into our condominium apartment. We settled into the same routine we had in Great Falls, feeding Nancy three times daily. I would usually have my dinner downstairs, and Nancy liked to have me take her in the wheel chair and she would sit next to me in the restaurant.

In the activities room we attended an art class which was offered to all residents of Fox Hill. Nancy painted a very nice still life of some fruit. Although she had been painting for many years, this was the first time I was ever actually with her as she painted, and now I was a big help to her because of how disabled she was from the ALS. Since they were all just beginners, the other people in the art class were very impressed with what she had painted.

Living now in Maryland rather than Virginia, we had to get a new nursing group. We quickly came to like the new team of nurses very much, and one of them would come in at least three times a week. There wasn't a whole lot they could do, but they would clean Nancy up, and they taught Borka how to do everything, too.

We had barely been at Fox Hill for two months when one of the most significant events of my life took place. Borka usually fed Nancy in the morning, but on Friday, June 19th at 8:00 a.m. I decided I would do it. As I was feeding her, Nancy stopped breathing. I yelled to Borka and ran to get the oxygen mask. It didn't do any good, and it was clear that she was passing away. We called the nurses who came over right away, and they started filling out a lot of forms. Even a policeman came who asked a lot of questions, and he also filled out some forms.

This was the first time I had ever been with someone when they died. I felt all right. I even envied Nancy. I have always had a very positive attitude towards death ever since Syria told me about Jack Williamson's death experience, which I described in Chapter 12. Nancy's struggle was now over. She would soon be with the angels, and then she would move on. I didn't think too much about myself and my future at this time. I just knew there was a lot to be done.

Nancy's Funeral

Kathy and Ken came over, and they took over the job of notifying everyone. David and his family arrived on Tuesday. I made plans with the funeral home to have the funeral Wednesday at 11:00 a.m. with a viewing the night before. Fortunately, I had picked out a cemetery plot just two months earlier.

Kathy did a wonderful job organizing the viewing and the funeral. Many of Nancy's paintings were displayed, including the one she recently did at Fox Hill. Nancy had been taking dulcimer lessons for about five years, and her teacher played the dulcimer at the funeral. After I spoke briefly, each of the grandchildren (except the youngest, Dexter) gave very nice eulogies about how much they each loved and appreciated their grandmother ("Mamoo," as they affectionately called her). Zevin, David's nine-year-old son, had to get up on a stool to speak at the lectern. He was so cute. And I had tears in my eyes as each of our three children gave eulogies about how much they loved their mom.

Alan Merten, president of George Mason University, posthumously presented Nancy with the Mason Medal. Some months earlier Nancy and I had been selected for this award, which is given annually to an outstanding individual or couple in recognition of support of the University. I had received my medal at the on-campus graduation exercises a few weeks earlier, but Nancy had not been able to attend, so it was very nice that Dr. Merten would come to her funeral to make this award.

Paul Mannes, an old friend of the family and Ken's brother-in-law, conducted the service, and he gave a beautiful homily. Mark Thurston spoke at the burial site. There were about three hundred people at the funeral, many of whom came up to me over the next several months and told me what a beautiful and inspirational service it was.

Jeffrey Siegel had been scheduled to give a piano concert at Fox Hill on June 25th. He was a longtime friend of ours and had given many concerts at George Mason University and one at our home the previous year. Despite all that had just happened, he came anyway to Fox Hill, and he dedicated the program to Nancy. Every time he performed a new piece, he said it was one of Nancy's favorites. All the residents really enjoyed the program.

Not long after Nancy's passing, Borka left to be with her family in Florida. She had promised that she would stay with us as long as Nancy was still alive, but now it was time for her to move on to the next phase of her life. I started having support in taking care of my place through the Fox Hill staff. A woman started coming up once a week to clean the apartment and do my laundry, so all I had to do was make my breakfast and keep things picked up. I began going downstairs to one of Fox Hill's restaurants every day for lunch and dinner. Friends and family began coming by frequently to join me for dinner.

Kathleen helped me get rid of a lot of Nancy's things. She put on a party where about thirty of Nancy's friends came and they were given pieces of jewelry, clothing, and purses. I had never realized how much stuff Nancy had brought over from the old house. We ended up having two estate sales—one at the Great Falls home just after we moved, and one at Fox Hill for Nancy's things.

Once Nancy was gone, I think I appreciated her more than ever. We almost always agreed on everything, and we had a lot of fun raising the children. Discipline issues were generally left up to me. I can still remember her saying to the children, "If you don't shape up, I'll tell your father."

We always agreed on the houses we wanted to buy, but I left the furnishing and decorating up to her. We also agreed on the many trips we took. For over twenty years she did a very good job as my secretary in my accounting practice, and I don't recall any arguments. We also had a lot of fun going to social functions such as charity events, political balls, and parties in our home at Deerfield Pond Court in Great Falls. Nancy would dress to the nines, and she would help me get properly decorated. But I also got a lot of joy and satisfaction in looking after her.

Recommitting to My Health—
Physically and Spiritually

Right after Nancy died I started meditating on a regular basis. At around 7 a.m. I read from a spiritual book for about five minutes, and then I meditated for about thirty minutes. I used the "soft belly" technique recommended by Dr. Gordon. It calls for the meditator to breathe deeply and focus on the rising and falling of the stomach. When the mind wanders, one keeps focusing on some spiritual affirmation such as, "Know that God is within me."

I attended a Unity Church retreat in August of 2009, and we discussed healing oneself. The instructor said that it was important to focus on healing yourself during meditation, but to be patient since it might take a year to notice results. And so during meditation I started focusing on my lungs as I breathed deeply. I also started using an affirmation such as "Heal me, O Lord, that I may do thy will."

In March of 2010 I noticed that my breathing was much improved. I was no longer using oxygen at night and rarely got out of breath when I exercised. I no longer had to use oxygen on the golf course, and in April I played five eighteen-hole rounds of golf in a week without oxygen when I made a visit to the Vintage Club in California. For several years I had been playing only nine holes of golf at a time. Of course, for those flights to and from California, I did use oxygen on the airplane, but to a much lesser extent than I had in previous years. I was even able to eliminate one drug therapy. My doctor had given me some new expensive medication for my breathing and after several weeks I stopped using it.

In addition to the meditation, I should also give credit for this healing to several other things. My homeopathy treatments, additional physical exercises I had been doing, and a personal healing that a woman did for me at an A.R.E meditation session.

New Beginnings

About two months after Nancy died, the depression which I had been feeling for a year started to lift. The many friends I was making at Fox Hill were a big help, and I became involved in planning social events for the group. For example, I took nine people to a performance in the Amadeus Concerts series, with which I have been involved for many years. Everyone who went from Fox Hill told their friends how wonderful it was, and we had good attendance from Fox Hill at each successive concert.

Our Fox Hill residents also took bus trips at least once a week to museums and other places of interest. At least twice a week I did water aerobics with a group. This really improved my walking and balance. Once a week I worked with the physical therapist on many of the exercise machines. I started playing golf again with three other men from Fox Hill at a little public course nearby. I was playing pretty well and scoring in the mid–forties for nine holes.

Most of us single people at Fox Hill do get lonely, which is a form of depression. We miss having someone telling us what to do, and we also miss having someone to look after. I find it helps to be with people as much as possible, so I always go downstairs for lunch and dinner where I can be with other residents.

I have attended very few social functions except those that are family related. I don't like to go to social functions by myself and have to drive home at night after a few drinks. On the other hand, at family parties someone will give me a ride, or I will spend the night. But one exception was a special event at Mount Vernon. Bob and Carew Lee, who live at Fox Hill and are long time supporters of Mount Vernon, drove me there for a black tie event in March of 2010. I had a great time seeing a lot of my old friends, and a week later I received two photographs of me from Jim Rees, the director. I was quite amazed at how well I looked in one picture, talking to Alan Merten, president of George Mason University. (See photo at the beginning of this chapter.)

Experiences with School and Church

In early September of 2009, I became a student in Mark Thurston's first three–credit course at George Mason's Center for Consciousness and Transformation, which is described in the previous chapter. I had attended a couple of his graduate courses in the spring semester of 2009, but those were shorter courses and this autumn course was a full, four–month experience. The name of this undergraduate course was "Consciousness, Meaning and Life Purpose," and it met every Wednesday from 1:30 to 4:15 p.m. There were twenty–seven students in the class, and we frequently broke up into small groups to share ideas. Among the papers that the other students and I had to write were an essay on happiness and another about one of our dreams and how we interpreted it using methods Mark had taught us in class.

Another interesting activity was a psychological inventory we took. It was called "Strengths Finder," which determines our most essential strengths. My top five themes were Empathy, Adaptability, Belief, Developer, and Connectedness. In reviewing my life, I felt that these themes accurately describe the kind of person I am.

In January of 2010 I signed up for Mark's next undergraduate course which was called "Meditation and Mysteries of the Mind," and it had about the same number of students as the previous course. We all learned a lot about the practice of meditation and research findings about its value, and I'm sure many of the students used this course as a stimulus to start meditating on a regular basis. After the course, one student wrote, "The course opened doors into profound levels of self-understanding, giving me the tools I needed to explore and mature successfully in my undergraduate career." Another student reported about her experience of learning how to do brief sessions of mindfulness practice, "Never before has a three minute lesson of deep breathing and awareness given me timeless skills to live more meaningfully and confidently in all that I do."

Soon after moving to Fox Hill I decided to start going to church again. First I attended a local Presbyterian church a few times, and then I visited the same Unity Church that Nancy and I went to thirty years ago. It is only a twenty-minute drive away from Fox Hill. That first visit in thirty years was very inspiring, and I met a couple who also hosted an Edgar Cayce study group in their home weekly. About forty years ago I attended two of those type of groups; but when I soon visited this one at the home of the Unity couple, I discovered it was by far the best. All the people in that study group had very good vibes, and the meditation experience was outstanding.

Reflections

In reviewing my life, I remember quite a few role models who have had a major influence on my life: my uncle Lyle, a professor of comparative religions at Duke University, Hugh Lynn Cayce at the A.R.E., and Jim Gordon at the Center for Mind Body Medicine, to name a few. Now it seems that it's my turn to be a role model and give advice to those who seek me out. One of them is a nephew who has read a first draft of this book. We've had a number of in-depth conversations recently, which I think have been very meaningful to him. Another nephew has done a lot of meditating, and I have taken him to Unity Church. Two other young men who have marriage problems are meeting with me periodically.

In looking back, I feel I've had a very happy and meaningful life. I think the happiest times were childhood, college years, and early married life. When I was older, many wonderful things happened. I started a business which generated a lot of money for me, my family, and the De Laski Family Foundation. We bought beautiful houses, and we took a lot of wonderful trips. But something about me didn't really appreciate all of this because I was always worrying about details. For example, if I was on a cruise, I was always thinking about our schedule, or our beautiful homes always needed some work or improvements. I was constantly thinking about the stock market, even if I was doing well. If I had it to do over, I would spend a lot more time thanking God and my angels for my good fortune.

I'm certainly glad I set up the De Laski Family Foundation. This has given a lot of meaning to my life, but meaningfulness is not the same as happiness. When I am gone, others will carry on the foundation. I think I might experience the most happiness by just doing things for others. I was recently on a Unity Church retreat, and the leader of a guided meditation instructed us to think back to our earliest childhood memory. Immediately I thought of my experience in the hammock which I related in Chapter 1. Again I told the Voice that I loved him and wanted to come up and be with him. And again he said that he had more for me to do.

Appendix 1

Sample of Government Accounting Charts

RATE TYPE: TARGETED

CONTRACT REVENUE SUMMARY

DIVISION: 01-Corporate   AS OF THE PERIOD ENDING 12/31/02

CONTRACT ACCT #	CONTRACT VALUE	PRIOR YEARS FEE	PRIOR YEARS REVENUE	CURRENT PERIOD REVENUE	COSTS	YEAR-TO-DATE FEE	PROFIT %	YTD REVENUE	CONTRACT TOTALS REVENUE	% COMP.	BACKLOG
1000	2909500.00	0.00	0.00	229680.00	1249187.50	124987.50	10.01%	1374175.00	1374175.00	47.22%	1535325.00
1001	400000.00	29987.00	400000.00	0.00	0.00	0.00	0.00%	0.00	400000.00	100.00%	0.00
1002	800000.00	17700.00	800000.00	0.00	0.00	0.00	0.00%	0.00	800000.00	100.00%	0.00
1003	6000000.00	107313.00	1230000.00	151695.00	1903537.50	114612.50	6.02%	2018150.00	3248150.00	54.13%	2751850.00
1004	250000.00	0.00	0.00	36000.00	235462.50	14537.50	6.17%	250000.00	250000.00	100.00%	0.00
1005	660000.00	0.00	0.00	25000.00	224250.00	22425.00	10.00%	246675.00	246675.00	37.37%	413325.00
1006	750000.00	0.00	0.00	60000.00	336375.00	28625.00	8.51%	365000.00	365000.00	48.66%	385000.00
TOTALS	11769500.00	155000.00	2430000.00	502375.00	3948812.50	305187.50	7.73%	4254000.00	6684000.00		5085500.00

	COSTS	FEE	PROFIT %	REVENUE
<OVER> UNDER APPLIED Fringe Benefits	-162.50	N/A	N/A	-162.50**
<OVER> UNDER APPLIED Overhead	1625.00	N/A	N/A	1625.00**
<OVER> UNDER APPLIED General & Admin	562.89	N/A	N/A	562.89**
PER GENERAL LEDGER	3950837.89	305187.50	7.72%	4256025.39

REPORT DATE: 04/25/02 11:56

Supertech

RATE TYPE: TARGETED

CONTRACT COST SUMMARY FOR THE CONTRACT TO DATE
(INCLUDES CONTRACTS ONLY)

DIVISION: 01-Corporate

AS OF THE PERIOD ENDING 12/31/02

CONTRACT ACCT #	DIRECT LABOR	ODC 43	ODC 44	ODC 45	ODC 46	OTHER ODC'S	TOTAL DIRECT COSTS	FB (SEE A) %	OH (SEE B) %	OTHER POOLS (SEE C) %	G&A (SEE D) %	TOTAL INDIRECT COSTS	TOTAL COSTS
1000-001	475000	45000	0	0	0	115000	635000	166250	285000	0	162937	614187	1249187
1001-001	165000	0	0	0	0	0	165000	57750	99000	0	48263	205013	370013
1002-001	285000	0	0	0	0	0	285000	226000	171000	0	100300	497300	782300
1003-001	1270000	125000	0	0	0	30000	1425000	444500	762000	0	394724	1601224	3026224
1004-001	105000	0	0	0	0	0	105000	36750	63000	0	30712	130462	235462
1005-001	100000	0	0	0	0	0	100000	35000	60000	0	29250	124250	224250
1006-001	150000	0	0	0	0	0	150000	52500	90000	0	43875	186375	336375
TOTALS	2550000	170000	0	0	0	145000	2865000	1018750	1530000	0	810062	3358812	6223812
<OVER> UNDER APPLIED INDIRECT COSTS							N/A	-162	1625	0	562	2025	2025
ACTUAL COSTS							2865000	1018587	1531625	0	810625	3360837	6225837

Appendix 2

Highlights from the Philosophy of Edgar Cayce

As Edgar Cayce puts it in this short passage below, being clear about one's spiritual ideal—a core value and direction in life—is the most important factor along the spiritual path.

> The more important, the most important experience of this or any individual entity is to first know what IS the ideal—spiritually. (357-13)

Meditation is a crucial discipline for us to practice. It provides a way to make a direct connection with the Higher Mind that resides in us all.

> Meditation is *emptying* self of all that hinders the creative forces from rising along the natural channels of the physical man to be disseminated through those centers and sources that create the activities of the physical, the mental, the spiritual man; properly done must make one *stronger* mentally, physically . . . (281-13)

Dreams are an invaluable source of guidance and self-understanding, and Cayce advocated taking the time and energy to study and interpret them.

> A dream is a *natural* experience! It's *not* an unnatural! Don't seek for unnatural or supernatural! It is the natural—it is nature—it is God's activity! His associations with man. His *desire* to make for man a way for an understanding! (5754-3)

*The theory of reincarnation isn't just for curiosity or speculation. Cayce sees it as valuable only if its view of the "continuity of life" makes us a better person in today's world—in **this** lifetime.*

Only that which produces or makes for experiences that may make a citizen a better citizen, a father a better father, a mother a better mother, a neighbor a better neighbor, is constructive.

And to find that ye only lived, died and were buried under the cherry tree in Grandmother's garden does not make thee one whit better neighbor, citizen, mother or father!

But to know that ye spoke unkindly and suffered for it, and in the present may correct it by being righteous—*that* is worth while!

What is righteousness? Just being kind, just being noble, just being self-sacrificing; just being willing to be the hands for the blind, the feet for the lame these are constructive experiences.

Ye may gain knowledge of same, for incarnations *are* a *fact*! How may ye prove it? In thy daily living! (5753-2)

Every one of us has innate intuitive or psychic abilities.

How develop the psychic forces? So live in body, in mind, that self may be a channel through which the Creative Forces *may* run. How is the current of life or of modern science used in the commercial world? By preparing a channel through which same may run into, or through, that necessary for the use in the material things. So with the body mentally, physically, spiritually, so make the body, the mind, the spiritual influences, a channel—and the *natural* consequence will be the manifestations. (5752-2)

Appendix 3

Highlights from the Philosophy of Guru Maharaji

From his address at the UN 60th anniversary:
Peace needs to be in everyone's life. Of all the things we have tried in this world, there is one thing we have never given a chance. That one thing is peace. If we want to hope for something, maybe we could hope in our heart that peace will come in our life. The peace that we are looking for is within. It is in the heart, waiting to be felt, and I can help you get in touch with it. It is not the world that needs peace; it is people. When people in the world are at peace within, the world will be at peace.

From "Grace and Gratitude" at the Vaishakhi Celebrations, 13th April, 1992:
I know very well that it is very easy to get lost in this world. But when my Master gave me this Knowledge, I did not know how much grace he has bestowed upon me. I actually did not realize what a grace has been showered upon me. But now as the days are passing and as I experience this Knowledge, this bliss, I have the feeling in my heart, how my Master really saved me from this illusory world. I can say nothing more. Actually he rescued me in the real sense. How much grace was bestowed upon me! Because it takes no time to get lost in the maze of this world.

This is such a world in which there is darkness everywhere.

And that darkness devours a man. It runs after man to eat him up. And man loses his wits. He becomes heartless. He does not listen to his heart. He loses his intellect and becomes crazy. He is unable to listen to the call of his heart. But what my Master imparted to me enabled me to go inside to that perfect place. Now, I don't need to go to the Ganges because the Ganges is within me too. I don't have to go to the temple, because there is that real temple within me. I don't need to go to the Church. He showed me the church inside of me and such a saga which goes along incessantly with each of my breath. He gave me a lamp and its flame, its light reaches every nook and corner and dispels the darkness within me, for which I shall ever remain grateful in my life, in my heart as long as I am alive.

From the Prem Rawat Foundation:

Every living human being has something wonderful happening inside. Within each person is a supreme beauty. Within each person is peace, joy, the feeling of the heart.

I offer inspiration, reminding people of the beauty of existence; I remind people that life itself is a gift. I encourage people to know that it is possible to open windows of understanding so they can be fulfilled. I see each human being as complete. Within each one shines a sun so bright that it can make any darkness go away.

What I am proposing is that within each individual is the domain where peace can be found. This is the message that I feel is sorely needed in this world. How important it is for that one message to be accessible to everyone.

More than just words, I offer a practical way to feel the contentment that is already within. My message is neither new nor old—it is timeless. The peace, the contentment, that we seek is within. It was, is, and always will be. Now is the time to turn within.

What I offer is a gift from one being to another. I want to make this possibility available to people. And if they want to pursue it, I want to help them however I can.

Appendix 4

More Details about Our Travels

In 1999, we took a trip to France and Italy which was sponsored by the Duke University alumni group. We first flew to Paris and toured the city for three days—plus a side trip to Giverny to visit the historic home of Claude Monet and the gardens made famous by his paintings—paintings which Nancy later re-created in her art studio at home. We next took a high speed train to the Rhone River where we boarded a ship for a cruise through the south of France.

But the trip didn't end with our arrival at the Mediterranean Sea. Although I thought this ship was better suited for river cruises than the open sea, we nevertheless sailed across to Italy. It was rough going, and Nancy and I were apparently the only passengers who didn't get seasick—in fact, we have been fortunate enough to have never gotten seasick. However, once the group made it though that tough stretch, we had a lovely time at various ports-of-call on the west coast of Italy. Especially memorable was our excursion inland to Florence where we saw extraordinary museums, and then our trip to Pisa to see the Leaning Tower. We then took a bus to Rome where we spent several days enjoying all the historic sites. I was learning that in Europe nothing is truly "historic" unless it is at least 1500 years old!

It wasn't long after that tour in France and Italy that we were back in Europe again. The following year we took a two-week garden and castle cruise sponsored by the American Horticultural Society. This very extensive tour went around the British Isles and Ireland. We started by flying into London and taking a bus to Dover. We then boarded the cruise liner and sailed west, stopping soon thereafter at Sark, a small island in the English Channel about fifty miles west of France. Although Sark is part of the British Isles, it was occupied by the Nazis for five years during World War II. They used it as a resort for older officers, and they liked to claim that because of Sark they had occupied part of England. One striking fact about Sark is that it is a car-free island—only bicycles, animal drawn carts, and tractors are allowed! We next stopped to see famous gardens on the Isles of Scilly, an archipelago just off the southwesternmost tip of Great Britain. I learned that one is never to say "Scilly Isles."

Next came Ireland, and we sailed around to its western shore, stopping for ports-of-call to see noteworthy castles and gardens. Sailing clockwise all the way around Ireland, we came back to the Irish Sea and finally arrived in Dublin. I was very surprised at how modern this city was, with crowds of well-dressed young people walking around with brief cases. I was told that many American computer companies have facilities in Dublin.

From Dublin we continued on across the Irish Sea to Wales, and then north to the beautiful Orkney Islands. In visiting some of these isles we would take a small boat to the shore, and if it was high tide then we had to wear boots which were called "wellies." Coming back to the mainland of Scotland, we visited Loch Ness, near Inverness. (Nancy swears she saw the Loch Ness monster and has a picture to prove it.) Finally, the tour ended up in Edinburg where we spent several days seeing more gardens and castles. In fact, all told on this trip, we visited eighteen gardens and ten castles.

Even though the tour arranged by the American Horticulture Society ended here in Scotland, Nancy and I wanted to see more. We had decided that since we were already in Europe, we should create our own extension tour. And so, from Edinburg we flew to Geneva and embarked on a one-week bus tour through Switzerland and Lichtenstein. Because in the ski resort areas it was the off-season, we were able to stay in the best hotels on short notice, and we frequently walked around on snow even though it was July. We concluded our trip by having dinner in Zurich with some of the relatives of our son-in-law Edward. It had been a great trip, and we had visited many places I had never even heard of before.

We were surely going to be ready to see more of Europe very soon.

The next good opportunity came through our involvement with Mount Vernon. For many years Nancy and I have been involved with the Mount Vernon Ladies Association, which owns and maintains George Washington's home on the Potomac River just south of Washington, D.C. In 2002 we were part of a tour group that explored the ancestral roots of George Washington in England. It was a fascinating history lesson to discover Washington's ties to the very country against which he fought for our independence. However, many of the highlights for me on this trip were spots that were not directly related to George Washington. I was very pleased that we got to visit Blenheim Palace, the birthplace and home of Winston Churchill, and we also visited his later home, Chartwell. And there was a very memorable overnight stay at Leeds Castle. What a historic place. Built in 1119, it was transformed in the 16th century by Henry VIII for his first wife, Catherine of Aragon. And later Elizabeth I was imprisoned here for a time before her coronation. It seemed like a pretty luxurious prison to me.

We had had such a good time with the Mount Vernon group that two years later, in 2004, we participated in another of their trips, this one to France to explore the roots of Lafayette. In addition to the sites of Paris, we had a chance to visit the home of Lafayette, about two hours' drive outside of the city. We went a little beyond just Lafayette–related sites on this trip. We got a private driver to take us to Bruges, Belgium which is primarily known as a shopping mecca. Of course Nancy had a great time. The next day we went on to Amsterdam where the main thing I remember is driving through the Red Light District. For a distance of about three blocks, scantily dressed ladies stood in their rooms in front of their windows, trying to entice possible customers. I assumed that when something started to happen they would draw the curtains. We also visited the home of Anne Frank, and then we went on to see the largest shipping area of flowers in the world. The warehouse was the length of over three football fields, and we had to ride around in a golf cart to see it all. After these three memorable days in Amsterdam, we flew home.

Between our two educational tours with the Mount Vernon group, we had continued our pattern of seeing Europe with various groups to whom we have a connection. We decided to try a cruise being sponsored by the Vintage Club, our winter home community in California. Every two or three years the club plans a private tour for its members. Soon after we joined the club and bought our first home there, they announced a cruise in the North Sea, but we declined that one because we had just been there. But in 2003 they planned a cruise around Spain, and then to Portugal, and finally to southern France, with a train trip to Paris. That one sounded very appealing to Nancy and me.

Now we were seeing a whole new part of Europe. We spent several days in Barcelona then sailed to Cadiz where we visited a farm that raised and trained bulls. We toured the farm, saw several bull fights, and had a fancy meal with our Vintage Club friends. At other ports–of–call there were bus rides to Bilbao and Oporto in Portugal. When we got to Lisbon, I was amazed at the traffic jams— but the immense congestion was not from cars, only bicycles.

Our last cruise stop was Bordeaux in France where we toured two wineries, one of which was Margeaux, whose wine I have collected and loved for many years. After we arrived in Paris by train, we extensively toured the Louvre, and the next day we went to Moulin Rouge for a fancy dinner and show. Another great trip for Nancy and me.

Travel Adventures Closer to Home

But not all of our travel has been to Europe. In 1999 we went on a memorable cruise much closer to home—a tour through all of the Great Lakes, starting in Toronto. It was actually the inaugural cruise for the re–establishment of Great Lake cruises, which had been suspended since the 1930s. Because our group was the first in decades, there were big ceremonies at each port-of-call. The largest ceremony was at Saginaw, Michigan, where film crews showed up, and I ended up seeing myself on TV while sitting at a bar with a fellow passenger.

The Great Lakes cruise also stands out in my mind because of a curious coincidence—truly a synchronistic event—linked to the timing of this trip. The cruise ended in Chicago on the day before an important meeting was scheduled with William Blair & Co, one of the Deltek underwriters as the stock went public. They had their headquarters right there in Chicago. A presentation was being given to a number of stock analysts and investors in order to interest them in buying Deltek stock. Our chief financial officer, Alan Stewart, was there, but it turned out that Ken (the president of Deltek at this time) couldn't make it. In the synchronicity of events, I was right there and able to represent us and make a presentation at the meeting. Afterwards, some of the people who had listened to me came up to chat, and I was asked whether I came from Virginia by car, rail, or plane. They were quite shocked to learn that I had come by boat. (Since my presentation resulted in some stock sales, I have playfully wondered if I should have charged Deltek for my travel expenses.)

That Great Lakes cruise was a wonderful way to see a part of America that was new to Nancy and me, and soon thereafter we decided that we wanted to see more of America. The opportunity presented itself in 1997 because we wanted to take our 1992 Mercedes to our first home we had just bought at the Vintage Club in California. So in December, we drove south from Virginia toward New Orleans. Touring that renowned city, I found that Bourbon Street was disappointing, but I found the graveyards very interesting. Because the water table is so close to ground level, bodies are interred in vaults above ground.

Leaving New Orleans, we traveled along Interstate 10 through Texas. I thought San Antonio was especially beautiful, and I particularly enjoyed visiting the Alamo. It's a long way across west Texas, and finally arriving in El Paso we stayed in a very nice hotel. The next morning we visited the entry points along the Mexican border, and then we continued west on Interstate 10, driving through New Mexico. I'll never forget the horrible smell of the emus—a very unusual bird—as they filled up acres and acres around Las Cruces. We made our way on into Arizona, and that night stayed at the Biltmore in Phoenix. It was just one more day's drive, and we arrived at our home in Indian Wells at the Vintage Club. We had been on the road for nine days. The long drive convinced us that we liked a Mercedes as a touring car, but we wanted to get a newer model. So when we got home in the spring, we bought Nancy a new 1998 Mercedes.

This nine-day cross country trip wasn't our only excursion to see America. In 2001 we decided we wanted another car at our desert home, and I also wanted to take four cases of my best wine to California. So we drove out in my 1992 Lincoln Mark VIII, and this time we saw yet another part of the country—traveling through Tennessee and southern Arkansas before finally connecting with Interstate 10 in Texas. Along that route we visited The Hermitage (Andrew Jackson's home), and in Nashville we toured the Country Music Hall of Fame and Museum.

In Memphis we visited Graceland, Elvis Presley's home, and stayed at the Peabody Hotel. This hotel is very famous because since 1932 at twelve noon the bellhop escorts about eight mallard ducks from their home in the penthouse to a fountain in the main lobby where they swim and have lunch. People come from miles around to see this ceremony.

We found southern Arkansas to be very run down, and it seemed that life was very hard for people there. When we checked into a Ramada Inn, we found there was no place to eat, but we found a Chinese restaurant across the street. They couldn't give us wine because it was a dry county, but they said I could bring some in from my car if I kept it under the table in a brown bag. So there we were drinking a $300 bottle of wine in paper cups from a bottle under the table. The next day we drove on and connected with Interstate 10, following the same pathway back to Indian Wells that we had used four years earlier.

But it was the trip back to Virginia the following April that provided us with our most extensive and adventuresome travels of America. We bought a new Lexus to replace our Mark VIII and drove back to Virginia by the northern route. What an amazing trip it was. We got to see some of the most beautiful geography to be found anywhere in the world. First we went to Yosemite National Park where we spent two days, and then we drove up to Lake Tahoe. From there it was on to Portland, Oregon, where we stayed overnight with some Vintage Club friends, and I visited one of Deltek's regional offices which is there in Portland.

The next day we drove up to Vancouver where we spent several days sightseeing. We next went to Seattle and stayed with some other Vintage Club friends. The following day we left our car at their home, and they drove us to the port in Seattle where we boarded a cruise ship for a week's trip to Alaska. We went up the Hecate Strait to Sitka, Ketchikan, and Juneau. We saw some museums at ports–of–call and many large beautiful glaciers. When we returned to the "lower forty–eight" United States, we drove east across Washington and spent two nights at Coeur d'Alene, Idaho. Nancy rode in the golf cart with me while I played the famous golf course which has a floating island for its green on the 14th hole. It's quite a remarkable golf hole and I can understand its notoriety. That floating island can be moved to essentially create a different golfing challenge as the length of the hole changes. All of us that day in our foursome hit our tee shots in the water.

The next day we drove to the edge of Yellowstone National Park and spent the night in a motel, then proceeded through the Park past Old Faithful and on to Cody, Wyoming. This is a cute little town, although I had never heard of it. I always remember it because my daughter's family has a dog named Cody. The next day we drove to Keystone, South Dakota and saw Mount Rushmore. As we headed east after Mount Rushmore, Nancy was driving along Interstate 90 and a policeman stopped her for doing 86 miles per hour when the speed limit was 75. She talked herself out of a ticket, but I felt kind of good because whenever I drive Nancy is always telling me to slow down.

Before heading south, we went a little way further on Interstate 90, crossing over the border into Minnesota so that Nancy could say she had been in that state. Then we came back to South Dakota and headed south to Sioux City, Iowa, where we spent the night. The next day we continued south, jumping over to Nebraska and Kansas so we could also say we had been in those states. We arrived in Kansas City and visited the Hallmark Card headquarters where they had a very nice tour. We went on about half–an–hour's drive east to the home of President Truman in Independence, Missouri, and then drove on to St. Louis where we spent the night.

The next day we crossed the Mississippi River and drove on toward Louisville, Kentucky, where we spent the night and toured the site of the Kentucky Derby. And as we were drawing nearer to Virginia, we were now approaching places that we had visited several times before, and so we knew where we wanted to stay. We called ahead and made a reservation at the Greenbrier Hotel in West Virginia, a fabulous hotel where we had celebrated several anniversaries about ten years earlier. When we checked in, they told us the main dining room was full but we could eat in the sport's bar. I told them that we had come over 5,000 miles in thirty days to get there. So they reconsidered and let us eat in their special dining room which usually cost $100 extra.

Being at the Greenbrier was a great environment for us to reminisce about our many road trips around America. Nancy likes to drive, and we try to split the time equally. Our usual rhythm is that she always lets me drive in the morning because I frequently get a little sleepy after lunch. By the time we had completed this thirty–day northern route across America, we could both say that we had been in all 50 states except North Dakota and Hawaii. In 2006 we took a 17–day cruise to Hawaii from San Diego, and so now North Dakota is the only state we haven't been in.

I was discovering that it's possible to have a vacation trip take me somewhere I need to go anyway. And so our next cruise was a more creative way than usual to get from our home in northern Virginia all the way out to southern California for the winter. Nancy and I flew to Ft. Lauderdale, where we boarded a cruise liner that took us into the Gulf of Mexico, through the Panama Canal, and then north to Costa Rica, Guatemala, the coast of Mexico and finally arriving in Los Angeles after sixteen days.

Appendix 5

Highlights from the Proposal to Establish the Center for Consciousness and Transformation at George Mason University

Overview

There is an opportunity for George Mason University to become a leader in the new and growing field of consciousness and transformation by the creation of the Center for Consciousness and Transformation. This Center will be unique—offering in-depth, interdisciplinary studies in consciousness, holistic health, human potential, creativity, mindfulness, conflict resolution, personal transformation, and transformational leadership. The Center will have a bold mission: to be a catalyst for transformative individual, organizational, and social change through education, research, and practice concerning the impact of states of individual and group consciousness on leadership, physical and mental health, conflict transformation, and the creative arts.

The Center for Consciousness and Transformation will offer courses toward an undergraduate minor as well as Master's and doctoral coursework. New courses developed by the Center will be integrated with courses already in place in various academic units and departments on campus. A wide range of disciplines and fields will influence the work of the Center including philosophy, psychology, religious studies, conflict resolution, communication, education, arts and arts wellness, leadership studies, and health and human sciences. The Center will be housed in New Century College because of its emphasis on interdisciplinarity and its successful history in sustaining collaborative efforts with a wide range of academic disciplines. New Century College is a comprehensive integrative studies degree program located in the College of Humanities and Social Sciences. New Century College will steward the program as a University responsibility and will maintain an active advisory group drawn from participating units.

About the Center

Global Model for Other Universities

The Center will be a model globally for other major universities, demonstrating how they can establish a program for their learning communities in the multi-disciplinary fields of consciousness and transformative practices. Along with Mason's global reach and technologies of distance-learning—the distributive campus model—the Center's research and courses will be positioned to directly reach an audience worldwide. The Center will spearhead a dialog among other Mason and non-Mason institutes, centers, and organizations committed to research, teaching, and transformative practices, especially in the fields and disciplines of leadership, physical and mental health, conflict transformation, and the creative arts. Using various means of technology, the Center's publications and materials will be disseminated widely.

Interdisciplinary Approach

The interdisciplinary Center will train, educate, and learn from young adult students at George Mason who are preparing themselves for careers and leadership in their chosen fields—providing a perspective of what consciousness and transformative practices offer to these respective disciplines. An interdisciplinary minor, certificate programs, and concentrations within existing Master's degree and doctoral programs all provide for a basis of interdisciplinary entrepreneurship throughout Mason.

The Center will collaborate with George Mason faculty from a wide range of degree granting units to develop new courses related to consciousness and transformation. Additionally, the Center will also foster informal opportunities on campus that facilitate collaborative learning communities among students, faculty, staff, and alumni. The Center will have a Director, Senior Fellow, and a Program Manager who will be employees of the University.

Conclusion

The Center provides an extraordinary and timely opportunity for George Mason to rapidly become a leading academic institution in the fields of consciousness and transformative practices. With an emphasis on theory, research, teaching, and practice, this comprehensive Center will attract scholars, practitioners, and students from diverse disciplines and fields around the world. Mason has an uncommon advantage and a bright future in being a catalyst and facilitator of transformational change throughout the world.

George Mason University and the de Laski Family

The University has benefited from a long and growing relationship with several members of the de Laski family. The de Laski family support has been instrumental in the University's ascendancy in higher education in our nation and globally. With the family's support, the University initiated an innovative summer music academy. Kathleen de Laski serves on the Board of Visitors, providing leadership and valuable counsel to the University. An academic bridge was built between George Mason University and Mount Vernon with the de Laski family playing a central role.

With the generous support of the family foundation, the University is expanding and renovating the performing arts facilities on the Fairfax Campus. We now have the opportunity to further the impact of our collaborative work by building a world-class center dedicated to the legacy of the de Laskis' work on consciousness and transformation.